Changing Citizenship

Changing Citizenship

Democracy and Inclusion in Education

Audrey Osler and Hugh Starkey

Open University Press

Open University Press
McGraw-Hill Education
McGraw-Hill House
Shoppenhangers Road
Maidenhead, Berkshire
England SL6 2QL

email: enquiries@openup.co.uk
world wide web: www.openup.co.uk

and Two Penn Plaza, New York, NY 1012–2289
USA

First published 2005
Reprinted 2008

A catalogue record of this book is available from the British Library

ISBN-10 0 335 21181 X (pb)   0 335 21182 8 (hb)
ISBN-13 978 0 335 21181 4 (pb)   978 0 335 21182 1 (hb)

Library of Congress Cataloging-in-Publication Data
CIP data has been applied for

Typeset by BookEns Ltd, Royston, Herts.
Printed and bound in Great Britain by Bell and Bain Ltd, Glasgow

Contents

Acronyms and Abbreviations

AAUW	American Association of University Women
ACHPR	*African Charter on Human and Peoples' Rights*
AFP	Agence France Presse
AP	Associated Press
BBC	British Broadcasting Corporation
BNP	British National Party
CGG	Commission on Global Governance
CRC	United Nations *Convention on the Rights of the Child*
CRE	Commission for Racial Equality
DES	Department of Education and Science
DfEE	Department for Education and Employment
DfES	Department for Education and Skills
DFID	Department for International Development
DTI	Department of Trade and Industry
EC	European Commission
ECECR	*European Convention on the Exercise of Children's Rights*
ECHR	*European Convention on Human Rights and Fundamental Freedoms*
EDC	Education for Democratic Citizenship
EMAG	Ethnic Minority Achievement Grant
ESRC	Economic and Social Research Council
EU	European Union
GCSE	General Certificate of Secondary Education
HRA	Human Rights Act
ICCPR	*International Covenant on Civil and Political Rights*
ICESCR	*International Covenant on Economic Social and Cultural Rights*
ICHRP	International Council on Human Rights Policy
IMF	International Monetary Fund
LEA	local education authority
LRA	Lord's Resistance Army
MP	Member of Parliament
NASUWT	National Association of Schoolmasters Union of Women Teachers
NATO	North Atlantic Treaty Organization

NCSL	National College of School Leadership
NGO	non-governmental organization
Ofsted	Office for Standards in Education
OHCHR	Office of the UN High Commissioner for Human Rights
OAU	Organisation of African Unity
PLASC	Pupil Level Annual School Census
QCA	Qualifications and Curriculum Authority
RACA	Raising African Caribbean Achievement project
RRAA	Race Relations [Amendment] Act
SAT	Standard Attainment Test
SEN	special educational needs
SEU	Social Exclusion Unit
TLRP	Teaching and Learning Research Programme
UDHR	Universal Declaration of Human Rights
UN	United Nations
UNCHR	UN Commission on Human Rights
UNDP	United Nations Development Programme
UNESCO	United Nations Educational, Scientific and Cultural Organization
WSF	World Social Forum

Acknowledgements

We wish to thank all those colleagues and friends who have supported us during the writing of this book.

In particular we acknowledge those colleagues at the Centre for Citizenship Studies in Education at the University of Leicester, particularly Professor Ken Fogelman, Dr Tehmina Basit, Barbara Hall, Tasneem Ibrahim and Dr Chris Wilkins. Also, Ph.D. students and experienced colleagues Colm Ó Cuanacháin and Anne Hudson for their ideas and reflections on citizenship and human rights education. Special thanks to Dr Helen May at the Centre for Citizenship and Human Rights Education at the University of Leeds for her invaluable assistance during the final stages of preparing the typescript and for ensuring that it reached the publisher on time.

Our grateful thanks to Fiona Richman at Open University Press for her tolerance and understanding when we experienced various upheavals during the writing process, not least of which was both of us changing jobs.

The authors and publishers also wish to thank a number of people for their agreement to use material that we have previously published elsewhere. The editors of *Educational Review*, 55(3): 243–54 for our use in Chapters 5 and 6 of material adapted from 'Learning for cosmopolitan citizenship: theoretical debates and young people's experiences'. Chay Osler and the editors of *Learning and Behavioural Difficulties* for the use of his statement on his experiences of exclusion in Chapter 4. The editors of the *European Journal of Education*, 33(2): 143–59 for use in Chapter 7 of our article 'Education for citizenship: mainstreaming the fight against racism?'.

We also acknowledge the Office of the United Nations High Commissioner for Human Rights (OHCHR) for the text of *The Universal Declaration of Human Rights* taken from their website and the United Nations Children's Fund (UNICEF) UK for allowing us to reproduce their simplified version of the UN *Convention on the Rights of the Child*.

Introduction

Education has a critical role to play in enabling us to respond to the processes of globalization. It is important that people have the chance to understand the links between their own lives and those of others, both globally and locally. Across the world, in established democracies as well as in newly democratized states, there is renewed interest in education for citizenship and human rights. The challenge facing curriculum planners, school leaders and teachers is to provide young people with appropriate experiences which allow them to make sense of international politics and interdependence while at the same time enabling them to feel that they can make a difference and participate in shaping our common future.

Education in democratic states has always been, either explicitly or implicitly, about strengthening democracy. Education has been viewed as a way of preparing young people to understand the society in which they live, how it functions, and to contribute to it in various ways. In other words, it has long been about preparing the young for their future roles as citizens. The emphasis has been on preparation to exercise future democratic rights, including the right to vote, in a responsible manner. For those who were not expected to take up positions of responsibility or power, the school subject of 'civics' emphasized responsibilities and respect for those in power, and was designed to encourage a sense of uncritical patriotism. In contrast, the education of elites has laid considerable stress on preparing the young for their responsibilities as future leaders. Education for democratic citizenship is based on the premise that all can contribute to shaping society's future, starting in the present.

Citizenship is changing. There is growing consensus that education for national citizenship is an inadequate response to growing global interdependence and that it is becoming increasingly important that everyone is prepared to participate in an increasingly globalized world. The challenge is to enable citizens to participate at a time when many people feel powerless and we are uncertain how to shape the future agenda. This sense of powerlessness and helplessness is magnified by our increased awareness of inequalities and injustice across the world.

Changing Citizenship is a response to this educational challenge. Within the globalized and multicultural communities that characterize today's societies, the concept of citizenship is pivotal. Educators, politicians and the media are using the concept in new contexts and giving it new meanings. While not wishing to deny its complexity, we believe that fundamentally citizenship is about making a difference. It is about working with others in the quest for the good society.

We are concerned not only with the status of citizenship, but also with citizenship as a sense of belonging. Citizenship can unite a diverse population, but the term is often used in ways that are exclusive. For example, in many countries, refugees and migrants are presented in popular and political discourses as groups who stand in opposition to citizens. We are interested in how citizenship can be practised in a variety of contexts to promote human rights and equality. We propose the concept of education for cosmopolitan citizenship as a means of understanding citizenship as it is experienced in diverse communities and in multicultural settings, whether these be local, national or global. We argue that education for cosmopolitan citizenship, informed by human rights, is appropriate for all schools, whether or not there is visible diversity in the community. Such education can strengthen democracy and contribute to the process of globalizing social progress and justice.

Part 1 of *Changing Citizenship* addresses processes of globalization and their implications for citizenship education. Citizenship is a concept at the intersection of many theoretical frameworks. *Changing Citizenship* therefore draws on a range of disciplines including sociology, political science, philosophy and human rights law. Chapter 1 examines various concepts of citizenship, considering their strengths and limitations. It explores the relationship of citizenship to nationality, cosmopolitanism, identities and belonging. In Chapter 2, we examine human rights as the principles underpinning democracy and development, exploring the role of education in achieving these goals. Chapter 3 examines children's status and rights as citizens, considering the contribution that children can make to debates about education and improving schools.

In Part 2, we examine, in Chapter 4, the right to education and the related concepts of rights in and through education. Drawing on our research into exclusion from school, we consider how schools might be made more accessible, acceptable and adaptable to diverse groupings of children. Chapter 5 examines learning for cosmopolitan citizenship as a way of enabling young citizens to recognize their common humanity and build a more inclusive society. We propose a model of citizenship learning and identify features of a programme of education for cosmopolitan citizenship, looking critically at the citizenship education programme for England. If the school curriculum is to be effective it needs to be aware of and to build on young people's learning in families and communities. Chapter 6 draws on our research with young people to explore their identities and sites of learning for citizenship beyond school. In Chapter 7 we discuss how antiracism is essential to an inclusive democracy, examining European policy frameworks and the ways these are applied at national levels in Britain and Sweden.

Part 3 examines how the school as an institution needs to change in order to ensure education for citizenship and democracy. Chapter 8 looks at the features of democratic learning and provides case studies of primary and secondary schools which have taken steps to build a school community based on human rights and democratic participation. Often teachers express concerns that children's rights are emphasized with little thought being given to responsibilities. In Chapter 9 we examine the relationship of rights and responsibilities, concluding with a set of pedagogic principles. In the final chapter, we examine the changing discourses of school leadership, drawing on the voices of headteachers to consider their role in education for citizenship and diversity and as citizens. Those school leaders who have made a commitment to equality and diversity provide us with valuable models of leadership as citizens and for citizenship.

PART 1
Changing Citizenship

1 Cosmopolitan Citizenship

Ugandan rebels burn family alive
Over 300 people were killed when the notorious Lord's Resistance Army (LRA) made a surprise attack on a camp for displaced people near Lira, in northern Uganda. The LRA surrounded the camp shortly before nightfall. They overcame the camp's defence forces, using grenades and powerful weapons. Residents who took shelter in their homes were burnt alive. 'They came running, surrounded the camp and starting setting huts on fire' said Molly Auma, a 26-year-old mother of three. She was shot and had her right-hand fingers blown off by a grenade. Samuel Ogwang, a 30-year-old shopkeeper, told [the] Agence France Presse (AFP) news agency that his wife had been killed and three of his children wounded. 'My parents were burnt alive in one of the huts. I buried 10 of my relatives yesterday before I brought these children to hospital'.
(www.bbc.co.uk, 22 February 2004; *The Guardian*, 23 February 2004; *Mail and Guardian online*, 16 March 2004)

This attack happened on Saturday 21 February 2004. Within 24 hours, international news agencies, including the British Broadcasting Corporation (BBC) and AFP began arriving at the scene, filming the camp and collecting evidence from survivors at the local hospital. By Sunday evening reports of the atrocities were being broadcast across the world.

Changing citizenship

Many citizens in the UK and in countries across the world were undoubtedly shocked and disturbed by these reports from the Lira camp in Uganda. The concerns of citizens, which are often focused on local and national issues, have expanded as local and national media report events in previously remote areas. The immediacy of the media coverage encourages citizens to feel implicated in some way in the lives of those whose story is being told.

This consequence of globalization suggests that approaches to citizenship need to be reconsidered. Citizenship is changing as citizens have greater opportunities to act in new international contexts. Citizenship involves making connections between our status and identities as individuals and the lives and concerns of others with whom we share a sense of community. We are increasingly able to make these connections and feel solidarity with others at local, national, regional (e.g. European) and global levels. There are now more ways of being a citizen than have perhaps previously been recognized.

The BBC report from Lira, Uganda, highlights a number of features that illustrate the context in which debates about citizenship and education are now taking place. First, it demonstrates the shrunken world of globalization. Within hours of the event, a BBC team had reached the remote refugee camp and started relaying an illustrated and edited report that was shown on the main TV evening news in Britain. The story, including eyewitness accounts, political background and visual evidence, was posted on the BBC website and transmitted on the BBC World Service. The BBC was not alone on the scene. Reporters from two other agencies, AFP and Associated Press (AP) were also collecting evidence. The electronic news media made available reports and pictures of these shocking events to people directly in their homes around the world. Newspapers and websites provided a fuller picture and background details for concerned citizens.

Second, news editors believed that BBC viewers in Britain would be interested in this massacre of refugees happening on another continent. The surviving witnesses are named in the report. Their personal tragedies are considered important enough to be of interest to citizens whose own lives are unlikely to be touched directly by these events, at least in the short term. This suggests that, as human beings, many of us have a feeling of connectedness to other humans in distress, or indeed in times of celebration, wherever they are located. Empathy, compassion and political action are not constrained by borders and boundaries. Feelings of concern and interest in the situation of other people on another continent derive from what we will refer to as a *cosmopolitan* vision.

Third, the background to this story illustrates issues of humanitarian law and human rights as the context in which we are writing about citizenship. The civil war between the government of Uganda and northern rebel groups has resulted in the displacement of over a million people. Such mass movements of people fleeing war have been a feature of the world in recent decades. Some of the victims of war become refugees, migrating across borders. A relative few reach richer countries, such as the UK, where they may seek settlement and possibly asylum. In Uganda, aid agencies, supported by funds from individuals and governments, supply essential food to camps for displaced persons. Ugandan non-governmental organizations

(NGOs) are also working to resolve the conflict. The Refugee Law Project, based at Makerere University, has interviewed hundreds of witnesses in an attempt to understand the causes of the conflict (Refugee Law Project 2004). The International Criminal Court in The Hague has started to investigate the LRA for war crimes. The LRA is said to have abducted some 20,000 children and brutally exploited them as soldiers and as sex slaves.

Thus, in the longer term, events in a remote African refugee camp may well have an impact on people in Britain. The instabilities caused by civil wars impact on global politics. Such conflicts hold back economic and social development. They result in large-scale migrations of populations, at first within the region and then beyond it, as workers and families seek safety in more stable and prosperous regions such as Europe.

Fourth, citizens have a capacity for action and may wish to respond to the massacre and the humanitarian situation in northern Uganda. In doing so they demonstrate a cosmopolitan mindset, showing concern for fellow human beings. Citizens have a range of options for action and potential intervention. They can inform themselves by accessing further details and analysis. They can use the information to express an opinion to the media, to an elected representative or to the Ugandan government. They can contribute to an aid agency working in Uganda. They can join or become active in a group campaigning for development and peace. All these options are open to young people as much as to older citizens. For example, there is a remarkable global campaign by a young Canadian, Ryan Hreljac, who created his own charity, Ryan's Well, to provide clean water to communities in Uganda, Zimbabwe, Kenya, Malawi, Ethiopia, Tanzania and Nigeria (Greenfield 2004: 8).

Finally, the full story of the conflict in Uganda includes the exploitation by the LRA of children as soldiers and sex slaves in ways that are gross violations of international human rights standards, particularly the United Nations (1989) *Convention on the Rights of the Child* (*CRC*). The significance of these standards in understanding citizenship is a major theme of this book.

Understanding citizenship

Citizenship is a site of political struggle. It is frequently defined as having two essential aspects, first a status and a set of duties and secondly a practice and an entitlement to rights. While these are certainly key elements, they do not take into account the fact that citizenship is probably most immediately experienced as a feeling of belonging. We suggest therefore that citizenship has three essential and complementary dimensions. It is a *status,* a *feeling* and a *practice.*

Citizenship as status

Citizenship is perhaps most often understood as *status*. The world is organized on the basis of nation states and almost all of the world's inhabitants are legally citizens of a state, whether it be demographically huge, like China and India, or tiny, like Vanuatu or Belize. Whatever the political regime, nationals of a state are citizens with an internationally accepted legal status that gives them some rights and usually also some duties. The rights available to citizens of autocratic states or dictatorships, including their political rights, are likely to be very restricted. In such states, duties, such as military service, may be onerous. In liberal democracies, statutory service to the state may be no more than the requirement to sit on a jury if chosen. Citizenship, in this sense, is simply the status of being a citizen. It describes the relationship of the individual to the state. The state protects citizens through laws and policing. It provides some collective benefits such as security, a system of justice, education, health care and transport infrastructure. In return, citizens contribute to the costs of collective benefits through taxation and possibly military service.

In many cases the status of 'citizen' has been achieved as a result of struggle against oppressive political control. For example, in France, the subjects of an absolute monarch achieved the status of citizen through insurrection in the 1789 Revolution. The twentieth century saw numerous successful campaigns across the world for freedom from colonial rule. In these contexts the word 'citizenship' has very positive connotations associated with freedom, equality and solidarity. Citizens are defined by their capacity to think of themselves not as passive subjects of an all-powerful ruler or government, but rather as individuals who can challenge their rulers and ultimately make a difference.

British people, however, tend to be far less confident about their legal status as citizens. They have become citizens by statute rather than by struggle. There are still debates as to whether British people can really call themselves citizens or mere *subjects* of the crown. The widespread consciousness of being British subjects has persisted into the twenty-first century. In fact, in Britain the status of 'citizen of the United Kingdom and colonies' does not go back for centuries but was created by the British Nationality Act of 1948. This ascription of the status of citizen was a key element of a new and restrictive immigration policy. It stemmed from the determination of the Labour government to distinguish between British subjects living in the UK and British subjects in British controlled colonies who were eventually denied free access to Britain. The mechanism was the institution of a distinction between British subjects (mostly outside the UK) and British citizens (mostly within the UK).

The term 'British citizen' was first introduced under the Immigration Act 1981 as a means to exclude Commonwealth citizens from freely entering the UK. It is not perhaps surprising therefore that in Britain the term citizen neither resonates positively nor is it clearly understood since the legal concept is unclear. For example, while citizenship has been developed to exclude categories of people from a right to residence, the right to vote is not exclusive to British citizens: 'Since the rights and responsibilities of British citizenship are not restricted to British nationals, the legal concept is not clearly defined. For example, Commonwealth and Irish citizens resident in the United Kingdom enjoy voting rights in local and national elections' (Smith 1997: xi).

In any country, the achievement of democracy and citizenship is an ongoing struggle, in the sense that the full realization of civil, political and social rights for all, balancing freedoms with equality, is always likely to be an aspiration rather than a fact. In Britain there have been many struggles for rights and for recognition of entitlements to rights but these have rarely been undertaken in the name of citizenship. Indeed, in persistent nationalist discourses the link between citizenship and nationality is used to exclude. In an extreme case, echoed in an attenuated but barely disguised form in the British popular press, the British National Party (BNP) promotes a sharp distinction between worthy British people and unworthy refugees, asylum seekers and immigrants.

Xenophobic political groups play on nationalistic feelings, strengthening and focusing on a division between us and them, between citizens and foreigners. Such nationalist discourses are based on a claim that the status and privileges attached to national citizenship, such as rights with respect to housing, employment and health, should not be available to migrants. In liberal democracies such restricted and nationalistic views may be widely circulated, exerting pressure on elected representatives who in many cases respond by supporting more restrictive immigration laws and definitions of citizenship. Citizenship as status is thus subject to political and legal definition and in this context has become a major site of struggle in all democracies.

Citizenship as feeling

Citizenship is a feeling of belonging to a community of citizens. However, even when individuals have the status of citizen, they may identify to a lesser or greater extent with a particular state. Although governments, communities and the media may promote feelings of national identity through national holidays, sporting events, jubilees, parades and public service broadcasting, individuals are likely to vary in the degree to which they feel they are part of the nation.

Although democratic states aspire to treat all citizens alike on the basis of equality, individuals and groups may have difficulties in accessing services. So, for example, in Britain parents of children with special educational needs (SEN) report difficulties in securing their children's right to education. Other groups may access services but not on the basis of equality. For example, in England, black community groups express concern at the differentials in achievement between different groupings of children. Overall, 48 per cent of students gained five or more A* to C GCSE grades in 2000, but students of Caribbean heritage were well below this, with just 27 per cent achieving these exam grades nationally. This national statistic masks huge local variation (Tikly *et al.* 2002). If individuals are not accessing services on the basis of equality, or they believe they are not doing so, they are likely to feel excluded. Experience of discrimination undermines a sense of belonging. A sense of belonging is a prerequisite of participative citizenship. If it is missing, so too is a sense of citizenship. This has implications both for those who feel left out and for the wider community and its elected representatives.

For many citizens, it may be easier to identify with a particular place or region. An individual may declare: 'I feel at home in Birmingham' or 'I feel proud to come from Yorkshire'. Our research with young people, reported in Chapter 6, supports the notion that feelings of identity and citizenship are frequently situated in local communities. Education, particularly a formal national curriculum, is one means for promoting identification with and positive feelings towards the nation state. With globalization and migration, increasing numbers of citizens are educated in more than one state. Programmes of student mobility and international exchanges encourage this trend and one result may be identification with more than one nation state.

Moreover, as well as pressure to develop national identities through education there is resistance. Many people, including teachers, who have the status of citizen, do not find it easy to identify with the nation or with national symbols. We have noted reluctance among British teachers and student teachers to endorse the use of national symbols, such as the flag, in school contexts. They perhaps feel that such symbols represent unthinking patriotism, discredited imperialism or an exclusive nationalism.

Some citizens who seek to belong may nevertheless be excluded. In the 1960s E.R. Braithwaite, the author of the novel *To Sir, With Love*, summed up the kinds of barriers to citizenship to which he was subjected:

> In spite of my years of residence in Britain, any service I might render the community in times of war or peace, any contribution I might make or wish to make, or any feeling I might entertain towards Britain and the British, I – like all other colored persons in Britain – am considered an 'immigrant'. Although this term indicates that we have secured entry into Britain, it describes a continuing condition in which we have no real hope of ever enjoying the desired transition to full responsible citizenship.
>
> (Braithwaite 1967, quoted in Fryer 1984: 382)

Braithwaite reminds us that for some citizens even the choice to identify with a particular group can be denied. Citizenship as feeling is often considered to be a question of identity. But even the choice of identity can be denied. Self-defined identity can be overruled by an excluding society. Braithwaite's observation that 'full responsible citizenship' was denied black settlers still has some resonance today for particular minority groups. Many British citizens continue to be viewed as outsiders, as can be observed in more recent debates about the allegiance of British Muslims (Commission on British Muslims and Islamophobia 1997, 2004; Jawad and Benn 2003).

Formal and informal barriers to full citizenship on the basis of gender and/or ethnicity continue to exit in many societies. They have been well documented in the case of the USA:

> Becoming citizens of the [American] commonwealth has been much more difficult for ethnic groups of color and for women from all racial, ethnic and cultural groups than for mainstream males. Groups of color have experienced three major problems in becoming citizens of the United States. First, they were denied citizenship by laws. Second, when legal barriers to citizenship were eliminated, they were often denied educational experiences that would enable them to attain the cultural and language characteristics needed to function effectively in the mainstream society. Third, they were often denied the opportunity to fully participate in mainstream society even when they attained these characteristics because of ... discrimination.
>
> (Banks 1997: xi)

According to this analysis, access to citizenship requires more than a legal status, though this is an essential first step. Developing this thesis further, Banks (2004: 5) observes:

> Becoming a legal citizen of a nation-state does not necessarily mean that an individual will attain structural inclusion into the mainstream society and its institutions or will be perceived as a citizen by most members of the dominant group within the nation-state. A citizen's racial, cultural, language, and religious characteristics often significantly influence whether she is viewed as a citizen within her society.

It is clear that the attitudes and behaviour of majority groups may determine whether or not minorities are able to feel included. Access to citizenship therefore requires a commitment by the state to ensuring that the education of all its citizens includes an understanding of the principles of democracy and human rights and an uncompromising challenge to racism in all its forms.

Further evidence that individual citizens may not necessarily feel included or valued, in spite of formal and perhaps legal guarantees, is provided in a study of British young people of South Asian heritage. The author concludes that:

> Asian young people generally felt that they were not being treated equally and that they were in practice second-class citizens. They also felt that their parents have, on the whole, tolerated prejudice, discrimination and harassment, particularly when they were working hard to integrate in education, business and other fields. Compared with the 1970s, young Asians in the 1990s were asserting their Britishness and were more articulate and more aggressive in their approach to highlighting unfair treatment by the institutions of society.
>
> (Anwar 1998: 191)

It is clear that the young people studied by Anwar had a clear understanding of citizenship. They perceived equality and fairness to be hallmarks of citizenship and were naturally aggrieved when it was denied to them. They felt that they did not have access to the full range of rights available to citizens to the same extent as members of the majority. In asserting their British identity they demanded that others respect their status as holders of rights and citizenship in Britain. However, individuals and institutions may resist inclusiveness and change and put up barriers to full participation. This in turn leads to the necessity to be more assertive in the struggle for equal rights. There will be conflicts and tensions within society and these are the legitimate and necessary subject of education for citizenship, which is therefore inevitably controversial.

Citizenship as practice

Citizenship is also defined in terms of *practice*, associated with democracy and with human rights. Citizenship refers to an awareness of oneself as an individual living in relationship with others, participating freely in society and combining with others for political, social, cultural or economic purposes. Active citizenship is facilitated by awareness of and access to human rights. It is not dependent on belonging to a particular nation state, though it may certainly be facilitated or restricted by membership of a state. Individuals can practise citizenship as holders of human rights, working individually, perhaps, but usually with others to change the way things are. It is this awareness of a capacity to influence the world, sometimes referred to as a sense of agency, which leads citizens to exert themselves on behalf of others.

Seen in this perspective, citizenship is not confined simply to a formal status in relation to a nation state. Nor is it confined to those able to exercise the right to vote. The scope of citizenship has expanded as new groups have demanded to be included among those who make decisions concerning their lives. The formal status of entitlement to political or voting rights has often proved insufficient to be felt as citizenship or to enable the practice of citizenship. Voting rights for women need to be followed by campaigns for real equality. Minorities may gain formal and legal equality of rights but this is rarely sufficient to guarantee equity in practice. To achieve real equality usually requires further campaigns.

Rights are, nonetheless, the essential starting point for citizenship. Rights provide the possibility to practise citizenship and to feel a sense of belonging. As we show in Chapter 3, children and young people are citizens by virtue of their entitlements to rights and their capacity to practise citizenship. They may rarely participate in the kind of activity organized by political parties, such as canvassing, leafleting or participating in formal policy debates. They may well, however, join campaigning groups and take part in marches or demonstrations, perhaps with their parents or friends. They commonly raise funds for good causes, often with the encouragement of their school or the media.

In the most mature democracies, some aspects of the practice of citizenship appear to be in decline. This is most notable in the decline in voter participation in elections. It can be argued that the start of the twenty-first century saw a crisis of democracy in those states that have the longest traditions of democratic governance. The first national elections of the century in the USA, Britain and France were notable for record levels of abstention. The US election of 2000 did not produce an indisputably fair outcome as the nation waited for the recounting of votes with 'hanging chads'. The 2002 presidential election in France became a referendum on democracy, as the candidate of the far right gained more votes than the socialist challenger and reached the final round.

As a response to the shock presence of a racist and xenophobic anti-democratic candidate in the final round of the presidential election of 2002, a French publisher produced a special guide to citizenship in a format similar to a tourist guidebook. It suggests how citizens can have an influence, as thoughtful consumers, as intelligent voters and as activists. It attempts to rouse an apathetic public:

> So, let us no longer ignore abuses of human rights or the environment and let us not allow the future of the world to be decided without us or be imposed on us. Let us react! Let's use our 'con-

sumer power' by being aware of what we buy. Let us use our 'citizen power' by voting and by keeping an eye on the way power is used. And let us use our 'activist power' by mobilising whenever a right is abused or threatened and, indeed, in order to extend rights.

(*Le Guide du Routard* 2002: 13 our translation)

The writer has a threefold conception of citizenship as practice in a European liberal democracy. Economic citizenship is exercised by acting as a responsible consumer. It may be expressed by purchasing fair-trade products or those less likely to harm the environment. Political citizenship involves voting, but also keeping informed and questioning those in power. It relies on the free availability of diverse sources of information, including the press and the internet. Active citizenship includes working with others to defend or promote human rights and the environment.

There is a dynamic relationship between citizenship as status and citizenship as practice. Citizens have human agency. They feel they can make a difference. They exercise their rights by taking action. They act to defend the rights of others. They perceive citizenship, because it is based on diversity and equality, to be about inclusiveness (Lister 1997). The practice of citizenship involves solidarity with others.

Evolving citizenship rights

Citizenship is a historical and evolutionary process associated, in Europe, with successive political struggles for rights (Marshall 1950; Klug 2000). The development of rights within nation states is closely associated with struggles for equality and for freedoms – that is to say, for citizenship. In the course of its evolution, citizenship has taken different forms and emphasized rights, duties and sense of community in varying degrees.

In Marshall's analysis, citizens first won a status that guaranteed civil rights – that is, the rule of law providing protection from arbitrary arrest and detention and certain personal freedoms. The next stage was to provide further safeguards in the form of the requirement that rulers be elected, and a third wave of citizenship rights is associated with the rights to an adequate standard of living and to education and health services.

Civil and legal rights enable citizens to feel relatively secure by ensuring personal freedoms of conscience, of religion and of movement, and an impartial system of justice based on the rule of law. The second wave of citizenship rights, political rights, was required to prevent authoritarian rulers and racist regimes, unencumbered by constitutional constraints, from deliberately undermining the security provided by civil rights. Citizens with political rights have the power to choose their rulers through elections. In a liberal democracy it is assumed that the minority, whose candidates did not achieve power, will consent to be governed and that the majority will guarantee the rights of minorities. Struggles for political rights involve the extension of voting rights and democracy.

The underlying principle of third-wave rights is that the right to human dignity can be effectively denied in situations of extreme poverty, illiteracy and illness. However, the provision of an entitlement, on an equal basis, to social rights has proved politically controversial and problematic. Socialist or communist regimes have offered equal social rights, but only at the expense of a denial of some fundamental freedoms.

Narratives of citizenship

A number of narratives of citizenship help to shape political debate. Beiner (1995) labels three major traditions or strands of citizenship as *liberal, communitarian* and *civic republican*. Each model has its strengths and its limitations and we argue that the context of globalization requires us to critically appraise these traditions and to develop new models. We propose that the concept of cosmopolitanism, unfashionable for much of the twentieth century, has much to offer and should be revisited. We suggest that a new narrative is gaining strength and that *cosmopolitan* citizenship is a worthy aspiration.

Liberal narratives of citizenship emphasize the importance of rights and freedoms in helping individuals to develop their potential by escaping the confines of social status, traditional roles and ascribed fixed identities. In other words, it emphasizes citizenship as possibility. Citizens are potentially free to choose their own identities and loyalties. They can find fulfilment in choosing their own destiny irrespective of family or cultural pressures. The *National Curriculum 2000* is arguably established on liberal principles. It provides an entitlement to learning with the intention that students find individual fulfilment. Learners should: 'develop knowledge, understanding, skills and attitudes necessary for their self-fulfilment and development as active and responsible citizens' (DfEE /QCA 1999a: 12).

The liberal tradition of citizenship stresses the rights of citizens. Rights are entitlements and universal human rights are universal entitlements in the sense that any human being can claim them. Since 1948, civil, political and social rights have been enumerated, carefully defined and codified in the *Universal Declaration of Human Rights (UDHR)* (UN 1948; see Appendix 1). Of the 30 articles, the first 20 are broadly civil rights, Article 21 consolidates political rights and Articles 22–30 are essentially social rights.

In order for rights to be guaranteed, however, there needs to be a legal framework and a court system to enforce their upholding. These are currently available essentially at national level, though there are also European courts and international courts. Constitutional instruments may well refer explicitly to international human rights instruments as underpinning national law and institutions. For instance, the Human Rights Act 1998 incorporated the *European Convention on Human Rights* (*ECHR*) (Council of Europe 1950) into UK law. That said, a legal guarantee is helpful but not sufficient to ensure that barriers to rights and citizenship are removed and social justice prevails.

Political pressure from civil society is also important, as is education. Laws and human rights, as Nobel peace prize winner, René Cassin, pointed out in a speech to teachers, are complemented by educationalists helping to promote public understanding (Alliance Israélite Universelle 1961).

While a liberal perspective stresses individual human rights, it also has its limitations. It does not necessarily ensure that equality is given due consideration, let alone achieved. It may even be taken to suggest that society is merely a collection of individuals.

The *communitarian* approach emphasizes group solidarity rather than individualism. It stresses the benefits of a sense of identity conferred by a cultural or ethnic group. It is prevalent in nationalist movements and struggles. Those aspects of citizenship education programmes that stress national identities may be considered communitarian. The limitations of this view are that it may confine individuals within predetermined ethnic or cultural identities with which they do not necessarily feel at ease. It may deny citizens the freedom to determine their own way in the world and develop as cosmopolitan citizens with multiple identities and loyalties.

The *civic republican* tradition of citizenship stresses the political community as an institutional framework capable of peacefully containing and working out the inevitable conflicts that arise in human societies. It emphasizes responsibilities to the community as a public sphere regulated by the state and attempts to confine identities of class, ethnicity, religion or culture to a so-called private sphere where the state does not restrict freedoms. A significant weakness of this view is that the distinction between public and private cannot be sustained in practice. In reality, the state is often expected to intervene in the affairs of households and religious or cultural groups under its obligation to uphold human rights and protect the vulnerable. Governments are expected, for instance, to outlaw and punish domestic violence, protect children and regulate broadcast media.

It is clear that we need to draw on and synthesize elements of all these narratives of citizenship in order to propose a programme of education for citizenship in a globalized world. A vision of a world community where national, ethnic and cultural boundaries are blurred or porous and where hybridity is increasingly the norm requires a common standard and this is potentially available in a common understanding of human rights. Even where education for democratic citizenship is an element of a *national* curriculum, it must be recognized that the characteristics of nations are not fixed but dynamic. Formal education plays a key role in helping young citizens imagine a national community, and it can also help them to imagine a global community.

Citizenship and nationalism

Writing during the First World War, the philosopher John Dewey recognized the extent to which nationalism, mediated through state education, had obliterated previous Enlightenment traditions based on cosmopolitanism:

> So far as Europe was concerned, the historic situation identified the movement for a state-supported education with the nationalistic movement in political life – a fact of incalculable significance for subsequent movements. Under the influence of German thought in particular, education became a civic function and the civic function was identified with the realization of the ideal of the national state. The 'state' was substituted for humanity; cosmopolitanism gave way to nationalism.
>
> (Dewey [1916] 2002: 108)

Dewey argues that the European Renaissance and Enlightenment movements had provided the basis for the development of a consciousness of the interconnectedness of humanity. He considers that this cosmopolitan world view was prevalent in the nineteenth century until ideologies of nationalism, perhaps inspired by the German nationalism that had strongly developed in his lifetime, refocused the loyalties of the people towards the nation rather than the world. Crucially, Dewey notes that across Europe, education was nationalized at the end of the nineteenth century. The state took control of education from religious and charitable foundations and made it compulsory. The role of teachers was redefined so that they became agents of a national state. They were expected to show loyalty to the state and promote patriotism. Thus the educational goal of introducing young people to a humanistic curriculum became subservient to a more instrumental, national curriculum. In Dewey's words, 'the "state" was substituted for humanity; cosmopolitanism gave way to nationalism'.

Dewey's analysis helps to explain the role of education in promoting nationalism as a dominant ideology throughout much of the twentieth century. In many circumstances cosmopolitanism has been presented as unpatriotic and as being in opposition to nationalism. Indeed, at various times, schooling and formal education have played a key role in disseminating visions of citizenship based on nationalist agendas.

The influence of ideologies opposed to cosmopolitanism is still very much alive. Nationalist political parties promote an identification of citizenship with an affective attachment to a single nation state and a sense of duty towards a particular nation and its members, however defined. Nationalist discourses encourage xenophobia because they make a sharp distinction between national citizens and foreigners.

Cosmopolitan citizenship

Nonetheless, cosmopolitanism survived strongly enough to provide an alternative grand narrative to that of nationalism, notably following the discrediting of ultra-nationalism as responsible for two world wars. A cosmopolitan vision underpins the *Charter of the United Nations* signed in 1945. The United Nations (UN) is an organization of independent nation states but its vision is undoubtedly humanistic. The preamble to its *Charter* proclaims: 'faith in fundamental human rights, in the dignity and worth of the human person, in the equal rights of men and women and of nations large and small' (UN 1945). This essentially cosmopolitan vision of a peaceful world based on justice and equality challenges world views based on domination or on antagonism between peoples.

Cosmopolitanism is a philosophy developed during the period of the Enlightenment, notably by Immanuel Kant (1724–1804). It is an extension of liberalism, the moral philosophy underpinning liberal democracy, which is concerned with 'upholding the dignity and inherent rights of individuals, understood as instantiations of a *universal* humanity' (Beiner 1995: 2). As we have noted, a liberal narrative of citizenship stresses the equality of all human beings with respect to their rights. At its most basic, the cosmopolitan citizen is one who 'views herself as a citizen of a world community based on common human values' (Anderson-Gold 2001: 1).

This challenges purely nationalistic conceptions of citizenship that emphasize the primacy of the national community. It suggests that the notion of community can be extended so that its limiting case is a community composed of all human beings. Such a community can be envisaged within a religious or a humanist perspective.

This simple formulation nonetheless begs the question of what is understood by a world community and what is to be included in the idea of common human values. We have argued that human rights, as set out in international instruments, constitute a standard derived from common human values:

As teachers we are likely to find our everyday professional lives easier to manage if we have firm principles on which to base our judgements and decisions. Whatever our personal religious or philosophical beliefs or our background, it should be possible for us to find common ground, on questions of values, with the vast majority of our students and their families if we refer to transcendent values such as those enunciated by representatives of international organizations and the world community. These transcendent values are expressed in declarations and conventions on human rights.

(Osler and Starkey 1996: 14)

Human rights are based on the assertion that human beings are equal in their entitlement to rights and to respect for their basic human dignity. A consciousness of human rights as universal entitlements has as its corollary an awareness of a world community comprising all human beings. This community also has institutions, particularly those of the UN.

Cosmopolitan citizenship does not deny the validity and indeed the importance of a national perspective; rather, it recognizes universal values as its standard for all contexts, including national contexts. It stresses those things that unite human beings rather than what divides them. It is epitomized by a global outlook: 'The cosmopolitan ideal combines a commitment to humanist principles and norms, an assumption of human equality, with a recognition of difference, and indeed a celebration of diversity' (Kaldor 2003: 19).

Citizenship is changing. There are a number of reasons why a limited understanding of citizenship as merely a function of nationality is no longer adequate. One of these is that globalization has enabled the development of a consciousness that identity is multiply situated. In other words, identity is far from the monolithic concept that nationalists promote. The narrow definition of citizen in relation to nationality is increasingly at odds with realities on the ground. Globalization and international migration have produced transnational communities and culturally diverse societies.

Since the mid-1980s refugees and asylum-seekers have become a very significant group of migrants within Europe. Western European states received 695,000 applications for asylum in 1992 at the height of the war in the former Yugoslavia (Castles and Davidson 2000). Although the figure dipped to 233,000 in 1996 it rose to nearly 400,000 in 1999 as a result of the war in Kosovo. Even in 2003, with the continuing conflict in Chechnya, 288,000 asylum applications were received in Western Europe, of which about 50,000 were for the UK (news.bbc.co.uk, 24 February 2004).

Simultaneously there is substantial voluntary migration of those seeking better employment or education. Indeed, one of the founding principles of the European Union (EU) is mobility of labour and the encouragement of student mobility. Increasing numbers of EU citizens migrate to a warmer climate in another state at the time of retirement. Individuals across the world now commonly hold multiple citizenships and may own two or more passports. As a consequence of all these migration trends taking place all over the world, societies have become culturally diverse and have had to change and adapt to the new demographics.

There is also resistance to demographic change brought about by migration, and hostile reactions to migration and changing cultures serve to undermine or destabilize democracy. Nationalist discourses are not confined to nationalist parties. Mainstream parties of right and left may court popular approval by asserting or implying that some citizens have a greater claim to belonging because they share a common culture and that those sharing this (national) culture are more entitled to the benefits of society than others. The promotion of such an inequitable view is profoundly undemocratic as it places conditions on entitlements to rights.

In the twenty-first century, personal identity is no longer necessarily tied to political belonging to a single nation. People's identities are multiple and this requires a reconceptualization of citizenship. Citizenship in a globalized world is increasingly internationalist and multilayered (Lister 1997: 196). A prominent example of this is the writer Edward Said. As his obituary in *The New York Times* put it:

> Mr. Said, who was born in Jerusalem during the British mandate in Palestine and emigrated to the United States when he was a teenager ... was an exemplar of American multiculturalism, at home both in Arabic and English, but, as he once put it, 'a man who lived two quite separate lives,' one as an American university professor, the other as a fierce critic of American and Israeli policies and an equally fierce proponent of the Palestinian cause. Though a defender of Islamic civilization, Mr. Said was an Episcopalian married to a Quaker ... From 1977 to 1991, he was an unaffiliated member of the Palestine National Conference, a parliament-in-exile.
>
> (Bernstein 2003)

Although Said was exceptionally talented, his multiple identities are exceptional only in that they are common public knowledge. By acknowledging that all of us can claim complex identities, it follows that citizenship 'requires a politics that plays itself out in a multiplicity of settings, from neighbourhoods to nations to the world as a whole' (Sandel 1996: 351). Citizens need to be able to think and act as multiply situated selves and education plays a crucial role in this process.

Cosmopolitan citizenship and education

Education for *cosmopolitan* citizenship is a key concept for this book. Cosmopolitan citizenship in a liberal democracy is not an alternative to national citizenship, nor is it even in tension with national citizenship. It is a way of being a citizen at any level, local, national, regional or global. It is based on feelings of solidarity with fellow human beings wherever they are situated. It expands horizons and stands opposed to narrow and exclusive definitions of citizenship:

> Education for cosmopolitan citizenship must necessarily be about enabling learners to make connections between their immediate contexts and the global context; it encompasses citizenship learning as a whole. It implies a broader understanding of national identity; it requires recognition that British identity, for example, may be experienced differently by different people. It also implies recognition of our common humanity and a sense of solidarity with others. It is insufficient, however, to feel and express a sense of solidarity with others elsewhere, if we cannot establish a sense of solidarity with others in our own communities, especially those others whom we perceive to be different from ourselves.
>
> (Osler and Vincent 2002: 124)

Cosmopolitan citizens process their multiple identities. In other words, they actively reflect on the communities to which they belong and the links that join these communities. In so doing, cosmopolitan citizens recognize others as essentially similar to themselves and arrive at a sense of citizenship based on a consciousness of humanity rather than on allegiance to a state:

> This process of recognizing oneself in the *other* leads inevitably to a cosmopolitan citizenship. This citizenship, independent of political structures and institutions, develops each individual in the understanding that one's culture is multiple, *métis* [hybrid] and that each human experience and existence is due to the contact with the *other*, who, in reality, is like oneself.
>
> (Cuccioletta 2002: 9)

That said, the context in which we are educating for citizenship is one where cosmopolitan ideals and nationalistic discourses clash, vie for attention and cause turbulence, conflict and confusion. Cosmopolitanism and nationalism coexist within nations and also within the consciousness of citizens who are subject to media and other influences that may lead them to adopt less generous dispositions. On the day of the publication of the story of the massacre in Uganda which opens this chapter, the British press was also running stories designed to create xenophobic feelings, particularly with respect to refugees and asylum-seekers.

The issue of migrants and asylum-seekers, which is, of course, a global issue, reveals dramatically the limited conception of citizenship enshrined in the legislation of the most liberal states. This is a highly contentious area as it is argued that a liberal view of human rights makes it difficult to justify privileging the needs of fellow human beings within a national polity over those in objectively considerably greater need in other countries (Nussbaum 1996). Cosmopolitan citizens are concerned both with the quality of civic life within their own national boundaries and with human rights violations or oppression wherever they occur. Thus they may be concerned that national immigration controls and regulations for the reception of asylum-seekers may effectively deny the right to dignity to newly arrived fellow inhabitants of a national territory.

It is still the case that the main political space where citizens can have a direct influence is the national state. Pragmatically, citizens are likely to have more leverage over a government that depends for re-election on their votes than over foreign governments or international organizations. That said, citizens can campaign both within and beyond national boundaries. Indeed it can be strongly argued that 'national citizenship and our national government are important to us chiefly to the degree that they become the instruments by which we exert our influence in the international community of nations' (Ignatieff 1995: 76).

Cosmopolitanism is a world view that celebrates human diversity. It is a way of looking at the world from a perspective that accepts that all human beings are equal in dignity and in rights. People everywhere have equal entitlement to consideration and to respect. Cosmopolitan citizenship is a way of thinking, feeling and acting as a citizen. Cosmopolitan citizens act locally, nationally and globally. They make connections between issues, events and challenges at all levels. They critique and evaluate within contexts of cultural diversity. They have a sense of solidarity with those denied their full human rights, whether in local communities or in distant places. They accept shared responsibility for humanity's common future. They are confident in their own multiple identities and develop new identities as they encounter and relate to other cultural groups.

Cosmopolitan citizens recognize that fellow citizens are entitled to equal rights whether they come from the same street or neighbourhood, from the same city or nation or indeed from anywhere in the world. This feeling of community and shared humanity, however, is something that has to be experienced and learnt. It requires an understanding of what community may mean when extended to the whole world. Cosmopolitan citizens need to learn which values are culturally specific and which are universal. Moreover they have to develop skills for participation and a mindset that welcomes cultural diversity. In short, cosmopolitan citizens are not born, they become cosmopolitan citizens through formal and informal education.

2 Human rights, democracy and development

Inequalities in the world

In his millennium report, the Secretary General of the UN, Kofi Annan, invited his readers to imagine the world as a village of 1000 people. He graphically describes the characteristics of today's human population:

> Some 150 of the inhabitants live in an affluent area of the village, about 780 in poorer districts. Another 70 or so live in a neighbourhood that is in transition. The average income per person is $6,000 a year, and there are more middle income families than in the past. But just 200 people dispose of 86 per cent of all the wealth, while nearly half of the villagers are eking out an existence on less than $2 per day.
>
> (Annan 2000: 14)

The world is demonstrably a very unequal place where just 20 per cent of the population (the 200 villagers in Annan's report) control the vast majority of the wealth. Nearly half the world's population experiences severe poverty. Huge disparities in wealth and income are matched by extremely unequal life chances, both within states and between them. Returning to the UN Secretary General's analogy of the village, we discover that:

> Life expectancy in the affluent district is nearly 78 years, in the poorer areas 64 years – and in the very poorest neighbourhoods a mere 52 years. Each marks an improvement over previous generations, but why do the poorest lag so far behind? Because in their neighbourhoods there is a far higher incidence of infectious diseases and malnutrition, combined with an acute lack of access to safe water, sanitation, healthcare, adequate housing, education and work.
>
> (Annan 2000: 14)

The grossly inequitable state of the world is a cause of tensions. Such inequalities create social conditions that can spawn violent political conflicts. This is increasingly taking place within as well as between nations. The consequent instability has repercussions across the world, as civilians flee from war zones. Moreover, while civil wars and inter-state conflicts continue, there is little chance of promoting economic and social development. Annan went on to observe: 'There is no predictable way to keep the peace in this [global] village. Some districts are relatively safe while others are wracked by organized violence' (2000: 15).

The anarchy that prevails in increasingly numerous failing and failed states (Gray 2001) and the rise of ethno-national governments prepared to organize and commit genocide (Chua 2003) appear to be a by-product of globalization. In those parts of the world where government scarcely exists, ruthless organizations like the LRA, cited in Chapter 1, can exploit children and civilians locally and terrorize fellow human beings at home or abroad as part of a political strategy. Poverty and inequality are barriers to citizenship and lead to instability. Indeed, it is hard to be optimistic about the future of the global community, given the current unjust and unequal state of the world.

Annan (2000: 15) challenges the world community to act in order to secure its survival: 'Who among us would not wonder how long a village in this state can survive without taking steps to ensure that all its inhabitants can live free from hunger and safe from violence, drinking clean water, breathing clean air, and knowing that their children have real chances in life?' As Annan suggests, it is in the interests of all states and their peoples to promote peace, development and democracy in order to ensure our survival. We need to protect and promote a society based on freedoms and human rights. This is, after all, the aspiration of all people according to the *Charter of the United Nations*. While peace, democracy and human rights are established in some parts of the world, they are threatened by instability in others.

Globalization and its consequences

Globalization has produced winners and losers. The winners gain employment, consumer goods and services, and opportunities to make money. The losers fall victim to social exclusion. Neo-liberal economic agendas deliberately undermine the social protection mechanisms that trade unions have won for members and the measures that states have put in place to protect fragile sectors of their economies. In this sense, globalization has, in many cases, greatly increased the forms and scope of social exclusion (Robertson 2003).

Globalization is contested in so far as it has involved governments of nation states adopting a neo-liberal economic agenda. The International Monetary Fund (IMF) has exerted huge pressures to privatize on countries desperate for international investment. Neo-liberalism privileges macro-economic performance over the rights and welfare of citizens. It is often accompanied by structural adjustments to national economies that close or transform significant sectors of the economy and result in unemployment or worsening conditions for workers. As the deregulation that accompanies neo-liberal economic programmes removes the safeguards and protection that trade unions achieved in the twentieth century, inequality increases. The most economically powerful citizens find new ways of increasing their wealth and incomes. These inequalities are a source of instability and conflict. Globalization can be seen as 'a wild process involving interconnectedness and exclusion, integration and fragmentation, homogenisation and diversity' (Kaldor 2002).

This neo-liberal model of globalization is not inevitable, but it has been dominant. Although by definition globalization simply 'refers both to the compression of the world and the intensification of consciousness of the world as a whole' (Robertson 1992: 8), such a sober definition does not do justice to the effervescent effects of globalization on people's lives.

Citizens in liberal democracies have real power to influence and change governments. They bear ultimate responsibility for taking forward the UN consensus agenda of justice, peace and social progress. However, in a context of globalization, governments of nation states are not the only powerful entities. Transnational institutions, particularly financial corporations, exercise economic pressure on governments and constrain their freedom of action. There is considerable academic debate on whether this means that the importance of the nation state is undermined. For instance, it is claimed that the power of the state is reduced because: 'a multiplicity of social circles, communication networks, market relations and lifestyles, none of them specific to any particular locality, now cut across the boundaries of the national state. This is apparent in each of the pillars of sovereignty: in tax-raising, police responsibilities, foreign policy and military security' (Beck 2000: 4).

This claim that the importance of the nation state is being undermined is sometimes overstated. National governments still exercise control over and responsibility for most aspects of their economy and society. It is true that there is increasing pooling of sovereignty in the EU, but national governments remain the most significant authority with respect to taxation, policing and foreign policy, including military deployment. This was clearly illustrated in the case of the 2003 Iraq war when each European government made its own decision to participate or not in spite of membership of the UN, the EU and the North Atlantic Treaty Organization (NATO).

Beck is one of a number of commentators who argue that globalization has undermined democracy and human rights because transnational corporations have diminished or removed the power of the nation state to deliver social progress to its citizens. New transnational forms of active, indeed militant, citizenship are developing among those opposed to the contemporary power and influence of transnational entities. They perceive the vast multinational corporations to be rapidly homogenizing the world, destroying its diversity, and threatening democratic and welfare rights that have been achieved through the struggle of previous generations (Robertson 2003).

The consciousness of the challenge of injustice and inequity in the face of apparently overwhelming economic forces is a space in which new forms of democracy and hence new forms of citizenship are developing. The World Social Forum (WSF) that started in Porto Alegre, Brazil in 2001 has attracted thousands of participants from hundreds of social movements to its annual meetings. It aims to provide a space for developing alternatives to neo-liberal globalization under the slogan 'Another World is Possible'. Its members belong to movements that practise political action independently of political parties. Active citizenship, in the sense of individuals aiming to exercise real influence on decisions, is possibly more widespread in the twenty-first century than at any previous time in history. It has indeed been argued that globalization requires or engenders democratization as a by-product (Robertson 2003).

There is empirical evidence to support the case that globalization and democratization are developing concurrently. The United Nations Development Programme (UNDP) reports that across the world there has been a movement towards accountable government, freer and fairer elections, better-protected human rights and a greater role for organizations within civil society (UNDP 2002: 10). Between 1980 and 2001, 81 countries took significant steps towards democracy, including 33 military regimes that were replaced by civilian governments. The number of states holding multi-party elections more than doubled over the period. A free press existed in 125 countries, with 62 per cent of the world population.

Another important indicator of democratization is that from 1990 to 2001 the number of countries ratifying human rights conventions and covenants increased dramatically. The UN *Convention on the Rights of the Child* 1989 has been accepted universally. The number of countries ratifying the *International Covenant on Economic Social and Cultural Rights* (ICESCR) and the *International Covenant on Civil and Political Rights* (ICCPR) grew from 90 to nearly 150 (UNDP 2002).

These are encouraging signs of an increasing acknowledgement of the importance of respect for human rights and of democracy as the political system most likely to preserve freedoms and promote equalities. However, it is not the case that there will necessarily be smooth progress towards democratic governments across the world. Democracy faces many threats and only the combined efforts of committed citizens will ensure its survival, let alone its progress.

Alternative globalization movements, like the WSF have the potential both to renew democracy and citizenship and also to undermine it. A discourse that caricatures and attacks transnational economic corporations rather than governments for reversing social progress risks minimizing the power of elected governments. It is a short step to implying that forms of democracy based on national parliaments are irrelevant. Thus anti-globalization protestors, members of one of the most original and active democratic political movements of the early twenty-first century, may collude in a discourse of globalization that may actually persuade people to accept their lot fatalistically (Hirst 2002).

Fatalism is arguably the greatest threat to democracy and a vision of a just and peaceful world society (Keane 2003). Feelings of powerlessness and lack of agency provide a political space for authoritarian movements. Active citizenship based on struggle and on rights stands opposed to apathy. Citizens have scope to exercise power and influence in support of peace, justice and social progress. However, the pursuit of these goals requires understanding and this gives a crucial role to education.

Apathy and fatalism are not the only threats to established democracies. The attack on the World Trade Centre, New York, on 11 September 2001, launched by activists educated in Western universities and taking advantage of freedoms of movement, of communication and of association, was 'an attack on the fundamental principles of freedom, democracy, the rule of law and justice' (Held 2001).

Perhaps the major lesson of 11 September is that frontiers and geographical distance no longer protect the privileged populations of the North. Echoing McLuhan, Plesch concludes that 'the global village has shrunk to Earth Avenue' (2002: 8). In other words, those committed to justice and peace in the world by working for human rights, have as neighbours those for whom terror is a political weapon. This juxtaposition makes democracy and civilization fragile. One of the greatest challenges to democracy is to remain focused on human rights whilst creating structures that protect civilian populations from terrorism.

This challenge applies at local, national and global levels. The opportunities and the threats are finely balanced:

> Many hoped that the September 11 terrorist attacks would inspire global unity in confronting the challenges of national and international governance ... But there is an equally strong possibility that the attacks and their aftermath will further weaken global

institutions, undermine human rights and exacerbate social and economic fragmentation.

(UNDP 2002: 9)

In fact the threats to democracy and human rights are very real. Amnesty International has identified strong forces working against the UN agenda of justice and peace through human rights. In a study of 155 countries, it recorded that in 2003:

- extrajudicial executions were carried out in 47 countries;
- victims of torture and ill-treatment by security forces, police and other state authorities were reported in 132 countries;
- prisoners of conscience were held in 44 countries;
- people were arbitrarily arrested and detained without charge or trial in 58 countries.

(Amnesty International 2004)

Indeed, a number of states that pride themselves on being liberal democracies, such as Israel, the UK and the USA, are among those states identified by Amnesty as undermining human rights not only by failing to control such abuses but also by deliberately condoning them as part of a strategy for combating terrorism. The threats to liberal democracy are global and they may include policies designed to promote security. Citizens need to be vigilant in protecting human rights and civil liberties from violations from their own governments as well as from external agencies.

Human rights, peace, democracy and development

Within Western democracies, the term 'human rights' is often linked in the media and in the public imagination to violations of civil and political rights exposed by organizations such as Amnesty International or Human Rights Watch. During the Cold War, communist governments expressed distrust of liberal conceptions of human rights, stressing collective social and economic rights as having priority over individual political freedoms. We argue that neither position does justice to the power of a culture based on the human rights covered in the 30 articles of the *Universal Declaration* (see Appendix 1). Human rights are indivisible and interdependent, and it is erroneous to claim priority for certain rights over others. Recognition of human rights is a prerequisite for any social interaction that is not subject to the pressures of abusive or arbitrary force. Any negotiation with respect to business or to daily life depends on an acceptance of the rule of law and the renouncing by individuals and groups of coercion by violence.

Human rights are proclaimed as universal principles. There is a consensus view by all the governments of the world that this is the case. At the World Conference on Human Rights in Vienna in 1993, 171 states, representing 98 per cent of the world's population, signed a Declaration and Programme of Action which reaffirmed in Article 1:

> the solemn commitment of all States to fulfil their obligations to promote universal respect for, and observance and protection of, all human rights and fundamental freedoms for all in accordance with the Charter of the United Nations, other instruments relating to human rights, and international law. The universal nature of these rights and freedoms is beyond question.
>
> (UNCHR 1994: 194)

This is also the view of the thousands of NGOs across the world, many of them working in partnership with governments and with the UN as key actors in what has come to be called 'global civil society' (Keane 2003). The World Conference on Human Rights was attended by over a thousand NGOs, meeting alongside governments in the NGO Forum. The 2000 participants adopted many recommendations, beginning, like the governments, with a statement reaffirming the universality of human rights: 'It is strongly and unequivocally affirmed that all human rights are universal and are equally applicable in different social, cultural and legal traditions. Claims of relativism can never justify violations of human rights under any circumstances' (UNCHR 1994: 230). The UN is thus able to claim legitimately that the rights embedded in the *Universal Declaration of Human Rights* 'have gained prominence as a universally recognised set of norms and standards that increasingly inform all aspects of our relations as individuals and as collective members of groups, within communities and among nations' (UN 1998).

The goals of the UN as set out in its Charter provide guiding principles to cosmopolitan citizens:

> We the peoples of the United Nations [are] determined:
> - to save succeeding generations from the scourge of war, which twice in our lifetime has brought untold sorrow to mankind, and
> - to reaffirm faith in fundamental human rights, in the dignity and worth of the human person, in the equal rights of men and women and of nations large and small, and
> - to establish conditions under which justice and respect for the obligations arising from treaties and other sources of international law can be maintained, and

- to promote social progress and better standards of life in larger freedom.

(United Nations 1945)

The four aims of the UN are, then: peace through the avoidance of war; human rights and equality; universal respect for international law; and social progress. These have more recently been expressed as the three global priorities of *peace, democracy* and *development* (UN 1998). Peace, including respect for international law, democracy and human rights, and social progress and development all require a commitment to human rights by states and an understanding of human rights by individuals. The UN *Declaration on the Right to Development* (1986) recognized the key importance of this economic and social collective right. At the World Conference on Human Rights of 1993 this was reaffirmed and linked to democracy as the expression of the concept most likely to ensure the third goal of the UN *Charter*, namely, social progress: 'Democracy, development and respect for human rights and fundamental freedoms are interdependent and mutually reinforcing. Democracy is based on the freely expressed will of the people to determine their own political, economic, social and cultural systems and their full participation in all aspects of their lives' (UNCHR 1994: 195).

The achievement of peace, development and democracy requires a culture of human rights and this in turn can be powerfully promoted through education. This was expressed by one of the architects of the *Universal Declaration*, René Cassin, in an address to teachers:

When [teachers] teach about human rights, when they convey to their pupils the notion of their rights, their dignity and their duties as citizens and human beings, then they are carrying out a task that complements wonderfully the work that we have achieved at the highest level ... Legal force of itself is only a secondary safety valve: it is the education of young people and also of adults that constitutes the primary and real guarantee for minority groups faced with racial hatred that leads so easily to violence and murder.

(Alliance Israélite Universelle 1961: 123, *our translation*)

Cassin's argument is twofold. First, rights are only meaningful when people know about them and understand them. Second, it is the culture of a society more than the law itself that creates the conditions for democracy and for social peace. The law contributes in its turn to the creation of such a culture. For example, in Britain, anti-discriminatory legislation, notably the Race Relations Act 1976, which outlawed both direct and indirect racial discrimination and gave powers to a Commission for Racial Equality, has contributed to a social climate that supports struggles for racial justice

(Parekh 1991a; Blackstone *et al.* 1998). Despite limitations and flaws, the law has enabled a climate to develop in which direct discrimination and overt manifestations of racism are no longer a regular feature of daily life.

One of the earliest tasks of the UN was the drafting of a definition of fundamental human rights and this was achieved in the space of three years. The *UDHR*, proclaimed on 10 December 1948, proposes a vision of a 'human family', that is to say a global community. The preamble affirms that all human beings on the planet are entitled to equal dignity and bear equal rights. Recognition of this equality, it asserts, is the basis for 'freedom, justice and peace in the world'.

The creation of the UN did not outlaw nationalism, but it did start to create a climate in which nationalist ideologies based on racism, xenophobia, colonialism and abuse of human rights could be challenged as inimical to the internationally accepted principles embodied in the *UDHR*. By acknowledging the essential dignity and equal entitlement to rights of all human beings, human rights provide a set of principles that enable diverse societies to flourish rather than fragment. As a culture of human rights has developed across the world, and as a globalized media reveals previously hidden injustices, oppression, exploitation and arbitrary use of violence, so demands for justice and social progress are no longer confined to concern for fellow nationals.

The acceptance of human rights as basic standards for all states has implications for political systems. Human rights are most likely to be safe-guarded in a pluralist, liberal democracy, and democracy is effectively a right under Article 21 of the *UDHR*, which addresses participative govern-ment based on 'periodic and genuine elections which shall be by universal and equal suffrage'. The fact that many states still fail to hold free and fair elections does not detract from the universal principle that citizens have a right to participate in genuine elections.

Within Europe, human rights have been given a legal guarantee under the *European Convention on Human Rights* (*ECHR*) (Council of Europe 1950) which by 2004 had been ratified by the 44 member states of the Council of Europe, including the 25 member states of the EU.

The formal title of the *ECHR* links human rights and 'fundamental free-doms'. US president Franklin Roosevelt first publicly enunciated four freedoms in a speech to Congress in January 1941: 'we look forward to a world founded upon four essential human freedoms. The first is freedom of speech and expression – everywhere in the world. The second is freedom of every person to worship God in his own way – everywhere in the world. The third is freedom from want … The fourth is freedom from fear …' (Roosevelt 1941). This speech is echoed in the preamble to the *Universal Declaration*, which proclaims 'freedom of speech and belief and freedom from any fear and want' as 'the highest aspiration of the common people' (UN 1948, see Appendix 1).

The *UDHR* claims these freedoms to be essential to a vision of the good society defined from below (the 'highest aspiration of the *common people'*). The first two are civil liberties, essential in a democracy. Freedom from fear is about security and rights with respect to the legal system, such as freedom from arbitrary arrest and the outlawing of torture and inhuman and degrading treatment. Freedom from want implies a system of welfare with regards to basic needs such as clean water, food, housing and medical care.

The *ECHR* (Council of Europe 1950) guarantees fundamental political freedoms, essential for a flourishing democracy and civil society, notably:

- freedom of thought, conscience and religion (Article 9);
- freedom of expression (Article 10);
- freedom of peaceful assembly and association with others (Article 11).

Together these freedoms underpin societies and a world order based on an aspiration to justice and peace.

Education and a global culture of human rights

Liberal democracies are potentially fragile, in particular where apathy and fatalism allow strongly nationalist or xenophobic parties to gain political control, as happened notoriously in Germany in 1932–3. One antidote to this threat is education. This is recognized in the *UDHR*, which calls on governments, schools and individuals 'by teaching and education to promote respect for these rights and freedoms'. Education, citizenship and human rights are indivisible and mutually reinforcing parts of a system designed to promote peace through justice and fundamental freedoms.

The interdependence of democracy, human rights and education is stressed in the preamble to the *ECHR* which suggests that fundamental freedoms 'are best maintained on the one hand by an effective political democracy and on the other by a common understanding and observance of the human rights upon which they depend' (Council of Europe 1950). A 'common understanding and observance' of human rights depends significantly on education. One of the primary purposes of state education systems is to transmit common values and principles. In liberal democracies these include the fundamental rights and freedoms on which a democratic system depends.

The United Nations Educational, Scientific and Cultural Organization (UNESCO) is the specialist agency of the UN that promotes education and a culture of human rights. Its Director General, Koichiro Matsuura, reflected on the potential of education both to promote human rights and alternatively to support goals that are antithetical to those of the UN. Education is an instrument of state policy and xenophobic or belligerent governments will use it to promote their own ends:

> We have to note that, unfortunately, education has not always and in all circumstances served to liberate peoples from the barriers of ignorance. It hasn't always helped them to affirm their dignity nor to map their own destiny freely. It has also served, and continues to do so, to bolster ruling elites, to exclude and even, it has to be said, to ferment conflicts. And this is precisely because education is not just a means of acquiring knowledge, but also a vehicle for moral and ideological training available to any social organisation.
>
> (Matsuura 2000, *our translation*)

Matsuura goes on to question whether education in the spirit of the UN is compatible with equally powerful claims to the freedom for communities to determine their own culture. He observes that it is often women and girls whose human rights are denied when claims to cultural specificity outside the frame of reference provided by international standards are pursued. They may be denied access to education or to the best quality education available, particularly when resources are limited. Other discriminatory practices operating within schools, such as low expectations of female students and the use of textbooks which reinforce gender stereotyping, are sometimes justified as being in keeping with community norms and cultural practices. Such direct discrimination against girls of school age, particularly in poorer countries, is paralleled by discriminations experienced by minorities in both richer and poorer states whose cultures may not be taken into account by the dominant majority.

Matsuura notes that rights to equality clash with claims to cultural expression. He responds by reaffirming the importance of acknowledging the universality of human rights:

> In spite of the vast number of systems of values, surely a common corpus of values is acknowledged in the Universal Declaration of Human Rights? The respect of this text by all human communities will in any case determine whether humanity can control its own destiny. And this is precisely the crusade being undertaken by UNESCO.
>
> (Matsuura 2000)

Human rights principles may not directly resolve clashes, but they do provide a framework within which conflicts can be negotiated. Claims to the right to cultural expression may well be triggered by a perception that there is no recognition of equality of rights. A human rights framework asserts this equality as the basis for interaction. The resolution of conflicts of rights is likely to require intervention from those with skills of intercultural evaluation or, in the last resort, judgements of the courts.

The creation of a global culture of human rights appears to be the only means by which the universal goals of peace, development and democracy can be achieved. Other radical solutions, such as state socialism, have been tried but have failed to deliver both development and freedoms. Education has a crucial role in promoting a culture of human rights. In turn, such a culture has profound implications for educational structures and priorities.

The concern to promote a global culture of human rights is international, but it is equally relevant and applicable at national and at local level. For example, the UK government, in passing the Human Rights Act 1998, sought to promote a culture of rights, based on a 'shared understanding'. A government minister expressed this as follows:

> The new culture that we want to build is one in which the Human Rights Act gives us a shared understanding of what is fundamentally right and wrong, a culture where people recognize the duties that citizens owe to each other and the wider community and are willing to fulfil them – and one in which public authorities understand that the Human Rights Act defines what the basic rights are.
> (Hansard (House of Lords) 2000a)

While the building of such a culture at national level can be the responsibility of both government and NGOs, the building of such a culture in microcosm, at school level, is a prime responsibility of headteachers and school governing bodies. Parts 2 and 3 of *Changing Citizenship* explore ways in which this culture can be promoted and considers the benefits to schools of adopting such an approach.

Globalization means that democracy now operates on many different levels. Citizens participate in democratic processes at all levels from the global to the local. The nation state is no longer the only locus for democracy. In other words, citizenship is local, national and also global. As we explore, notably in Chapter 6, individuals, including young people, practise citizenship within local contexts such as the neighbourhood and the school and they may also be involved in movements and campaigns on international issues. Citizenship in this global context supports democracy and human rights as necessary conditions for sustainable development, social progress and peace.

3 Children as citizens

Introduction

Debates about the changing nature of citizenship generally exclude more than 40 per cent of the world's population, namely children.[1] When political theorists consider the processes of democratization or policy-makers discuss ways of revitalizing democracy, little thought is given to the interests and concerns of children and young people. Politicians may not feel pressure to prioritize the interests of a group of citizens who do not have an entitlement to vote. Even when citizenship education is placed on the agenda as a means of strengthening democracy, children and young people are rarely consulted about their needs. As we explore in Part 2 of *Changing Citizenship*, the young have tended to be seen simply as consumers of citizenship education, rather than as partners in a project to strengthen democracy.

This is not to suggest that children and young people are neglected by social policy-makers or commentators. Stories which link young people, particularly adolescents, with antisocial behaviour and crime are common in the media. Indeed, the supposed deficiencies of the young serve as a proxy measure for the general health of the nation (Griffin 1993; Osler and Vincent 2003). Young people are often portrayed as threatening yet politically apathetic. This deficit model of the young is then applied in education and particularly in the construction of citizenship education programmes (Osler 2000c; Starkey 2000; Osler and Starkey 2000). Young learners are not yet widely recognized as partners who need to be consulted. At best they are viewed as citizens-in-waiting who need to be inducted into their future role. All too often, however, they are seen as needy individuals whose incompetence needs to be addressed.

As we have illustrated in Chapter 2, efforts to develop and strengthen citizenship education and efforts to democratize and revitalize public institutions are taking place in contexts which remain in many ways profoundly undemocratic. Poverty, war and conflict combine to increase levels of inequalities across the globe. Children and young people, learning about justice, equality and human rights, remain acutely aware of injustice and inequalities in their local communities and in the wider world. It is important that education programmes acknowledge the gap between democratic ideals and students' everyday realities. The challenge is to encourage students as citizens to take responsibility for addressing the gap between the democratic ideal and the reality. Education for citizenship is an important element in the project of strengthening and revitalizing democracy, but the success of the project also depends on the determination of governments, politicians and civil society to address inequalities and injustices. Young people cannot be expected to solve all the world's problems, but they have a vital contribution to make in helping to shape the future.

This chapter examines children's status and rights as citizens, identifying issues which need to be addressed if we are to ensure greater democracy and inclusion in education. We examine the implications of the UN *Convention on the Rights of the Child (CRC)* 1989 for education policy. We are concerned both with the implementation of the *CRC* as a governmental human rights obligation and with its use to broaden and extend common understandings of human rights and children's citizenship.

We consider the significance to education policy and practice of recognizing children as citizens, drawing on research into children's participation in school decision-making and the use of children's voices in research reports to demonstrate how children have much to contribute to education policy and practice. We argue that through recognizing children as citizens and engaging with student voices, educators, policy-makers and researchers can increase their understanding of learning and teaching processes and of what constitutes a successful learning community. Moreover, by drawing on the *CRC* as a framework they can ensure that the principles of inclusion and non-discrimination are built into their agendas.

The chapter concludes by discussing changes in conceptions of childhood in recent decades, examining the extent to which children are now recognized as citizens in their own right, rather than as citizens-in-waiting. We reflect on ways in which the *CRC* has contributed towards changes in children's status and in legal and education policy frameworks, and consider the impact of these changes on our understandings of childhood.

A world fit for children?

In September 1990, in the same month that the *CRC* was adopted, the first World Summit for Children was held in New York, bringing together leaders from over 70 countries. An *African Charter on the Rights and Welfare of the Child* (Organization of African Unity 1990) was agreed that same year. The *European Convention on the Exercise of Children's Rights (ECECR)* (Council of Europe 1996) which focuses on procedural rights and seeks to support the

CRC and contribute to its implementation in member states of the Council of Europe, was opened for signature in January 1996 (Jeleff 1996). The *ECECR* entered into force in July 2000 and as of July 2004 had been signed by 24 states and ratified by 9 of these. Effectively, the *CRC* has put children's rights on national and international policy agendas (see Appendix 2 for a simplified version of the *CRC*).

In 2002, the UN held a Special Session on Children. World leaders made a further commitment to children's rights in *A World Fit for Children*. This document addresses ten key principles and pledges:

- the best interests of the child (putting children first);
- poverty reduction (investment in children and addressing child labour);
- an end to discrimination, recognizing that all girls and boys are born free and equal;
- development for all: protection, health and good nourishment are essential for human development; governments commit themselves to fight diseases and causes of hunger and to supporting safe environments;
- education for all; an entitlement to free, compulsory and good quality primary education for all;
- protection from harm and exploitation;
- protection from war;
- combating HIV/AIDS;
- respecting children's right to express themselves, listening to them and ensuring their participation;
- protecting the natural environment and protecting children from the effects of disasters and environmental problems.

The list addresses both civil and political rights and social, economic and cultural rights and reminds us how these are interdependent. Children will not be able to claim their civil and political rights (e.g. freedom of expression, non-discrimination) unless action is also taken to ensure basic needs and social, economic and cultural rights (health, adequate nutrition, basic security). The governments of rich countries have committed themselves to realizing children's rights at home as well as globally. This agenda is proposed by the UN but its implementation requires action by national governments, NGOs and by individual citizens. The principles apply to all children, whether they live in relatively prosperous or in developing countries. In particular, teachers have a key role to play in putting children first, ending discrimination and listening to their students.

UN *Convention on the Rights of the Child*

The *CRC* is now universally recognized. It has been ratified by 192 states and the remaining 2 (Somalia and the USA) have signed it, indicating their intention to ratify. The *CRC* came into being in 1989 although the drafting process began ten years earlier, in response to a formal proposal by Poland. From 1983, NGOs began to play a very significant role in the process. Although the industrialized countries were over-represented throughout the drafting process, this bias towards the North was offset by the particularly active participation of a number of developing countries, notably Algeria, Argentina, Senegal and Venezuela (Cantwell 1992).

At a base level, human rights are safeguards against governmental abuse of power. Yet they are clearly much more than this. They provide us with a standard against which we can evaluate policy development. We are interested in the ways in which the rights embodied in the *CRC* might provide a framework within which we can assess policies and their impact on children and young people's development as cosmopolitan citizens. So, for example, the right to education is specified in Article 28 of the *CRC* and the principles and values on which that education should be based are spelt out in Article 29 (see Appendix 3 for the full text of these articles). Together, Articles 28 and 29 provide us with clear guidelines for establishing education for citizenship. As the *CRC* is a universally recognized and accepted standard, its prescription is valid in any given national context.

Children's right to an education in line with the principles set out in Article 29 give legitimacy to educational programmes that may be contested by pressure groups with political or moral agendas. The principles provide a common standard for curriculum development, to ensure that children are prepared to live together, respecting equality and diversity, recognizing our interdependence at local, national and international levels.

Equally, the *CRC* is used as a tool for combating discrimination, since the rights specified apply to all children and young people under 18, without exception, and the state has an obligation to protect children from discrimination and to take action to promote these rights (Article 2). Generally, rights are not absolute, and the rights of any individual may be in tension with those of others. The *CRC* recognizes the specific needs of particular groups of children, such as those with disabilities (Article 23), those in public care (Article 20) and refugees (Article 22). Those responsible for providing education and other services need to assess the degree to which they are ensuring the equal rights of these particular groups of children and avoiding practices which lead to discriminatory outcomes. Article 3 requires schools and all other institutions to give primary consideration to the best interests of the child in any course of action taken. Effectively, the *CRC* can be seen as a policy tool through which all are empowered to exercise their equal human rights.

The *CRC* marks an important development in international law on children's rights since, unlike the Declaration which preceded it, a Convention is legally binding on all states which ratify it. A special treaty body, the UN Committee on the Rights of the Child, exists to support the process of its implementation. State parties are required to report to the Committee on the measures they have taken to implement the *CRC* two years after its entry into force and subsequently every five years (Article 44). The Committee can request further information from those states that fail to provide sufficient information and, under Article 45, can take into consideration reports from NGOs and other competent bodies. These measures are important, for the Committee can make suggestions and recommendations based on the reports it receives under Articles 44 and 45. NGO reports to the UN Committee on the Rights of the Child are thus potentially very influential. No government wishes to receive an unfavourable report from the UN Committee on its record in guaranteeing children's human rights.

In the UK, NGOs have collaborated to produce comprehensive reports to the UN Committee on the extent to which law, policy and practice comply with the principles and standards in the *CRC* (Lansdown and Newell 1994; CRAE 2002). Such initiatives provide a powerful example of how citizens can act to promote children's rights and open up debates about the status of children in society. For example, the first UK NGO report argued that: 'The first and most urgent task must be to ensure that legislation throughout the UK no longer tolerates physical or mental violence to children. Article 19 insists that children must be protected from "*all forms of physical or mental violence*"' (Lansdown and Newell 1994: 56).

In 2004, as the Children Bill went through Parliament, the 'Children are Unbeatable' campaign, which has among its supporters children's welfare and children's rights groups and a significant number of Members of Parliament, highlighted how current legislation affords children less protection from violence than adults, since courts have allowed parents the common law defence of 'reasonable chastisement' and acquitted parents of assault or cruelty even in cases where they have caused serious bruising through use of a belt or cane. What is interesting is that the debate generated by 'Children are Unbeatable' has been framed, at least in part, not only by reference to the need to protect children but also explicitly in terms of children's human rights and particularly their right to dignity. Campaigners have drawn attention to the fact that UK law is not in conformity with international standards and that other European countries have laws which ban parents from smacking children.

The Chair of the Committee on the Rights of the Child, Hoda Badran, commended the creative process by which the first UK NGO report was drawn up through the development of a network, the production of consultation papers and engagement with children and young people:

Non-governmental organizations have a vital part to play in this process, and this is expressly recognized in Article 45 which stresses that the Committee is entitled to seek their expertise on the implementation of the Convention ... [The process] represents a major innovatory contribution to the methodology of monitoring the state of children's rights within an individual country and as such may be of much interest internationally.

(Lansdown and Newell 1994: v)

Education researchers also have a key role in disseminating the results of their research, so that NGOs are able to draw on evidence relating to the implementation of children's rights in education.

The *CRC* provides an internationally agreed set of minimum standards for children, defined as all those under the age of 18 years. Children are now universally recognized as a group to which human rights law applies. The *CRC* is both an agenda for action and a means by which public understanding and education on children's rights can be developed. The very existence of the *CRC* has enhanced the position of children's rights internationally, and heightened public awareness of these rights. Since the end of the Cold War there has been increased cooperation between states on children's rights. Emergent democracies face a number of pressures, both internal and external, to address human rights issues, and international collaboration has helped support a climate in which the protection of children's rights remains a relatively high priority.

One of the special features of the *CRC* is that it integrates economic and social rights with civil and political rights, effectively recognizing the interdependence and indivisibility of these rights. Children's rights, as covered in the *CRC*, have been categorized as the three Ps: those of protection, provision (services, material benefits) and participation. The *CRC* recognizes that children, particularly those in exceptionally difficult conditions, need special protection, and that children may have group needs for which specific provision must be made. Moreover, children have the right to express their views (see Article 12 in Appendix 3) and to receive appropriate information and education to enable them to participate in decisions about their own lives and futures. Children are citizens, rather than citizens-in-waiting: 'Respect for children as human beings means they are no longer perceived as mere *objects* of protection but as *subjects*, bearers of human rights like all human beings. This new perception applies to the child as an individual as well as to children as a social category' (Verhellen 2000: 34).

The principle of indivisibility of rights established in the *CRC* is perhaps of particular importance to those states where widespread poverty prevents the majority of children from effectively claiming their rights. In practice, economic and social rights cannot be separated from political and cultural rights. Under Article 28, for example, states which have ratified the

CRC are required to engage in international cooperation to implement the children's right to education and to facilitate access to scientific and technical knowledge and modern teaching methods. It states that 'particular account shall be taken of the needs of developing countries'. Article 45, also concerned with international cooperation to secure the implementation of the *CRC*, permits the Committee to transmit reports from state parties which contain a request or need for technical advice or assistance to the UN Children's Fund and other competent bodies, and to include the Committee's observations and suggestions on such requests. Under the *CRC*, state parties who are unable to fulfil their obligations for social or economic reasons might request the support and cooperation of other state parties in order to secure children's rights.

Children's rights, education policy and research

In the UK, relatively little attention has been given to the concept of children's rights within mainstream education policy or research. For example, the Department of Education and Skills (DfES) rarely makes reference to rights in education in the context of England (Tomaševski 1999). This is in contrast with the rights-based approach to education which has been promoted by the UK government in the context of international aid policies (DFID 2000). In other words, a rights-based approach is recognized by the UK government as the basis for policy development, yet human rights principles are not systematically applied to the development of education policy in England.

Despite evidence which suggests that by consulting with young people education researchers and practitioners may be able to increase the effectiveness of teaching and learning, consultation processes which would give children a voice have, until recently, been given very little consideration by government agencies in England. However, the official report *Learning to Listen* (DfES 2003) suggests an encouraging departure from this trend, citing examples of government consultations on a range of issues, including the needs of young people in public care; the policy development of HM Treasury's Child Trust Fund; the development of effective leaflets about the Children and Family Court Advisory Service; and on priorities in rural areas, such as improved housing, transport and local services.

Unfortunately there is, as yet, no statutory obligation to consult with children in the process of educational policy development. The White Paper, *Schools: Achieving Success* (DfES 2001b) suggests that children in English schools will be consulted concerning the quality of schooling they receive:

> We will encourage students' active participation in the decisions
> which affect them, about their learning and more widely. School
> councils can be an important way of doing so ... The National
> Healthy School Standard involves pupils in policy development
> and gives them the opportunity to take responsibility for some
> aspects of school life and the school environment. Furthermore,
> Ofsted inspectors will now systematically seek the views of a
> school's pupils as part of its inspection. We will also find out the
> views of children and young people as we develop and evaluate
> policy.
>
> (DfES 2001b: 28)

The emphasis here is on *encouragement*, rather than obligation. There is, for
example, no proposal that school councils or other student consultative
bodies be made mandatory.

This commitment to engage young people in policy development and
school inspection procedures is not matched by any commitment to engage
them in school governance. Legislative reforms on the constitution of governing bodies are intended to allow greater flexibility in the appointment of
governors to meet a school's particular circumstances, but do not promote
student representation. Likewise, legislation relating to school exclusion and
exclusion appeal panels in England does not give students the right to
appeal. This remains with the parent or guardian. Indeed, since 2000, the
government has relaxed school exclusion procedures in England, making it
easier for headteachers to exclude and more difficult for parents to appeal.
We have argued that these regulations need to be amended so as to bring
them in line with Article 12 of the CRC and to ensure that learners who are
subject to disciplinary exclusion have a right to be heard (Osler and Vincent
2003). In Wales, as a result of a proposal put forward by the Children's
Commissioner, the Assembly has revised exclusion procedures, so that from
2004 secondary school pupils have a right of appeal (Shaw 2003).

Researchers concerned with giving children a voice in mainstream
schools have tended to make the case by arguing that promoting children's
participation, whether this be in decision-making processes or in learning
and teaching, will lead to more effective schooling. The case that children's
participation is a requirement under the CRC and that government has an
obligation to guarantee children's human rights has less frequently been
made. Indeed, a key publication which draws on the Economic and Social
Research Council (ESRC) project 'Consulting Pupils about Teaching and
Learning' within the Teaching and Learning Research Programme (TLRP)
simply presents a number of pragmatic arguments for consulting pupils and
giving them a voice. The researchers produce evidence to demonstrate that
learner participation can enhance school organizational, disciplinary and
administrative processes, individual learning and motivation, and peer

learning. The publication makes brief reference to children's rights and to the UN *CRC*, but suggests that policy initiatives prompted by the need to implement the *CRC* 'tend to rely on coercion' and 'can be superficial' (Rudduck and Flutter 2004: 101). We would argue that the process of extending rights to groups who have suffered disadvantage or discrimination has generally relied, to a greater or lesser extent, on legal provisions. So, for example, particular rights for girls and women in schools, including provision of equal pay for female teachers, have been realized as a result of the 'coercion' of the law. Longer-term and widespread cultural change is often brought about as a result of legal requirements.

We recognize the significant research which has taken place within the ESRC TLRP project on consulting pupils, but suggest that by underplaying the wider national and international significance of the principle of children's human right to participation the researchers missed an opportunity to give their work greater authority. There is also a danger that in overlooking the importance of the *CRC* as an international standard, researchers may not have identified or given sufficient weight to the specific voices and interests of those children that schools are more likely to marginalize, including those from specific black and minority ethnic communities, those with disabilities and those in public care. We argue that schools that are able to respond to the varied needs of these young people are also likely to meet those of mainstream learners. Research evidence suggests that unless these young people are specifically targeted, overall efforts to improve schools merely perpetuate existing inequalities and differentials in attainment (Osler and Hill 1999; Gillborn and Mirza 2000; Tikly *et al.* 2002).

There are three key reasons why children's views and perspectives need to feature centrally in research and policy development relating to citizenship and citizenship education. First, the *CRC* sets an important international standard on the participation rights of children and young people and has wide-ranging implications for education policy and practice (see, e.g. Newell 1991; Lansdown and Newell 1994; Osler and Starkey 1996; Verhellen 2000). As we have shown, the *CRC* acknowledges children's actual citizenship rights. Although young people under the age of 18 do not have the right to vote, they are nevertheless citizens and key stakeholders in consultation processes relating to citizenship and citizenship education.[2]

Second, research projects which have drawn on the voices of young people from marginalized groups, such as children with special educational needs or girls from specific ethnic minority groups, have sometimes challenged the assumptions of education professionals concerning those groups (Osler 1989; Tisdall and Dawson 1994; Osler *et al.* 2002; Osler and Vincent 2003). Such approaches may provide policy-makers with the opportunity to hear and take into account the voices of otherwise marginalized young people. In a sense we may even claim that these young people are enabled to influence policy and practice. By seeking out the views of children, including young children, researchers may uncover how social processes and educational practices operate to exclude or discriminate against certain groups (Troyna and Hatcher 1992; Connolly 1998).

Third, research and consultation with children may also inform teachers seeking practical solutions to everyday challenges facing schools. Researchers have shown how such consultation processes inform and strengthen school improvement strategies and support schools in addressing questions of discipline (Rudduck et al. 1996; Osler 2000a).

The notion of rights-based education allows us to examine education processes from the perspectives of a range of actors, including children, reflecting on rights, freedoms and responsibilities. Overall, the right of individual children to express an opinion about decisions which may affect them is not generally guaranteed in English education law. The *Code of Practice* regarding the education of children with SEN recommends that the child's views be taken into consideration. The *Code* attempts to enable children and young people to become 'active participant[s] in any programme of intervention proposed by the school or related services'. It notes that under Articles 12 and 13 of the *CRC*: 'Children … have a right to receive and make known information, to express an opinion, and to have that opinion taken into account in any matter or procedure affecting them. The views of the child should be given due weight according to the age, maturity and capability of the child' (DfES 2001a: Section 3, 27). However, as the *Code of Practice* does not have statutory status, the participation rights of children with SEN may still be denied (Sinclair Taylor 2000). It is possible to pay lip-service to the principle of consulting young people about their education, but if a child's best interests conflict with established practices and procedures, their voice may be disregarded. This is illustrated by our recent research study that seeks to give voice to a 15-year-old student with Asperger Syndrome who was unlawfully excluded from school (Osler and Osler 2002).[3] It illustrates how a 'successful' school with good examination results can neglect a student with a Statement of SEN and even deny an individual the right to education without being called to account. The student was experiencing stress-related epileptic seizures, generated in part by bullying. Yet he had a clear understanding of the type of support he needed to enable him to manage the threat of bullying and establish a secure learning environment. He had not broken any disciplinary code. Instead of taking the student's opinion into consideration the school chose to medicalize his problems, arguing that it was not equipped to cope with epilepsy and excluding him in contravention of statutory guidelines. Legal frameworks are essential and children need to have a right of appeal when their rights are denied. These legal frameworks need however to be supported by a culture in which children's participation rights are recognized.

A number of our research projects underpinned by the principles of the *CRC* have addressed students' own perspectives as a central aspect of data collection. Students' voices have also featured prominently in our research reports. The projects address a number of substantive and interrelated issues relating to democracy and inclusion: exclusion from school; race equality; the quality of student-teacher relationships; school violence and conflict management; girls' experiences of exclusion; and learning for citizenship. We are interested not only in the learning environment of the classroom and related issues of school ethos, but also in 'informal' community learning and its implications for teaching and learning in school. We report here on two studies which adopted very different approaches: the first examined exclusion from school and wider issues of school discipline, drawing on the experiences of five schools in two local education authorities (LEAs). The second was an action research project in one school, initiated by a teacher, which set out to explore how students could work together to address problems relating to relationships, conflict and aggression.

Student voice, learning and discipline

A common theme running through much of our work on inclusion and exclusion has been students' understandings of what constitutes a positive learning environment. It is not just students with SEN who may be able to suggest how learning environments might be improved to support the processes of teaching and learning. As part of a project which sought to identify strategies which schools and LEAs have adopted to minimize the use of exclusion from school, we asked students in inner-city primary and secondary schools about relationships in school; systems of reward and sanctions; specific problems which they faced and ways in which these might be effectively resolved.

The study included a statistical analysis of exclusions in one LEA, together with qualitative data collected from a number of LEAs and case studies of five individual schools (Osler 1997a, 2000a; Osler and Hill 1999). We found that schools which had successfully reduced exclusions had involved students as well as parents in discussing good behaviour and discipline. The findings, in the form of guidance to schools on developing an inclusive and equitable learning environment, were endorsed by then Education Minister Estelle Morris and disseminated to all secondary schools and directors of education in England (CRE 1997). A press report which highlighted that these schools had effective structures for involving children in decision-making, such as school and class councils (Osler 1997b), led Schools Councils UK to commission further research exploring the links between school councils and low exclusion rates (Davies 1998).

Our questionnaire was answered by 158 students in five primary and secondary schools (Osler 2000a). They made a number of recommendations concerning school discipline. They suggested that teachers should:

- give praise for good behaviour;
- listen to students;
- take trouble to sort out the underlying causes of disputes instead of dealing with the immediate effects of violent behaviour;
- recognize bullying, racial and sexual name-calling as real problems;
- care more;
- investigate before they punish;
- show respect for students.

They felt that headteachers/school management should:

- find ways of canvassing students' views through suggestion boxes, school councils, student newspapers, questionnaires and assemblies;
- set aside class time to discuss school council business and prepare for meetings;
- invite parents to attend lessons;
- organize individual tutorial time each term for all students;
- provide training for students in non-violent conflict resolution and peer mediation skills;
- organize support for those finding work difficult, including tutorial visits at home;
- discipline racist teachers;
- ensure student representation on the board of governors;
- train students as peer counsellors.

The responses show that the students make links between discipline, behaviour and learning. It is for this reason that they advocate extra support for those who are encountering difficulties. They also make links between student participation and disciplined learning environments, recommending that teachers should listen to students, canvas their opinions, offer greater support for school councils and enable peer counselling if they wish to improve school discipline. They expect teachers who break agreed standards of behaviour to be subject, as they are, to disciplinary procedures. Thus student voice and participation, learning and discipline are seen as interrelated.

The five case study schools differed in the degree to which they had developed formal structures which encouraged student voice and participation in decision-making. The three secondary schools and one of the primary schools had school or class councils, although in one of the secondary schools the council was not meeting as regularly as planned. The students had varied experiences of participation in school decision-making, which related to the type of school they attended, the formal structures in place and their own engagement in them. Nevertheless, students appear to value school councils as they enable them to address problems which concern them. As one pupil stated confidently: 'We make a difference'. In other words, such mechanisms appear to give pupils a sense of agency and a means by which they can contribute to processes of change (see also Hudson, 2005 and Chapter 9 of this volume). Students argued that involvement in decision-making increased motivation to achieve and made them feel a part of the school community. School councils are important at a symbolic level, demonstrating that the school is a 'listening school' (Thorne 1996). They also play a practical role in enabling students to effect change and acquire democratic skills, such as advocacy, listening and conflict resolution.

Curriculum, conflict and student voice

In an action research project which sought to address both teacher-student conflict and conflict between students in a boys' school, human rights were used as the framework through which students might find a voice and explore a range of identities (Carter and Osler 2000). Considerable concern has been expressed about the ways in which schools serve to construct and regulate masculine identities through the organization of the curriculum and modes of authority (Wolpe 1988; Connell 1989). The intensity of such concerns has been further heightened by research which has highlighted boys' apparent 'underachievement' in schools (Arnot et al. 1996). Debates have addressed the relationship between boys' academic performance, motivation and social behaviour. The issue of gender and academic performance is complex, affecting particular sub-groups of boys and girls in different ways and to different degrees (Arnot et al. 1998).

In the research school, aggression and verbal abuse between boys had become the norm and were viewed by staff as an irritating diversion, serving to hinder the processes of teaching and learning. Within the school, the behaviour of significant numbers of boys was perceived to be problematic by the staff. We wished to learn more about learners' perceptions of the difficulties. A group of ten self-selected students worked with the teacher-researcher over a six-month period to identify sources of aggression and consider how aggressive behaviour affected, and was in turn influenced by, the wider school community. They discovered that there were generally two types of response to aggression in others: either passive or aggressive. The boys worked to develop their skills and find a range of alternative responses. They were introduced to human rights principles and encouraged to put them into practice in the group setting. During a group discussion one student assessed his own development: 'I think I have calmed down and if someone annoys me I won't hit them like I used to. I might sometimes call them a name back but I will think before I react … I know I'm not exactly the best listener but I've tried to improve but I will need to keep working at it. I think I am more trusting and happier at school' (quoted in Carter and Osler 2000: 343).

The project was then extended to include a second teacher, a form teacher who worked using similar techniques with a class of 30 students. He used a set of materials designed by the teacher-researcher which allowed boys to examine relationships using problem-solving and group work. The tutor and the teacher–researcher met regularly to plan and discuss the work. A programme was planned and designed for the group using various established activities. The students began by drawing up a class contract, and worked on a series of games whereby they developed skills of active listening, cooperation, teamwork and problem-solving. Although in the small group students learned over a period of months to respect each other's rights, in the four-week project with the class of 30 students, rights were often only maintained when stressed by the teacher. Students took turns to observe the activities and at the end completed evaluation sheets. Interviews were also conducted with other teachers who taught the group to establish whether they were able to identify any differences in students' attitudes and behaviour.

A number of students were positive about the class programme: 'I feel really good when we talk about stuff in the group, I get out my frustration and feelings ... you don't get the mick taken out of you if you say something wrong, other people just explain it back to you ... it's nice to hear good things about myself ... it builds me up inside' (quoted in Carter and Osler 2000: 345). Some staff were critical of students' lack of judgement in knowing how to act properly or claim rights. This was reciprocated by most students feeling that they were never trusted to act well: 'They don't trust us to do anything properly. They treat us like babies and haven't even let us try. They don't want us to succeed, then they might have to treat us properly' (quoted in Carter and Osler 2000: 347). Another student, responding to a situation where he had been accused of unacceptable behaviour, wrote: 'One of this school's major faults is the *lack of voice a student is given* ... Some of the teachers are afraid to give a student the chance to explain himself' (quoted in Carter and Osler 2000: 347, emphasis added).

One of the limitations of this project is that it took place in a wider school environment in which authoritarian modes of control persisted and in which there was little trust between staff and students. Students were required to abide by rules and accept sanctions and practices in which they had had little say. Similarly, staff had had little opportunity to shape the institution and appeared to lack the confidence and skills to effect change. Nevertheless, the project suggests that initiatives which give students voice have the potential to address problems of conflict and aggression, giving students access to a wider range of identities and helping establish a climate of cooperation in which teaching and learning might take place more effectively.

Changing conceptions of childhood

Relationships between adults and children are changing as we develop new understandings of childhood. This is the context in which a student can observe: 'Some teachers forget we are growing up and just expect the childish things of little kids' (Carter and Osler 2000: 347). The CRC marks an important step forward in changing perceptions of childhood. In it, children are acknowledged as citizens and as autonomous holders of rights. However, it would appear that a climate where children are generally recognized as citizens has not yet been achieved.

In Europe until the nineteenth century, children were not generally recognized as a separate class from adults. They were regarded as the property of their parents and were expected to fulfil particular duties to them. Young children often played an important economic role, contributing to family work and supporting their parents in old age. They had few legal rights. As a result of industrialization and the increase of children's work outside the family, a series of measures was introduced during the nineteenth century to protect the children of the poor. Children's labour was perceived as a social fact rather than a social problem; it has been argued that protecting children was a means of protecting society from the destabilizing effects of antisocial behaviour resulting from mistreatment (Hart 1991).

During the twentieth century a shift in status of children from that of property to persons began to take place in a number of Western countries. The first international attempt to codify children's rights was made in 1924 when the Assembly of the League of Nations endorsed the *Geneva Declaration of the Rights of the Child* proclaimed by the NGO Save the Children International Union. This document, which was revised and expanded in 1948, formed the basis of the 1959 UN *Declaration on the Rights of the Child*, a statement of general principles for children's welfare and protection.

During the 1960s and 1970s, debates about children and childhood reflected a more widespread and rapid change in attitudes taking place in a number of Western countries. This period saw a further move away from the traditional view of children as the property of their parents. While some advocates of children's rights argued that they should be given the same rights as adults, others raised questions about the limits to the possibility of children's autonomy in relation to adults, both parents and teachers (Archard 1993). Mainstream human rights discourse started increasingly to be applied to children, with a focus on self-determination and participation, as well as the protection of the vulnerable: 'The liberationist movement challenged those who claimed the status of children could be advanced exclusively by conferring on children increased protection. The emphasis shifted from protection to autonomy, from nurturance to self-determination, from welfare to justice' (Freeman 1992: 3). Effectively, the debate about children's political rights was opened.

The legal context and children's rights

Any discussion of children's citizenship requires us to consider children's legal status and rights. Of course the *UDHR* applies equally to children as to adults, recognizing all as having an entitlement to human rights. As we have seen, the *CRC* makes explicit the fact that children are not only entitled to rights of provision (e.g. adequate food, health care and education) and to special protection but that they also have participation rights. In other words, it recognizes children as citizens with political rights. Despite the fact that the *CRC* has now been almost universally ratified, children's rights are often inadequately codified in national legal frameworks. Some 30 years ago, Hillary Clinton wrote:

> The phrase 'children's rights' is a slogan in search of a definition. Invoked to support such disparate causes as world peace, constitutional guarantees for delinquents, affection for infants, and lowering the voting age, it does not yet reflect any coherent doctrine regarding the status of children as political beings. Asserting that children are entitled to rights and enumerating their status does not clarify the difficult issues surrounding children's legal status.
> (Rodham 1973: 487)

Although there was much discussion and some activism relating to children's rights during the 1960s and 1970s, there was little consensus during these decades as to what 'the rights of the child' might imply. The experiments with radical alternative models of schooling which emphasized non-authoritarian, cooperative forms of education (Illich 1971; Lister 1974; Watts 1977) were responding to ideals of liberating children. Although this was sometimes expressed in terms of children's rights, the text of the 1959 UN *Declaration on the Rights of the Child* was rarely quoted. Children's rights were indeed 'a slogan in search of a definition'.

The *CRC* marked an important step forward in comprehensively defining children's rights. Among other things it acknowledges children's political rights and provides a framework within which a coherent doctrine regarding children's status as political beings can be debated. The emphasis on participation within the *CRC* is recognition that children are entitled to influence decisions that affect them. This is an explicitly democratic perspective, acknowledging and legitimizing children's participation in political issues.

While the *CRC* provides us with an important set of principles and standards for children's rights, we need to be wary about equating the existence of the *CRC* with the realization of these rights. The effectiveness of the *CRC* depends, first and foremost, on the raising of public awareness concerning its provisions. While legally binding on all state parties, the *CRC* cannot be enforced in the same way as domestic legislation. For this reason it is important that governments are persuaded of the importance of ensuring that, where national legislation currently fails to secure the minimum standards set in the *CRC*, appropriate legislation is enacted.

Some 30 years after Hillary Clinton's assessment, and despite the *CRC*, children remain a key group internationally whose interests and rights as citizens are yet to be properly secured. There remain many difficult issues concerning children's legal status. There is far from universal recognition among policy-makers that children are, in fact, political beings or that they are competent and ready to participate in political processes.

Fundamental to the *CRC* is the requirement (Article 3) that in all actions concerning children 'the best interests of the child shall be a primary consideration'. This is important as an agreed international standard in child-rearing which goes beyond the basic requirements of a number of national systems of legislation. One measure to enable and promote children's rights in this way is the appointment of an ombudsperson or Commissioner for Children. The function of such an official is to make a continuing assessment of the impact of changing society on the way children grow up and to promote children's interests. Children's Commissioners for Scotland, Northern Ireland, Wales and London have been established and the Green Paper *Every Child Matters* (HM Treasury 2003) includes a government commitment to a Children's Commissioner for England. This post was established by the Children Act (2004).

The Green Paper is interesting in that it highlighted official understandings of children's interests and status. It focused on children's protection and provision through a range of prevention strategies, but not on children and young people's participation rights. Yet some efforts were made to consult with young people on the Green Paper's contents. In the foreword, the Prime Minister emphasizes the origins of the proposed reforms, an official inquiry into the circumstances surrounding the death of a child, Victoria Climbié, at the hands of family members, after a process of mistreatment and abuse that went undetected by the authorities. The Prime Minister stresses the need for 'measures to reform and improve children's care' (HM Treasury 2003: 1). An emphasis on children's protection is reinforced by the government minister responsible for the report, Paul Boateng, who in his foreword states:

> We have to do more both to protect children and ensure each child fulfils their potential. Security and opportunity must go hand in hand. Child protection must be a fundamental element across all public, private and voluntary organizations. Equally we must be ambitious for all our children, whoever they are and wherever they live.
>
> (HM Treasury 2003: 3)

The emphasis is on care, not on rights or on children's engagement in decision-making about their own futures. There is no acknowledgement that in order to fulfil their potential, young people need to participate. Nor is it recognized that participation is, in itself, one means of preventing abuse and developing protection. There are no references in the Green Paper to the *CRC* and just one to rights. The notion that children's protection might be forwarded by ensuring their participation and giving them a voice is missing.

The report of the coalition of NGOs in England to the UN Committee on Children's Rights (CRAE 2002) echoed Freeman's (1988) call for a child impact statement for monitoring implementation of the *CRC*. This would require all those who draft legislation, policies and practices in areas such as taxation, social security, housing, social services, environment and education to assess the impact of their proposals on children and on the implementation of a full range of rights in the *CRC*.

In the UK, as Newell (1991) stresses, not all courts of law affecting children adopt a 'best interests' principle. He points out that while the Children Act 1989 went a long way to ensuring that social welfare institutions in England and Wales act in the best interests of the child, the same principle is not generally guaranteed in education and that 'there is no duty to observe the best interests of the child in education legislation' (1991: 9). Following the Children Act 1989 a number of publications (e.g. Gallagher and Cross 1990; Lindsay 1990; Rodway 1993) considered its implications on schools and LEAs, but this analysis has generally been limited to children with SEN and to those educated in residential settings. While attention has been given to the need to inform and involve such children in decisions which affect their lives and futures, much of the education guidance has been non-statutory and authorities have not therefore been bound by it. Consequently, the right of these and other children to have their opinions taken into consideration in procedures which affect them (Article 12) relating to their schooling has often been denied (Osler and Osler 2002).

Children's political and citizenship rights

This chapter has taken the *Convention on the Rights of the Child* as a framework for exploring children's political and citizenship rights. It has sought to demonstrate the value of the *CRC* as a working document for policymakers and researchers, indicating how research agendas informed by the *CRC* might be particularly useful in developing policy-related research which might enhance the position of children as citizens.

While the status of children as political beings and the legal frameworks to support their citizenship rights still require further development, the *CRC* has provided us with a starting point for debate and discussion around a common agenda. The *CRC* has the potential to further influence educational policy, law and practice. It provides clear steps to establish a human rights-friendly school.

The advantage of applying the *CRC* as international human rights law lies in its comprehensive delineation of the prohibited grounds of discrimination and the corresponding governmental obligations. The *CRC* recognizes discrimination as structural as well as interpersonal, allowing for institutional as well as individual responses towards promoting equality and inclusion. The research projects presented in this chapter suggest that increased student participation and democracy in schools can lead to an enhancement of the processes of teaching and learning in a number of ways.

At the beginning of the chapter we introduced three Ps running through the *CRC*: protection, provision and participation. In considering children as citizens we have focused on participation. We conclude with three further Ps for educators concerned with children as citizens: principle, pedagogy and policy.

It would appear that the *principle* of ensuring student participation, in line with the *CRC*, is likely to require firm legal frameworks. In education, as in other areas of social policy, children's participation rights need to be recognized in law. The law then has the potential to influence professional cultures, so allowing children's rights to become part of everyday practice.

By giving young people a voice, we can inform *pedagogy*. Students clearly value the opportunity to be consulted about decisions which affect them, and the development of school councils or other mechanisms which give students a voice has both symbolic and practical benefits. The research indicates that more democratic schools are likely to be more inclusive and better disciplined. Giving young people a voice within school, whether through specific curricular initiatives or through broader school structures, may enable them to address questions of identity, rights and participation and to resolve problems relating to conflict and aggression.

Researchers who draw on student voice can support the process by which children are engaged in *policy* debates. The research suggests that not only does the promotion of student voice have the potential to positively influence the learning environment, but it may also provide policy-makers with new insights.

Together the six Ps amount to both a research agenda and an agenda for action. These agendas are child friendly, internationally recognized and politically challenging. Once children and young people are recognized as having political (participation) rights their claims to engage as citizens and make a valuable contribution to communities and to schools and other institutions can begin.

PART 2
Learning for Inclusion

4   The right to education

Introduction

In countries like the UK, where there are adequate numbers of schools, the right to education is often assumed. Yet the existence of a school place does not, in itself, guarantee a child the right to education. As we have already noted in Chapter 3, the *Convention on the Rights of the Child* not only confirms the right to education, but also outlines particular entitlements within education, which should be available to all children without discrimination. The right to education entails governmental human rights obligations to make schooling accessible, acceptable and adaptable (Tomaševski 1999).

In this chapter we explore the concepts of inclusion and exclusion in education with reference to rights. Young people who are unable to claim their right to education may be unable to access a number of additional rights. For example, it may be difficult to access appropriate information or to participate in cultural and artistic activities. Equally importantly, they may be prevented from gaining the skills which ensure that they can enjoy future economic rights and participation. We draw on a number of research studies into exclusion from school to examine how children and young people experience the right to education. We consider the right *to* education and the related concepts of rights *in* and *through* education. We explore the various ways in which different forms of educational exclusion are, in effect, a denial of the right to education.

We argue that schools as institutions need to adapt to learners in order to guarantee a right to education for all. We draw on the voices of young people, the better to understand their experiences of school and, in particular, how schools can guarantee the equal right to education for all. It is by upholding these rights that schools will be genuinely inclusive, respecting difference and promoting equality.

Exclusion, discrimination and rights

The concepts of social inclusion and exclusion are commonly used in debates about injustice and inequality in education. Within the EU the term 'social exclusion' is used to denote the experiences of individuals and groups who have been marginalized through economic disadvantage, including the low paid and unemployed. The term is used in a similar way in the UK, with an emphasis on economic deprivation or marginalization. Those individuals or communities said to experience social exclusion are presented as disadvantaged and their deprivation is often seen as multiple, affecting housing, health, education and other services. Although the discourse of social exclusion is extended to cover pockets of deprivation in otherwise prosperous areas and, occasionally, to rural populations, social exclusion is more readily equated with inner-city populations and, by association, with ethnic diversity. The language of social exclusion is not that of human rights, so that exclusion is not expressed as a denial of social rights, nor is it generally defined by reference to discrimination.

The UK government's Social Exclusion Unit (SEU), established in 1997, provides an official definition of social exclusion: 'a shorthand term for what can happen when people or areas suffer from a combination of linked problems such as unemployment, poor skills, low incomes, poor housing, high crime, bad health, poverty and family breakdown' (SEU 2001: 10). Yet, the Department for Education and Employment (DfEE) in its key policy document, which makes explicit the link between educational exclusion and longer-term social exclusion, fails to define social exclusion (DfEE 1999a, 1999b). This document, entitled *Social Exclusion: The LEA Role in Pupil Support,* brought together for the first time strategies on behaviour management and measures that might be taken when these strategies were ineffective. There is no reference to children's rights in education.

Following the publication of the Stephen Lawrence Inquiry report (Macpherson 1999) an SEU report, *Minority Ethnic Issues in Social Exclusion and Neighbourhood Renewal,* recognized that 'people from minority ethnic communities are at disproportionate risk of social exclusion' because of their disproportionate concentration in deprived areas and because they 'also suffer the consequences of racial discrimination' (SEU 2000: 7–8). This reference to discrimination is exceptional. Despite the introduction of the Race Relations (Amendment) Act 2000, which requires public bodies not only to avoid discrimination but also to promote race equality, British government initiatives to address social exclusion have not given significant attention to racial discrimination. Nor have specific initiatives to promote a vision of an inclusive multicultural society been much in evidence (Alibhai-Brown 1999; Osler 2002).

Although the SEU report goes on to acknowledge that children from some minority communities are less likely to do well at school and to be excluded from school in disproportionate numbers, it does not suggest that, within the education system, any discriminatory processes may be at work. Nor has there been recognition from within the Department for Education that there is a link between social exclusion and discrimination. Despite a general acknowledgement by government of institutional racism in society, education ministers have generally avoided any reference to racism within the education service (Osler 2002). Indeed, there is suspicion of antiracism in education, as we discuss in Chapter 7. Bernard Crick, the Chair of the government's advisory group on 'Education for Citizenship and the Teaching of Democracy in Schools', suggests that those Home Office ministers who have endorsed antiracism in schools are 'perhaps not wholly conversant ... with good practice in actual classroom teaching' (Crick 2000: 143). He argues that education ministers are wiser in not adopting an explicit antiracist position.

Social exclusion remains an apparently neutral term, which does not place emphasis on the role of the state. Whereas governments have a responsibility to uphold the rights of individuals and, indeed, to prevent discrimination, social exclusion is defined without reference to rights and, therefore, without reference to the state. 'Linked' social problems, to use the words of the SEU, such as poor skills, low income, bad health and family breakdown may be explained without necessarily placing responsibility on the state. The use of the word 'exclusion' suggests that social polices may not have been inclusive, but the language, unlike the language of rights, does not place a direct obligation on the state to take steps to ensure adequate health care, housing and so on are provided.

Social exclusion is sometimes explained in terms of social differences. For example, the Crick Report implies that exclusion may be self-imposed, or that experience of exclusion may lead to self-exclusion. It argues that the curriculum 'should make students aware of the difficulties such exclusion can have on the individual and society and of the reasons why some people "opt out" of the moral social set-up' (QCA 1998: 3.19, 19). We recognize that individuals and groups may sometimes choose to opt out or to exclude themselves, but this should not obscure discriminatory elements that are sometimes present in the processes of social exclusion. If exclusion is presented largely as a lifestyle choice or if discriminatory elements of exclusion are overlooked, there is a danger that the complex nature of exclusion will not be understood and that measures to address it will be inadequate. In understanding exclusion it is important to be cognizant of problems such as the maintenance of vested interests, gender inequalities and structural and institutional racism. We argue that an in-depth understanding of social inclusion and the discriminatory processes which contribute to it requires an analysis of its causes at a structural level.

In a speech given at a seminar, *Challenges for Race Equality in the 21st Century*, Home Secretary David Blunkett acknowledges the positive benefits and strengths of diversity; the contributions of individuals from minority communities; and the limitations of public institutions, particularly the police and criminal justice system, to provide a fair service to all. Nevertheless, he presents diversity, rather than race equality, as the challenge:

> There are barriers to people building relationships across ethnic or cultural divides, especially against a backdrop of rapid change. But in working to break down these barriers we must not lose sight of the benefits. Our strength as a country has always come from our confidence in our sense of identity and belonging, and from our acceptance of our interdependence and mutuality.
>
> (Blunkett 2004)

The Home Secretary places emphasis on the responsibility of government to take a leadership role in achieving 'diversity with integration'. Yet the term 'ethnic and cultural divides' and the assumption that diversity is necessarily a barrier to the building of relationships are, in themselves, problematic. The assumption is that there are greater differences between people of different ethnic groups than within these groupings. Yet an individual may, for example, have more in common with someone of the same profession or someone who shares an interest in the same sport but is from a different ethnic group than someone who is from the same ethnic grouping but whose professional life or particular interests are different. The speech also places considerable emphasis on identity and belonging; one of the challenges is for political leaders and commentators to recognize that many individuals belong to many communities; their personal and family lives already encompass people of different cultures and ethnic backgrounds. Their very identities are based on the assumption that people can move between different communities and that the so-called barriers to which the Home Secretary refers are, in fact, fluid borders which are crossed regularly as part of everyday personal and professional life.

Social and educational policy in relation to inclusion and exclusion often operates within a framework in which there is an oversimplified and idealized understanding of what is a normal child or a normal learner. So, for example, just as the Home Secretary assumes 'ethnic and cultural divides' so some teachers also assume that children normally identify with one culture or ethnicity. Other groups, communities and individuals are then assessed against this unquestioned standard. Research suggests that a number of teachers assume that children of mixed heritage have fragmented home backgrounds and 'confused' identities (Tikly *et al.* 2004). Not only do such children experience racism from teachers and their peers, targeted at their mixed heritage, but this racism also acts as a barrier to achievement, particularly as teacher stereotypes lead to low expectations. These children's responses to racism and their unwillingness to accept stereotypical understandings of their identities can lead to professional perceptions of rebellious and challenging behaviour.

A further danger of an approach in which there is an oversimplified understanding of the 'normal' learner is that it stresses the differences between groups and communities and underplays the differences between individuals within both the 'normal' group and within other groups and communities. It is important to consider the complex ways in which race, class, gender and other categories intersect in order to produce specific group experiences and unique individual experiences.

Democracy, inclusion and rights

In a discussion of the tensions facing multicultural nation states in promoting unity and diversity through education, Amy Gutmann argues that a central goal of democratic education is to 'both express and develop the capacity of all children to become equal citizens' (2004: 71). Taking the example of the USA, she looks at the special claims that minorities make on the educational system in order to achieve this democratic ideal of civic equality. She examines the needs and claims of various groups, including indigenous populations, established and recent immigrant groups, linguistic minorities and historically oppressed citizens. Past and present inequalities need to be addressed through curricular design so that all members of the society are aware of the oppressions and contributions (past and present) of members of historically oppressed groups of citizens. She argues that democratic education must necessarily include this 'politics of recognition' out of respect for individuals and their equal rights as citizens. To ignore the experiences and contributions of these citizens is both an intellectual and ethical failure.

One of the strengths of the US constitution has been its elasticity, so that a limited and particularistic conception of citizenship, which was originally confined to white male property owners, has been extended to other groups. African Americans, Native Americans, white males without property, women of all racial and ethnic groups and more recent migrants have attained expanded rights over the years (Banks 1997). As we have seen in Chapter 3, one of the challenges facing communities across the globe is that of recognizing children as competent citizens and of extending our conceptions of citizenship to include children and young people. Just as other groups, such as minorities and women, have attained expanded rights and had these rights secured through legal mechanisms, so too must children. This has implications within a number of policy areas; our concern is education and how children's rights can be secured there.

In England, there is increasing rhetoric within government about the need to consult with young people. As we noted in Chapter 3, young people are expected to 'take responsibility for some aspects of school life and the school environment' (DfES 2001b: 28). This would seem to imply the development of democratic processes in schools, but in contrast to the situation in many other European countries, education legislation in England does not guarantee student representation in school decision-making (Davies and Kirkpatrick 2000; Osler and Vincent 2002). In practice, legal frameworks give emphasis to parental rights and the prevailing culture among education professionals reflects concerns about children's competence to participate in decision-making processes. The *Code of Practice* relating to children with SEN, although not statutory, recommends that such children should be given a say in decision-making. It makes direct reference to the *CRC* and highlights the contribution that children can make in the assessment of their own needs. There are no equivalent processes in place for children who are not designated as having SEN. Yet the *Code of Practice* quotes from official guidance relating to the Children Act 1989, cautioning that there is 'a fine balance between giving the child a voice and encouraging them to make informed decisions, and overburdening them with decision-making procedures where they have insufficient experience and knowledge to make appropriate judgements without additional support' (DfES 2001a: 27). The wording of the official guidance assumes incompetence. Professionals are cautioned against overburdening children and young people under the age of 19, regardless of their individual levels of understanding. In a prevailing culture in which professionals may themselves need support in recognizing children's competence, adults working with children are, in effect, further discouraged from recognizing that many young people do have sufficient experience and knowledge to make appropriate judgements. The emphasis is on children's insufficient experience rather than on teachers' professional responsibility, in line with the spirit of the *CRC*, to ensure that children and young people receive appropriate support in order to participate in decision-making.

Children who believe their right to education is not being upheld by the state are not able to appeal directly. Instead, it is the parent or carer who must seek redress. The government claims that children can exercise their rights through parents. Yet this implies, first, that the parent has the knowhow and resources to act on behalf of the child and, second, that there is no conflict of interest between parent and child. For example, in a decision as to whether a child needs a residential placement in order to guarantee access to education, a parent's perspective and preferences might not necessarily be consistent with the best interests of the child. Nor may the decisions of a local authority be determined solely by reference to the child's best interests, with other factors, such as local provision, professional preferences and resources determining the outcome. When a child is in the care of a local authority, decision-makers may experience a direct conflict of interests if the solution judged to be in the best interests of the child places a greater financial burden on the authority. Children need to have access to an independent advocate, such as can be provided though the offices of a Children's Commissioner, in order to effectively claim rights in education.

The emphasis on parental rights has severely detrimental effects on children in the care of the state. Where a child is looked after by a local authority, the authority acts as legal guardian. In such cases the chances of the guardian being faced with a conflict of interests are increased. We know that children in this situation are particularly vulnerable to early dropout and to disciplinary exclusion. For many children looked after by the local authority, their right to education is denied or severely restricted: three quarters of them leave compulsory schooling without any qualifications (DfEE 1999a). What is needed is a comprehensive legal framework and effective procedures to protect the rights of children. Children in the care of the state are a limiting case: if the laws and procedures are able to guarantee the rights of the most vulnerable young citizens then they are also likely to protect the rights of the wider child population.

Defining exclusion from school

In England, the term 'exclusion from school' is generally understood to mean disciplinary exclusion, either on a fixed-term or permanent basis. From 1995/6, when official numbers peaked at 12,467, official statistics indicated a downward trend in the annual number of permanently excluded students. Our research suggests that as schools cut the number of permanent exclusions, in line with government targets, the numbers of both temporary and unrecorded (unlawful) exclusions rose (Osler *et al.* 2000).

The report *Truancy and School Exclusion* (SEU 1998) highlighted the government's desire to address social exclusion by cutting the numbers of exclusions from school. An explicit link was made between school exclusion and longer-term social exclusion. Importantly, the government recognized that disciplinary exclusion and other forms of exclusion from school had similar impacts on children's education and on their school attainment. However, from 2000 the government relaxed school exclusion regulations. Official discourse on exclusion from school began to change and exclusion was increasingly linked to school violence. The downward trend in officially recorded exclusions was reversed in 2000/1, when the number of permanent exclusions rose to over 9,200, an increase of 11 per cent on the previous year.

A central feature of the government's plan to combat social exclusion by cutting the number of school exclusions had been replaced by growing official concern about the need to address youth violence and criminal behaviour. The official exclusion figures began to rise as official discourse focused on the need to tackle violent and disruptive behaviour. This change in official discourse can be explained, in part, by pressure from teacher unions, notably the National Association of Schoolmasters Union of Women Teachers (NASUWT). An NASUWT 2004 full-page recruitment advertisement, headlined 'NASUWT making a difference – pupil indiscipline' highlights six union claims, four of which relate directly to exclusion and one of which refers to 'false, exaggerated and malicious allegations by pupils'. The advertisement states that the NASUWT has:

- a strong commitment to protect members from disruptive and violent pupils and on average at least one ballot a week to support members in refusing to teach such pupils;
- secured a landmark victory in the House of Lords on teachers' entitlement to refuse to teach disruptive and violent pupils;
- achieved changes to the DfES' exclusion regulations and guidance to give more support to schools which exclude pupils;
- campaigned successfully for the removal of national exclusion reduction targets set for schools and LEAs.

(*Times Educational Supplement*, 27 February 2004: 20)

The focus on 'disruptive and violent' pupils and on ballots to refuse to teach those pupils whose exclusion from school is overturned by independent appeal panels highlights and reinforces a culture in which students are presented as problems and where teachers' interests are presented as in opposition to those of their students. While disruption is a common cause of disciplinary exclusion, incidents of violence towards teachers are relatively uncommon. Our research in Birmingham showed that the most common recorded cause of exclusion was disruption of lessons and disobedience (37 per cent of excluded pupils), followed by violence to other students (30 per cent). There were comparatively few examples of violence against members of staff (5 per cent) (Osler 1997a; Osler and Hill 1999).

The focus is on disciplinary exclusion, and other forms of exclusion, particularly exclusion as a result of factors such as bullying, caring responsibilities, truancy and pregnancy are consequently obscured (Osler and Vincent 2003). As the young people who experience these forms of exclusion do not tend to put direct pressure on teachers, their needs are often overlooked. An educational psychologist, interviewed in one of our research projects into exclusion, vividly explained how a girl may be in difficulties and effectively self-exclude without necessarily getting support, whereas aggressive behaviour (more prevalent among boys) demands an immediate teacher response and intervention: 'There is someone I am working with at the moment ... she's very emotionally distressed, as shown by crying, worrying, refusing to do her schoolwork and those sorts of things. While the school are concerned about her, it's not as pressing as a six-foot kid who's throwing desks about'. This same respondent went on to argue that self-exclusion, where a student is in school but not getting full access to the curriculum, needs to be seen as a behaviour problem and a cause for concern and action: 'At one end is the quiet reserved pupil who is not making any demands on the teacher. They are not accessing the curriculum but they are also not creating any behaviour difficulties. To me that is a behaviour problem and their needs are being overlooked' (quoted in Osler and Vincent 2003: 77, 78).

The example illustrates how a particular form of exclusion may fail to trigger adequate support, so denying an individual access to education. It illustrates how the ways in which teachers and schools define problems have implications for the allocation of resources and support. An inequitable distribution of resources is not only likely to have discriminatory outcomes but may also ultimately lead to the denial of the right to education.

Exclusion from school and special educational needs

A rights-based approach to the schooling of children with disabilities and SEN must necessarily examine whether that schooling is not only available but also accessible, acceptable and adaptable. A rights-based approach to inclusion will acknowledge actual or potential discrimination. Under the *CRC*, children with disabilities and SEN not only have the right to education, but like other children can claim rights in and through education. The Special Educational Needs and Disability Act 2001 places a positive 'reasonable adjustment duty' on schools and local authorities which is anticipatory. In other words, schools must adapt their practices, procedures and, under certain conditions, their facilities, to ensure that children with disabilities or SEN can access schooling. As then Education Minister Tessa Blackstone explained during the passage of the Bill through parliament:

> It will not be good enough for a school or LEA or local authority in Scotland to wait until a disabled child arrives on the doorstep. The approach must be to think ahead – always to have the rights of disabled children on the agenda ... For example, a school or LEA might be ordered to change a policy that prevented visibly impaired pupils from going into a science laboratory and, additionally, ordered to provide extra tuition to enable a child to catch up on things that he or she may have missed due to discrimination.
>
> (Hansard (House of Lords) 2000b)

So, for example, we might therefore reasonably expect schools to make adequate provision for a student with epilepsy, so as to ensure that they will not suffer discriminatory treatment simply because a school lacks adequate first aid support. It will be unacceptable for the school simply to argue that participation in certain lessons or activities poses a health and safety risk. There is an obligation to review provision to ensure that all appropriate steps have been taken to alleviate such risks. The school and LEA are responsible for ensuring that provision is made for all students to participate, including those with disabilities. Where disability discrimination occurs, cases can be brought to the county court in England and Wales and to the sheriff court in Scotland. A financial remedy is payable. Under the Act, failure to anticipate the needs of students with disabilities or SEN may well lead to unlawful discrimination.

In our case study of an Asperger Syndrome student, who was suffering from stress-related seizures, the school ruled that the student concerned could not participate in school trips or residential activities unless his mother accompanied him. The school also decided to exclude the student from mock examinations, on the grounds that a seizure might disturb other students. Under the Special Educational Needs and Disability Act 2001, now that a school has a 'reasonable adjustment duty' to accommodate to the needs of such students, it is likely that this ruling concerning school trips would be judged unlawful. It is also likely that the Act would today require the school to alter its examination arrangements, perhaps by providing an alternative venue, rather than deny the individual access to this important aspect of exam preparation (Osler and Osler 2002).

The anticipatory duties of schools, as set out in the Act, have far-reaching implications for school ethos and culture. Schools are expected to be inclusive and to act in the best interests of all students, guaranteeing that the education they provide is accessible, acceptable and adaptable. The institution itself may be required to change in order to meet the needs of individual students and secure their right to education.

Statutory guidance explicitly states that a decision to exclude a student should only be taken 'in response to serious breaches of a school's discipline policy; and ... if allowing the pupil to remain in school would seriously harm the education or welfare of the pupil or of others in the school' (DfEE 1999a: 31). Yet there is clear evidence that children with SEN are particularly vulnerable to disciplinary exclusion. Our research in Birmingham, the largest English metropolitan education authority, indicates that over half of those excluded from school were on the schools' special needs register (Osler and Hill 1999). A number of researchers have suggested that some children are excluded when what is required is assessment and provision of appropriate support (Norwich 1994; Parffrey 1994). There is certainly evidence that exclusion is often linked to poor acquisition of basic skills, particularly literacy.

Schools are required to improve standards so that students will be well-placed to make their contribution to an internationally competitive workforce. The British government's standards agenda has included a strategy of identifying the worst performing or 'failing' schools through the publication of inspection reports and league tables of students' performance. From the earliest years of schooling, children are subject to a long process of preparing and sitting for a series of national tests. The testing system has come under heavy criticism, but testing does not necessarily undermine children's rights. It is the use to which tests are put and the ways in which they may distort teaching which may result in discriminatory and exclusive practices in education.

Monitoring of learners' performance, by gender, ethnicity and class, can expose inequities. Test results can be used to inform teachers and school leaders of how successful they are in meeting the needs of different groupings of students, providing information which can then be used to redirect resources to meet the needs of those who require additional support. The targeting of resources to ensure equity is in keeping with the standards agenda, since schools will not raise their overall standards if particular groupings of students do not share the benefits of overall school improvement. Test results can be used to guarantee equity and to address discriminatory processes that might be operating within the system. In this sense they can be used to support children's right to education.

However, in England the tests are, first and foremost, a means by which schools can be held accountable to parents. The testing regime is one means by which the 'failure' of the school system can be addressed. Parents are portrayed as citizen-consumers, free to choose a school according to its examination results. The intention is to inform parents, so allowing some degree of choice. What has developed is a quasi-market in education, with successful schools attracting additional students and resources, and less successful schools, that experience falling rolls, receiving resource cuts. The expectation is that this strategy will bring those schools that are judged to be of an unacceptably low standard to an acceptable level. In reality, many parents may have little choice of school, since those schools that are judged to be successful are likely to be oversubscribed and families on limited incomes will not have the resources to transport their children to distant schools. Ranking by performance encourages selection of learners who are likely to perform well. It also encourages teachers to orientate their teaching towards enhancing student performance in tests. The effect is to institutionalize competition between schools. Resources are likely to be invested in students at critical grade boundaries such as C/D at GCSE (Gillborn and Youdell 2000) rather than invested in groupings who are not sharing the overall benefits of school improvement. This focus is likely to detract attention from the needs of students with disabilities and SEN, who are often more expensive to educate, and to discourage the investment of time and effort necessary to guarantee their rights.

In practice, it is possible for a school which is judged to be successful to neglect the rights of students with SEN (Osler and Osler 2002). Below is an account by Chay, a Year 11 student (aged 16) with Asperger Syndrome, submitted as evidence to a group of professionals discussing his case. It highlights his understanding of the low status of SEN provision in his school. It was written while he was excluded from school, not as a result of any breach of the disciplinary code but because the school was unable to adapt to meet his individual needs. Chay argues that the schooling provided was unacceptable, highlighting some of the pressures to which he was subject. These include a feeling that he was not consulted about his own learning needs; a sense of isolation and rejection; bullying; and a sense of failure and frustration that he cannot achieve. The account reveals that he does have the competence to assess many of his own needs, and that he understands the ways in which the school structures are operating to marginalize not just special needs students but also those teachers who are responsible for supporting them. From his perspective the education provided was neither accessible nor adapted to his needs.

Negligence?

I feel offended that the school has not asked me for my opinion on what I need. For this reason I have written this paper setting out my viewpoint. I've tried to do this politely, but I realize that it might be difficult for some teachers to accept, because my perspective is so different from theirs, and at this stage I feel very frustrated.

I want to learn but that right has been denied.

I feel that at the last meeting (at the beginning of January while I was still excluded from school) I was not listened to. I am shocked and dismayed that I have had to wait for three weeks following that meeting for anyone to so much as mention a mentor, even though that was agreed and promised at that stage. I tried to raise the subject and even went to see Mrs Y, the deputy head, about it, because she had previously been responsible for organizing mentors for Year Nine. She apparently knew nothing about it. I think it was a shame she was not at the meeting as she had spoken to both my mother and my aunt on the phone at the time of my exclusion and during it.

Obviously, my having epilepsy is no fault of the school but I have for too long been under the impression that the school thought that it was mine. Having seizures occurs when I am under stress and also, at the moment, while I am on the wrong medication. Seizures rarely happen at home. I would like the school to reflect whether they are in any way responsible for the seizures. Being weaned off tablets can be a slow and painful experience. It cannot and must not be rushed and I should like more understanding on the part of the staff, both teachers and first-aiders.

Excluding me from school because of the seizures was, of course, very wrong. I should like something, other than a long-awaited mentor, to make up for it. I should like decent, realistic and sensible advice from my teachers as well as my future mentor when s/he is selected on how I might deal with bullies, other than 'Ignore them!' or 'These are the best years of their life and they are spoiling them. Just remember that'.

I'd like to make similar comment with regard to Asperger Syndrome: I would like *all* my teachers to understand what this means and how it may affect my learning. I hope they will begin to consider this so that other students with this condition might be better understood. I hope my family will highlight this at the meeting which reviews my statement and I feel confident that Dr C will also do this.

Academically, I should like lots of support to enable me to achieve something in each subject which will be of value for my future. I would like a special needs assistant in some of my weaker subjects or all subjects if necessary. I feel this is particularly important as I missed the whole of December and my mock GCSEs as a result of the school's exclusion. It would be bad enough to be sent home on the grounds of bad behaviour but to be sent home and asked to stay away until my seizures were 'sorted out' is exceptionally distressing.

The special needs department deserves to feel part of the school and not just a little island which is overlooked by all except wretches like myself, escaped from a shipwreck. In maths there is a single special needs assistant to help a teacher in a class where the other students hardly ever want to learn. She has really got her work cut out because I understand that all in the class, save two, also have special needs statements.

I want to feel as if I am, at least to some small degree, good at something. I get encouragement at home and in the special needs department. Where is everybody else? I have been given the Foundation English GCSE exam paper, when even I know I can do better. I love English. I used to be praised for the stories I wrote in Middle School yet I have not written a single story in [this school] since Year Nine. If I can write a novel outside school, as I am doing, I should not be underestimated within school. Could a 'normal' student working on Foundation English translate *Beowulf*?

Da Comme of more undre mist-hleothelm
Grendel gongon; Goddes yrre boaer.

And what about reading? I have read Chaucer, Tolkien, Philip Pullman, Charles Dickens, Edgar Allan Poe ... I can quote from any one of these and yet at the moment I am feeling, in a word, quite 'thick'. Yet bullies would have everyone believe that I am. I have no way of demonstrating that I am not. How do you think that makes me feel? Does anyone care? I have set targets here for the school. I believe that it's now their turn to challenge me and enable me to get established in my future career, whatever that may be.

In short, I want to learn. If you were to ask 'What do you want done first?' I could not answer. If the seizures were to stop the school would have no excuse to neglect me and I would be less stressed. On the other hand, they will not stop until the school can support me and enable me to be less stressed. I can see that I have written a lot and I am sure I could make this longer. But really all this is a desperate cry for help. Now!

Testing regimes can undermine the rights of learners. Targets which require teachers to test all children, including those with certain types of learning difficulties, often put pressure on teachers to teach to the tests. This in turn may put pressure on particular students with SEN to conform, covering up any difficulties. Those who cannot keep up and who find the work too difficult may effectively self-exclude, dropping out of school (Osler and Vincent 2003). A regime of frequent testing and the consequent sense of failure are likely to undermine the confidence of those with learning difficulties. Schools are less likely, in these circumstances, to adapt their practices to meet the special needs of these children. In considering the needs of children with SEN it is important to consider whether the schooling available is accessible, acceptable and adaptable.

While the Special Educational Needs and Disability Act 2001 provides a legal framework to secure the rights of individual learners by requiring schools to become more accessible and adaptable, the wider policy context has served to undermine the rights of students with SEN. A number of researchers examining administrative frameworks relating to the education of students with SEN have noted tensions and contradictions between the stated commitment to inclusion and the quasi-market system which operates. Researchers examining the impact since 1997 of the Labour government's education policy, based on notions of 'stakeholder welfare', argue that: 'the layering of new policies that have as their notional objective "inclusion" on top of practices that have demonstrably contrary effects, serve to prevent inclusionary outcomes for children and young people who, for various reasons, fail to perform in this market' (Loxley and Thomas 2001: 299). They argue that dissonance has occurred because the policies have been implemented without addressing the overall legislative framework in education, introduced by the Thatcher government from the late

1980s, which was informed by a belief in the importance of individualism and the free market. Education is seen as a commodity rather than a right. Children's rights to education on a non-discriminatory basis are undermined by a legislative framework which does not recognize the principles of the *CRC* or provide adequate rights of appeal.

Exclusion from school and race equality

African Caribbean students are disproportionately represented among those who are excluded from school. When exclusion statistics peaked during the mid-1990s, black boys were six times more likely to be excluded than white boys. Black girls were also much more vulnerable to exclusion than their white female peers, with national statistics suggesting that they were eight times more likely to be excluded (Osler and Hill 1999). African Caribbean learners do not tend to fall into the general pattern of excluded students. White excluded students are likely to be disaffected, have poor attendance records and a history of trauma and low achievement. By contrast, African Caribbean excluded students are more likely to be of average or above average ability, although they may be judged by their school to be achieving below their full potential (Ofsted 1996).

Although the government set targets to reduce the number of exclusions by a third, no targets were set to address either the disproportionate number of boys formally excluded or the disproportionate number of black students excluded. Differential rates of suspension and exclusion between different ethnic groups are not peculiar to England. In New Zealand, for example, the suspension rate for Pakeha (white) students is 10.9 per 1000, compared with 35.8 per 1000 for Maori students and 19.3 per 1000 for Pacific students (Alton-Lee and Praat 2001).

The majority of teachers we interviewed for a study in the mid-1990s were unable to provide substantial explanations as to why African Caribbean students are disproportionately represented among those excluded from school. Some suggested, in the case of boys, that it was 'youth sub-cultures' and others mentioned discrimination in society, but were reluctant to elaborate on these answers. Some also argued that pressures to meet the demands of the National Curriculum had led to an approach where teachers often failed to consider whether or not the content of lessons built upon particular children's experiences or cultures. In other words, the education provided failed to adapt to their needs and did not conform to Article 29 of the *CRC*, which states that the education of the child shall be directed to 'the development of respect for [the child's] cultural identity, culture and values'. It might also therefore be, to a greater or lesser degree, inaccessible. It might lead some children to feel neglected or excluded and thus more likely to be disaffected. One teacher argued that teacher expectations are central but that the issue was nevertheless complex, and that curriculum and teacher training also play their part:

> The over-representation of African Caribbean boys (among those excluded) is a very complicated issue, but I think expectations make a big difference, and I think we do tend, however well intentioned, to see a black boy and think they are going to be trouble … And I have seen the faces – although we don't have many Afro-Caribbean children at our school – I have seen those that we do have react so positively if a book is read that has a different central character, one that they can empathize with.
>
> (primary deputy headteacher, quoted in Osler and Hill 1999)

One explanation for the over-representation of African Caribbean students within the exclusion statistics is racism. The suggestion is not that most teachers operate in overtly racist ways but that deep-seated stereotypes held by teachers and school governors may lead to black children being seen as having behavioural difficulties. All the evidence suggests that when schools access appropriate support the numbers of exclusions can be reversed. It is critical however that specific initiatives are adopted to address the over-representation of African Caribbean children. At a local level, it is important to ascertain whether any ethnic group is over-represented and to target resources and support to this particular group, in order to achieve equity. Our research demonstrates that schools which adopt a colour-blind approach are successful in cutting exclusion for all groups, but this does not address existing inequalities. The Race Relations (Amendment) Act 2000 places a positive duty on schools to promote race equality. This legal framework is critical in ensuring that schools adapt to the needs of all learners to ensure that the schooling provided is both accessible and acceptable to them. This requires schools also to review their provision, including their curriculum (Osler and Hill 1999; Dadzie 2000; Tikly *et al.* 2004).

Redefining school exclusion

Both professional and media discourses support the view that exclusion from school is largely a male problem and that the story of girls' schooling is more or less an unqualified success. Boys are presented as in difficulty. Exclusion from school is discussed in the context of concerns about male youth crime and boys' problems are presented in the context of a wider debate about an apparent 'crisis' in masculinity. In order to understand girls' experiences of schooling and exclusion we interviewed 81 girls aged 13 to 15 years in six localities across England. Our research suggests that definitions of school exclusion need to be extended to include the experiences of girls. In particular, it is important to understand exclusion from school as a wider problem than disciplinary exclusion and to extend it to include truancy, self-exclusion and other absence as a result of pregnancy, caring responsibilities and so on (Osler *et al.* 2002; Osler and Vincent 2003).

Girls' and boys' problems are categorized differently from each other, with consequent differences in the ways problems are measured and resources allocated. For example, suicide rates for girls and young women are low compared with those of boys. Yet if the problem is reconceptualized to acknowledge differences in suicide rates between ethnic groups and to address the widespread problem of self-harm among young women, the picture looks very different. Adolescent boys are more likely to commit suicide but girls and young women do attempt it. Three times more young women than young men engage in self-harming behaviour and the group most likely to do so are girls aged 13–15 years (Meltzer *et al.* 2001).

At school level, the professionals we interviewed recognized that similar behaviour is also perceived in different ways, according to whether the student in question is a boy or a girl: 'I think there is an assumption that if a female is showing aggressive behaviours, it doesn't really fit in with the stereotype, so there must be something wrong here … let's try and sort it out. But if a boy does the same thing then that's it, they're out' (educational psychologist). Alternatively, some girls may be punished for behaviour which is regarded as 'extreme': 'Girls are greater victims of inconsistencies: there is a degree of intolerance but also a degree of shock and horror; they do not have the ability to be "loveable rogues" ' (head of pupil referral unit, quoted in Osler and Vincent 2003: 67–8).

One girl, in describing the experiences of a classmate, highlighted how various forms of exclusion can be linked:

> There was this girl and she started to get bullied because she was very big built and they used to call her fatty and everything … but she wasn't. Then she started skipping days off school. They just thought she was skipping days off because she didn't like school. I think she missed 17 maybe 20 science lessons, then it was whole days, weeks and months. Then she left because she fell pregnant and then that was it. She's trying to get into college but she hasn't got any GCSEs and it'll be hard because she's got the baby. I really wanted her to have some more life. I wanted her to have an education … to just have something to help her but she never managed it. She's dyslexic as well but she's not statemented. She just thought to herself she was thick: 'I don't know nothing. I'm stupid', because people put her down and so she'd skip days off school.
>
> (Sam, quoted in Osler and Vincent 2003: 155)

Sam shows how bullying, absenteeism, unidentified SEN and, finally, pregnancy and motherhood, combined to exclude this student. The case she presents is in many ways typical of the way in which girls are excluded from schooling without necessarily having been subject to any disciplinary process. The girls spoke a great deal about bullying and described the exclusionary processes which girls show towards each other. Bullying was, for them, a key cause of exclusion, yet professionals failed to identify it as such.

Truancy was one form of self-exclusion which featured prominently in many girls' accounts. All but one of the girls reported that they had truanted at least once. A smaller but significant number reported missing extended periods of schooling. Girls reported two types of truancy. The first occurred when individuals were fearful of attending school. Truancy was also acknowledged as something which happened because the alternative appeared more attractive:

> I didn't really fit in, so I didn't want to go to school. Teachers wouldn't help me with my work. It really started from there.
> (Belinda, self-excluder being educated in pupil referral unit)

> 'Cause some [students] they have more fun sitting around someone's house ... mainly drugs as well, 'cause once you get into drugs and that, you just think 'Oh school's rubbish, you might as well go and have fun'.
> (Caroline, self-excluder with both fixed term and permanent exclusions, mainstream school)

Evidence from both girls and young women and the professionals who worked with them suggests that pregnancy is linked to school exclusion in complex ways. Although government guidelines expressly state that pregnancy should not be a reason for disciplinary exclusion, in reality it often marks the end of an individual's schooling. Many girls who become pregnant are often already alienated from school.

School exclusion needs to be redefined so as to build upon girls' experiences of schooling and behaviour patterns which are more commonly found among girls. Redefining school exclusion to include girls' experiences is critical. It is not merely a matter of semantics. Currently, resources aimed at disaffected learners are targeted at boys. Girls' behaviour and boys' behaviour need to be considered as part of a more complex whole. If exclusion is defined so as to include girls' experiences then it is likely that resources designed to address disaffection will be more equitably distributed.

Our research suggests that although exclusion from school can sometimes take the form of voluntary self-exclusion, girls often exclude themselves when their schools fail to adapt to their needs, or when the processes of learning are inaccessible. In such situations they are unable to claim their right to education or access rights through education.

Inclusion, rights and citizenship

The struggle for the right to education is an ongoing one for many. As we have seen from the examples of the girls quoted above, and from other examples in this chapter, educational exclusion routinely involves processes of multiple discrimination which are structural. The affected people, whether they are designated as having SEN or subject to stereotypical judgements based on gender or ethnicity, are often able to identify both the ways in which they are excluded and the changes which need to take place if their right to education is to be secured. Those young people who challenge discriminatory processes and stereotypes are often judged to be rebellious or to exhibit challenging behaviour. Yet students are often in a strong position to identify the ways in which schooling might better meet their needs. In other words, they have concrete suggestions on how schooling might be accessible, acceptable and adaptable. As we sought to illustrate in Part 1, citizenship itself is a site of struggle and the realization of children and young people's citizenship rights is ongoing.

Armstrong (2004: 114–15), in his study of the life stories of adults categorized as having 'learning difficulties' argues that:

> Far from being a state of *being*, 'citizenship' is perhaps better understood as a process of *becoming*. As such, it is constantly being contested and negotiated in social practice. It is concerned with the endeavours of individuals and groups to participate on equal terms and with dignity in the life processes of which they are a part … It is about belonging and being accepted on terms that are fair, humane and dignified.

In this way the struggle for the right to education can be seen as part of the struggle for citizenship. Full citizenship depends on accessing not only the right *to* education but a number of rights *in* education and *through* it. Thus the right to education is critical in the struggle for citizenship. It is only when schooling is made accessible, acceptable and adaptable to learners' needs that the right to education can be realized.

5 Learning for cosmopolitan citizenship

Introduction

Cosmopolitan citizenship is a *status* deriving from equal entitlement to human rights. Importantly, it is based on a *feeling* of belonging and recognition of diversity across a range of communities from the local to the global. It is a *practice* involving negotiation, equitable resolution of differences and work with others to promote freedom, justice and peace within and between communities. Cosmopolitan citizenship requires consideration of the meaning and implications of belonging to a world community and an appreciation of the nature and scope of common human values. It also requires an understanding of equality and diversity in local communities. Learning for cosmopolitan citizenship therefore requires the development of a global awareness, an understanding of and commitment to human rights, and opportunities to act with others to make a difference.

In the spirit of the *Convention on the Rights of the Child* (see Appendices 2 and 3) we argue that formal education systems should promote the kind of learning for cosmopolitan citizenship that helps young citizens to recognize their common humanity, make connections between their own lives and those of others and operate effectively in contexts of cultural diversity and change.

As citizens in a diverse world we require a set of principles against which we can critically reflect on our own culture, values, beliefs and behaviours and those of our fellow citizens. Cosmopolitan citizens do not accept that all cultural practices have equal merit. They do give sympathetic consideration to different cultural traditions and practices whilst subjecting all traditions, including their own, to critical evaluation in the light of universal principles: 'Pluralism does not mean a radical relativism. That would be self-defeating. One must stand somewhere. It is not possible to stand nowhere. But neither is an attempt to stand everywhere tenable. I can realise that all cultures have claims – *and* that all cultures are bounded and open to error' (Figueroa 2000: 55).

Consequently, cosmopolitan citizens learn to take a stand on the basis of cosmopolitan principles. They need to acquire skills of 'intercultural evaluation' (Hall 2000: 49). The only universally recognized standards currently in existence derive from human rights, particularly as defined by the *UDHR* (see Appendix 1) and the *CRC*. In a multi-faith society and/or secular society, these texts provide a framework from which a school or any other learning community can derive a set of explicit, shared values. From such a reference point it becomes possible to respect others while not necessarily valuing all aspects of their cultures.

In this chapter we present models of education for citizenship that are grounded in human rights principles and we use them to evaluate the programmes of study and schemes of work for citizenship education that have been developed for schools in England. We recognize that there is no society that can claim entirely to respect and implement human rights principles and no democracy that is fully realized and inclusive. It follows that terms like citizenship, community, democracy and human rights have meanings that are contested and are constantly subject to redefinition and appropriation. *Changing Citizenship* is itself an attempt to refocus the terms of the debate relating to citizenship education.

Human rights and education

The *Universal Declaration of Human Rights* and the *Convention on the Rights of the Child* identify education as a fundamental human right and define its aims and purposes, namely to strengthen 'respect for human rights and fundamental freedoms' (*UDHR*, Article 26.2; *CRC*, Article 29.1b, see Appendices 1 and 3). In other words, children have a right to education in human rights. Education for citizenship is primarily about understanding human rights as the core principles that underpin democracy and provide the basis of societies that value and promote justice and peace in the world.

In Chapter 3 we noted that the *CRC* provides a clear and agreed definition of the purposes of education. This expression is very much in line with cosmopolitan principles (Held 2004).[1] The *CRC* asserts that education should promote an awareness of the responsibilities that are incumbent on those who exercise rights in a democracy as well as 'the development of respect for human rights and fundamental freedoms'. It should prepare the child for 'responsible life in a free society'. This implies an education that promotes critical reflection and thinking. It also implies the development of a sense of agency and the belief that citizens can make a difference.

The *CRC* sees education as a means of promoting a 'spirit of understanding, peace, tolerance, equality of sexes, and friendship among all peoples, ethnic, national and religious groups and persons of indigenous origin'.

Education for equality is consequently a key concept under the *CRC*. Phrases such as 'all peoples' imply the goal of developing global awareness. This awareness includes, importantly, 'the development of respect for the natural environment'.

In reconceptualizing education for citizenship, our starting point, as we argued in Chapter 3, is the principle that, as actors in a political space, children are citizens. Under the *CRC* young people have the right to express opinions whenever and wherever this could influence decisions affecting them (Article 12). They have freedom to receive and impart information and ideas of all kinds and to form and act upon their own opinions and beliefs whether alone or with others (Articles 13–15). They also have rights to privacy and to the protection of their reputations (Article 16). Education for citizenship is therefore the education of citizens, not the education of citizens-in-waiting.

Citizenship and community

In Chapter 1, we presented citizenship as status, feeling and practice. The status of citizenship is, at one level, exclusive. The legal status of national citizen is exclusive in that it defines who is and who is not entitled to certain rights. However, we all belong to communities in which we can practise citizenship and, at another level, we are all citizens as holders of human rights. These rights are exercised in communities. Citizens practise their citizenship within and between communities. Democracy provides a political space in which citizens can enjoy freedom but where they are necessarily constrained because their fellow citizens have rights to security and rights to exercise their freedoms too. Learning for citizenship is learning to live in a community of citizens from diverse cultural backgrounds where all bear equal rights. Citizenship is founded on the twin concepts of equality and diversity, but the reality is that in any society there are great differences in the extent to which individuals and groups are able to exercise or achieve their rights.

The willingness of citizens to compromise their freedom of action within a wider group is likely to be determined by their sense of community. Communities provide feelings of security and conviviality and are a major locus of identity. These benefits of membership may be felt to outweigh the costs, which include accepting the rules of the community. Community is therefore a key concept within the definition of citizenship.

The concept of community has developed in the English language since the fourteenth century. Originally rooted in actual social groups, sociologically, politically or geographically defined, community later developed a sense of the quality of relationships and subsequently a sense of common identity and characteristics. Whereas our relationship to the state is formal and possibly instrumental, our experience of community is more direct and significant (Williams 1983). Community is invariably used in a positive sense as a warmly persuasive word. It has an affective force that leads us to feel that it is always a good thing (Bauman 2001).

Community is consequently used rhetorically and strategically for advantage. The very positive connotations of the word give it a potential for persuasion that has been used politically. For instance, in the 1980s an unpopular poll tax was introduced in Britain as the 'community charge'. The very persuasiveness of the word community means that it is a concept that should be viewed critically and with caution.

The discourse of community also belongs to a romantic intellectual tradition looking back to a pre-industrialized society seen as based on cooperation and consensus. One architect of the communitarian movement describes communities as 'social webs of people who know one another as persons and have a moral voice' (Etzioni 1995: ix). This definition may imply a vision of community that takes as its model the local neighbourhood or village. It takes no account of social difference and unequal power relationships that can lead to resentments and conflicts.

A communitarian perspective emphasizes cultural and ethnic group solidarity as capable of overcoming conflicts. However, such communities may put up physical or conceptual walls or barriers against other communities. The wall that constitutes the so-called 'peace line' in Belfast is a physical expression of a social situation. It prevents access between neighbourhoods and perpetuates a tradition of social separation between two 'communities' defined by reference to religion, culture, politics and interpretations of history.

Communities exist in a variety of forms, all of them potentially providing a feeling of safety in an insecure world (Bauman 2001). Neighbourhoods are communities of place. Churches, mosques, synagogues or temples bring people together around common values and rituals in communities of faith. Clubs, political parties and trade unions are examples of communities of interest. In practice, the way people exercise power over others in communities means that the sense of security may be illusory. For instance, sexual abuse or harassment and forms of racism are found within all types of community.

The concept of citizenship relates essentially to membership of a civic or political community. By definition, a political community involves conflicts including consideration of and struggle over 'the meaning and scope of membership of the community in which one lives. Who belongs and what does "belonging" mean in practice?' (Hall and Held 1989: 175). This is particularly acute in the case of nationalist ideologies, but the struggle for the definition of the soul of any political entity, whether a party, a nation or a transnational grouping such as the EU, invariably produces strong

emotions and tensions. Education for citizenship must acc̲
̲itably have to address concerns that arouse c̲

citizens feeling part of a national community, they should also recognize that their 'imagined community' (Anderson 1991) is in fact a 'community of communities':

> Citizens are not only individuals but also members of particular religious, ethnic, cultural and regional communities, which are comparatively stable as well as open and fluid. Britain is both a community of citizens and a community of communities, both a liberal and a multicultural society, and needs to reconcile their sometimes conflicting requirements.
>
> (Parekh 2000: ix)

The argument presented in the Parekh Report is that a liberal narrative is not sufficient, since individuals do not exist independently of their membership of communities. A communitarian approach is also inadequate as communities are not fixed in their membership or their characteristics: they are 'open and fluid'. So the imagined community of the nation needs to find a formula for reconciling its traditions of individual freedom with the reality that many of its members may prioritize responsibilities to their communities that exist within and beyond the boundaries of the state. Parekh proposes a reconceptualization of Britain both as 'a community of citizens' and as 'a community of communities'. The community of citizens is the political nation state whose members have rights and responsibilities within that polity and guaranteed by it. The community of communities recognizes the multicultural, multiethnic and multifaith dimensions of the state. In accepting that citizens have feelings of belonging both to the state and to communities whose boundaries may extend beyond the nation (the Jewish community or the Polish community, for instance) the state guarantees the freedom for individuals to determine their own identities. The promotion of this individual freedom is a core tenet of the liberal tradition and of human rights.

The world, too, can be conceptualized as a community of citizens and a community of communities. *The Charter of the United Nations* (1945) defines the obligations of member states as 'to practise tolerance and live together in peace with one another *as good neighbours*' (emphasis added).

The UN is often referred to in terms of a community of nations. The report of the Commission on Global Governance, produced for the fiftieth anniversary of the UN, was entitled *Our Global Neighbourhood* (CGG 1995). The title implies that the definition of community can be legitimately extended to encompass a sense of identity with any or all human beings as bearers of human rights. Even if it is not yet fully democratized, there is a political community at a global level. There are international institutions such as the UN and its agencies and there are transnational political movements and pressure groups such as environmental and debt relief groups, and umbrella movements such as the WSF.

Successful living together on the planet or within a nation or state requires a sense of citizenship and a sense of security provided by membership of communities. Communities require common feelings and experiences to hold them together. These can derive from:

- a shared symbolism;
- a feeling of belonging and entitlement to certain rights of membership;
- a sense of gratitude towards and responsibility for the well-being of the community.

(Parekh 2000: 50–1)

However, communities are dynamic social groupings capable of changing and evolving. The mechanisms for this include:

- questioning of the way the community is developing;
- evaluating its strengths and weaknesses;
- political debates between different factions over visions of the future;
- fluid boundaries and welcoming new members.

(Parekh 2000: 50–1)

Communities with fluid boundaries allow individuals to have a range of belongings, identities and loyalties. To achieve this may require struggle, as those holding or aspiring to power in communities may attempt to reify a community and define it as a closed and static entity. In the 2004 elections to the European Parliament, at least two political parties, the UK Independence Party and the BNP argued that Britain could not and should not welcome new migrants on the grounds that there was no room for them. BNP election literature drew a sharp distinction between 'Britain's culture, heritage and values' and its perceived antithesis, 'multiculturalism'. Espousing a policy akin to the notorious and discredited apartheid of Afrikaaner nationalism in South Africa, the BNP campaigned for a closed and static definition of national identity: 'We respect the right of every cultural and national group in the world to preserve their unique identity and heritage. Unlike the politicians, however, the BNP believes that we British should also have that right – the right to be ourselves in our own country living under our own laws and customs' (BNP 2004). Such essentialized definitions of communities are the product of political groups ideologically motivated to change social realities. They deny the possibility that diverse communities can coexist productively within a single state. They are often a cloak for much cruder expressions of racism. In central Europe, in the 1980s and 1990s, a similar vision implemented by nationalist parties in the Balkans led to 'ethnic cleansing' and genocide.

Communities and identities

Political campaigns for narrowly-defined national identities require critical consideration in any programme of education for democratic citizenship. Identity is individual, but it is also collective. Citizenship, as we have argued, involves a feeling of belonging and community provides this as well as being a source of collective identity (Jenkins 1996). Community is a symbolic construction where individuals belong *in* a locality or a sociocultural grouping and recognize that in that context they belong *with* each other (Cohen 1985). However, it does not necessarily imply uniformity of belief or practice.

Within communities, identity formation is associated with locale, networks and memory. These concepts also help further to define community. Locale relates to routine practices, familiar locations and specific people in the immediate sphere of practical activity within which we move. The sense of locale involves layers of social interactions from the family, to the neighbourhood, to the community. It is an important concept that encapsulates 'how an individual construes their relationship to the community they inhabit and how thereafter the person considers that their community relates to the wider world' (Preston 1997: 9).

Identity is constructed in relation to networks of people with whom the individual interacts, locally or at a distance, sometimes called 'social webs' (Etzioni 1995). Identities are also constructed with reference to memory, both personal memories and collective memories. Memories and memorials are present in communities in the form of stories, myths, traditions and symbols such as street names, statues or plaques. Such collective memories are often sites of struggle. Traditions can be invented and changed. History can be rewritten. Streets and buildings can be renamed. Statues can be taken down or relocated.

The political dimensions of identity can be positive or negative in a democracy based on equal rights. Some identity groups, such as political parties with an ethno-nationalist agenda, promote negative stereotypes, incite injustice and frustrate the pursuit of justice. Other identity groups help overcome negative stereotypes and combat injustice and inequalities. Reasons for joining with others on the basis of identity include:

- to publicly express what they consider to be an important aspect of their identity;
- to conserve their culture, which they identify with the group;
- to gain material advantage for themselves and their group;
- to work with others to combat discrimination or injustice;
- to receive moral support from others sharing some part of their social identity;
- to express and act upon ethical commitments that they share with a group.

(Gutmann 2003: 210)

Thus political movements based on identity can support or oppose a cosmopolitan view of citizenship. In learning for citizenship the actions of identity groups require critical intercultural evaluation. Identity is a very significant political phenomenon in a democracy and citizens need to learn about identity politics and be enabled to think about their own identities in political terms. We have tried to express this in a model we have developed of education for citizenship.

A model of education for citizenship

We summarize key features of our approach to education for citizenship and the relationship between its components in Figure 5.1 (Osler and Starkey 1996, 1999). It is based on a grid with two vertical and two horizontal dimensions. In the vertical axes we represent citizenship education as having a *structural/political* dimension and a *cultural/personal* dimension. The structural/political strand corresponds to citizenship as status. It includes an institutional element and may emphasize cognitive skills and understandings such as acquiring knowledge of the structures of society and politics. The other strand focuses on the cultural/personal dimension, or citizenship as feeling. This approach to citizenship education is about personal development, linked primarily to cultural choices. The two dimensions are complementary rather than in tension. Both may involve action or citizenship as practice.

Figure 5.1 Components of citizenship education

	Structural/political	Cultural/personal
Minimal	**Rights** understanding and experience of • human rights • democracy • diversity • inclusion • civil society, e.g. NGOs implies: **human rights education**	**Identities** feeling of belonging • either/or (tension) • both/and (hybridity) implies: **feelings and choices**

Maximal	**Inclusion**
	 • security: physical, social,
	   psychological, financial
	 • active participation
	 • commitment to democratic
	   citizenship
	
	 implies:
	 **building a more inclusive
	 democracy**
		Competence
		 • political literacy
		 • cosmopolitan world view
		 • skills to effect change, e.g.
		   language, advocacy,
		   mobilization
		
		 implies:
		 **skills for democratic
		 participation**

The two horizontal dimensions represent a minimal and a maximal approach (McLaughlin 1992; Richardson 1996). Minimal citizenship education provides just enough knowledge, reflection and experience for learners to come to see themselves as citizens. We contend that at a minimal level, citizens need to have knowledge, understanding and experience of the democratic basis of political life, particularly human rights. They must become aware of barriers to citizenship such as discrimination and the key role of voluntary organizations and civil society in achieving justice and inclusion. All these elements can be considered to be part of the structural/political focus of citizenship education. Simultaneously, as we suggest in the top right hand quadrant of the table, citizens also need to be able to reflect on and be comfortable with a range of personal identities and consider themselves part of various communities. At one level learners may experience a tension between their own identity and that of others (either/or). For example, ethnicity is sometimes seen as a fixed caegory, whereas in reality many people redefine their ethnic background over time. Cultural and religious identities are not fixed. Individuals may identify with many groups (both/and). Chapter 6 explores young people's multiple identities. This implies a learning environment where feelings and choices about identity are explored and developed. The feeling of belonging to communities is essential for citizenship and a primary task of education is to enable learners to develop new identities to add to those that they bring to the learning process. Explorations of identities are thus at the heart of education for citizenship. Inevitably this implies considerations of political struggles around the boundaries of citizenship and identity: 'There are still boundaries, but they are blurred by all the crossings. We still know ourselves to be this or that, but the knowledge is uncertain, for we are also this *and* that' (Walzer 1997 quoted in Archard 2003: 100).

This is however the minimal entitlement. The lower horizontal axis in Figure 5.1 suggests appropriately ambitious aims for citizenship education, which we refer to as maximal, implying that citizenship education must ultimately be judged on its outcomes, namely by the society it produces. While, for the purposes of introducing our conception of citizenship education, we have placed 'minimal' and 'maximal' positions as discrete elements in the table, in fact we recognize that there is a continuum.

In a democratic context, communities from the national to the local are expected to be inclusive of all their citizens. Structures and political processes can be judged on the extent to which they reduce barriers and produce participation and enjoyment of human rights and fundamental freedoms. Knowledge of rights will not in itself achieve rights. So at the maximal position, political structures support and promote such things as a basic income, security and opportunities for active participation. Political debates provide for confrontation between a variety of visions of the good society, and active citizens contribute to these visions and help to realize them.

At a cultural and personal level, citizens in a healthy democracy will equip themselves with the competencies they need for effective participation and active engagement with others. The development of multiple identities needs to be complemented by the development of various competencies, including political literacy and skills to effect change. These are best learnt through experience rather than through academic study alone. In short, our model proposes that learning for citizenship is best achieved if it is based on acquiring knowledge, reflecting on identity, living in a community and developing skills for participation.

We have used this model to evaluate programmes of education for citizenship in a number of contexts and for drawing up our own courses of postgraduate teacher training and continuing professional development. When we evaluated European action programmes to ascertain the extent to which they were contributing to the development of understandings of citizenship, we interrogated the project documentation using a brief questionnaire based on the four quadrants of our model of citizenship education. The questionnaire is shown in Figure 5.2 (Osler and Starkey 1999).

Figure 5.2 Achieving a balanced project

1 INFORMATION	3 IDENTITIES
• Is there a focus on specific information about democracy, human rights or European values?	• Does it explore/affirm various identities, including European identity? • Does it promote intercultural development?
2 INCLUSION	4 SKILLS
• Does it prepare participants for social/economic inclusion? • Does it have an equal opportunities focus, or one which addresses the specific needs of women/girls in claiming their citizenship rights? • Does the project have active methods/encourage participation?	• Does it develop skills for democratic participation, including skills of working through transnational links?

We were able to identify the extent to which elements in the projects corresponding to the four dimensions were present. We considered a project to be balanced and well conceived if it contributed to providing information, ensuring inclusion, reflecting on identities and developing skills. We were able to make evaluative judgements about projects such as a youth exchange between Poland and Northern Ireland: 'Like a number of other case studies in our research, it developed a sense of participants' own regional identities, as well as developing a sense of inclusion, a (new) European identity and information for democracy. The participants reflected on the different ways inwhich they were, or were not, part of something called "Europe"' (Osler and Starkey 1999: 205).

The project coordinator attested to the effect of the project: 'Through the experience with others they see themselves in a new way. They acquired an increased self-esteem and an openness towards others. They realised that as a living person they always need to learn, but also that they *can* learn' (quoted in Osler and Starkey 1999: 205).

We have developed a further evaluation tool that also helps define learning outcomes for programmes of education for cosmopolitan citizenship. Drawing on UNESCO's (1995) *Integrated Framework of Action on Education for Peace, Human Rights and Democracy*, we suggest that educated cosmopolitan citizens will be confident in their own identities and will work to achieve peace, human rights and democracy within the local community and at a global level by:

- developing skills to cope with change and uncertainty;
- accepting personal responsibility and recognizing the importance of civic commitment;
- working collaboratively to solve problems and achieve a just, peaceful and democratic community;
- respecting diversity between people, according to gender, ethnicity and culture;
- recognizing that their own worldview is shaped by personal and societal history and by cultural tradition;
- recognizing that no individual or group holds the only answer to problems;
- understanding that there may be a range of solutions to problems;
- respecting and negotiating with others on the basis of equality;
- showing solidarity with and compassion for others;
- resolving conflict in a non-violent way;
- making informed choices and judgements;
- having a vision of a preferred future;
- respecting the cultural heritage;
- protecting the environment;
- adopting methods of production and consumption which lead to sustainable development;
- working to achieve harmony between immediate basic needs and long-term interests;
- promoting solidarity and equity at national and international levels.

(Osler and Vincent 2002: 22)

Education for citizenship in England

The introduction of citizenship education to schools in England needs to be situated within a wider debate about the development of citizenship within Britain. As the Parekh Report (2000) noted, the context is a diverse and pluralistic Britain within a multicultural Europe and a globalized world.

Our model of the components of citizenship education (Figure 5.1) conceptualizes it as having two interrelated components, namely the structural/political and the cultural/personal. We argue for a holistic approach at all levels. In other words, the cultural and personal elements, which by definition involve the affective as well as the cognitive domains, must interact with all teaching and learning activities designed to promote knowledge and understanding. The importance of such considerations becomes particularly acute when account is taken of the diversity within any society. In England, the National Curriculum is a uniform framework, but those required to study it are a diverse group, not necessarily identifying easily or primarily with a particular nation.

The preparation for the introduction in 2002 of citizenship as a subject within the National Curriculum for England was undertaken initially by an advisory group set up by the Secretary of state for Education and Employment. The recommendations of this working party were published in *Education for Citizenship and the Teaching of Democracy in Schools*, often referred to as the Crick Report, after its chair, political scientist Bernard Crick (QCA 1998). The report provides a framework for conceptualizing education for citizenship and develops the basic content that is included in the formal programme of study to be covered by schools. Detailed guidance for teachers on curriculum planning for citizenship has also been made available (QCA 2001a, 2001b, 2002a, 2002b).

The introduction of citizenship education provided a unique opportunity to promote education for living in a diverse society sharing basic common values. The UK government has indeed highlighted citizenship education as a key means by which education for racial equality can be achieved (Home Office 1999). Yet, in its representation of minorities, and in its discussion of identity and diversity, the Crick Report shies away from a commitment to human rights as the basic values for democracy. Although political literacy is a central concept of the Crick Report, it falls short of asserting that a commitment to human rights principles and skills for challenging racism are essential attributes of a politically literate citizen (Osler 2000c; Starkey 2000). It recommends merely that students should develop 'a concern for human rights' (QCA 1998: 44).

The Crick Report makes no mention of racism when it presents the case for education for citizenship in the light of perceived threats to our democracy. Our analysis suggests that this important and in many ways valuable report may itself unwittingly reflect racism, particularly in its references to minorities, which tend to be treated as a homogeneous group (Osler 2000c).

In its discussion of national identity in a pluralist context, the Crick Report refers to 'due regard being given to the homelands of *our* minority communities and to the main countries of British emigration' (QCA 1998: 18, emphasis added). The implication is that members of minority communities tend to see the countries from which their families migrated, possibly generations before, as their 'homelands' rather than Britain. It precludes the notion of multiple or hybrid identities, and the recognition that an individual may have more than one 'homeland' and may identify themselves as *both* British *and* of a particular ethnic grouping.

The report focuses on cultural differences between ethnic groups rather than differences in relation to power or equality of educational outcomes. In fact there is no discussion of any differences in the participation rates or leadership roles of citizens. Race and racism, either institutional or interpersonal, receive no mention. Similarly there is no discussion of the different experiences of citizenship, or leadership, by women and men.

The Crick Report developed learning outcomes for Key Stage 3 (Years 7 to 9) and proposed study of the *CRC*, the *UDHR* and the *ECHR*. Study of the *CRC* was to be in the context of learning about English law as it was included alongside concepts such as *discrimination, equal opportunities, tribunal, ballot* and *trade unions*. The other two human rights instruments were to be introduced in the context of *prejudice, discrimination, xenophobia* and *pluralism*, though not *racism*, a term that is largely banned from any document or speech emanating from the DfES. Human rights as a concept was also linked to *overseas aid, development* and *charity*. What is missing is any recognition that human rights are about democracy and about shared core values. Moreover, the context is resolutely national, even when linked to aid and development. Human rights are not invoked in the context of the study of Europe or even of the UN (QCA 1998: 49–52).

However, the mention of specific human rights instruments disappeared in the definitive programmes of study, to be replaced by a more general formulation, 'the legal and human rights and responsibilities underpinning society' (DfEE/QCA 1999b: 14). There is official guidance, in the form of schemes of work for teachers, and this includes a unit on human rights at Key Stage 3 and one at Key Stage 4 (QCA 2001a, 2002a). At Key Stage 3 the emphasis is on the (British) Human Rights Act 1998, which incorporated the *ECHR* into UK law. The more fundamental document for understanding human rights, namely the *UDHR*, is not proposed until Key Stage 4 (Years 10 and 11).

A limited definition of citizenship

In order to convey succinctly the essence of citizenship as a school subject and to provide a broad sense of the expectations of the programme, the Crick Report provided 'a sound-bite summary of three senses or strands of Citizenship education' (QCA 1998: 63). This has been featured in slightly expanded form on the DfES website:

> *Social and moral responsibility:* Pupils learning from the very beginning self-confidence and socially and morally responsible behaviour, both in and beyond the classroom, towards those in authority and towards each other.

> *Community involvement:* Pupils learning how to become helpfully involved in the life and concerns of their neighbourhood and communities, including learning through community involvement and service.

Political literacy: Pupils learning about the institutions, issues, problems and practices of our democracy and how citizens can make themselves effective in public life, locally, regionally and nationally, through skills and values as well as knowledge – this can be termed political literacy, which encompasses more than political knowledge alone.

(QCA 1998: 40–1)

This schematic view of the content of education for citizenship has been widely taken up by those providing training programmes and promoting citizenship, but it has been subject to little critical analysis. In fact this 'sound-bite' formulation entirely fails to acknowledge globalization or even to recognize an international dimension. There is no sense of a wider world. The descriptor for political literacy mentions only the local, the regional and the national.

The limited view of citizenship is perhaps encapsulated in the phrase 'our democracy' in the definition of political literacy, which clearly confines the object of study to the UK. Although there is a clear intention that young people learn to make themselves effective within the system, there is no sense that the system itself is flawed by inequalities and economic and social exclusion. In other words, that the basic principles on which 'our democracy' is based, namely justice, human rights and the rule of law are not always fully upheld. Although 'power' is a key concept in the Crick framework, this is not translated into the specification of knowledge and understanding to be acquired.

Surprisingly, for a definition of citizenship, the emphasis in the summary is not on rights but rather on responsibilities and, arguably, deference. This is implied in the phrase 'morally responsible behaviour ... towards those in authority', as if behaviour towards those in authority was more significant than behaviour to others in the community. Community is defined essentially in terms of neighbourhood. Although the strands are said to be interrelated, the political nature of social responsibility and of community involvement is not invoked. In other words, the view of citizenship promoted by this summary differs greatly from the model of cosmopolitan citizenship and the model of children as citizens that we developed in Part 1. Far from being at the heart of this official schema, human rights are marginalized.

The programmes of study for citizenship in England are formulated very broadly. In fact there is little differentiation between the content prescribed for Key Stage 1, Years 1–3, the youngest learners, and Key Stage 4. Schools have the freedom to provide opportunities for young people to reflect on their identities, although the instructions are that 'pupils *should be taught* about the diversity of national, regional, religious and ethnic identities' (emphasis added). This is not the same as having opportunities to reflect on and discuss identities. Similarly, 'pupils should be taught about the legal and human rights and responsibilities underpinning society', but this vague formulation fails to ensure that undertakings with respect to the *UDHR* and the *CRC* are in fact respected.

Reconceptualizing citizenship

Citizenship requires a sense of belonging. To neglect the personal and cultural aspects of citizenship is to ignore the issue of belonging. Cosmopolitan citizens are confident in their own multiple identities and schools can usefully provide learning opportunities to explore and develop these (Osler and Starkey 2003). In Chapter 6 we present evidence from our research with young people that suggests that they are engaging as citizens and learning the skills for cosmopolitan citizenship within their homes and communities as well as in schools.

Cosmopolitan citizenship implies recognition of our common humanity and a sense of solidarity with others. It is insufficient, however, to feel and express a sense of solidarity with others elsewhere if we cannot establish a sense of solidarity with others in our own communities, especially those others whom we perceive to be different from ourselves. The challenge is to accept shared responsibility for our common future and for solving our common problems.

We suggest that citizenship education requires reconceptualizing in the context of globalization. Our research suggests that education for cosmopolitan citizenship enables young people to perceive themselves as citizens with rights and responsibilities locally, nationally and globally. This is not a process that can be realized exclusively at school. Learning also takes place in families and communities and teachers need to be sensitive to and aware of sites of citizenship learning beyond the school. By building on this community learning, schools can encourage learners to make connections between their various experiences and the knowledge they acquire through formal study.

6   Practising citizenship

Introduction

The way individuals practise citizenship depends to a large extent on their identities and on the way they perceive their roles in a range of communities. Our values, too, are an essential element of our identities and are likely to be shaped by experiences. Our identities are shaped by our social contexts and by those with whom we engage in what is essentially a dialectical process. Constructing an identity or identities is essentially a political process. This political dimension has been described as challenging to the political establishment: 'We live in a time when the very private experience of having a personal identity to discover, a personal destiny to fulfil, has become a subversive political force of major proportions' (Roszak 1979 quoted in Giddens 1991: 209). But this political dimension of identity is not always acknowledged in education for citizenship.

As young people struggle for their rights and for equal opportunities, they are involved in emancipatory politics. As they construct their identities they are engaged in what Giddens calls 'life politics': 'While emancipatory politics is a politics of life chances, life politics is a politics of lifestyle' (Giddens 1991: 214). Young people can experience power struggles and conflicts of an essentially political nature in their everyday lives. One important role of education for citizenship is to help them become aware of and understand the politics underlying their choices.

This chapter explores the identities and sense of belonging of young people in Leicester, a culturally diverse city in Britain. The demography of Leicester changed considerably during the 1970s as the city began to experience the migration of families from East Africa. The 1990s also saw changes in the population as refugees and asylum-seekers arrived. Many children in the city's schools have a family history of migration, their grandparents or parents having moved to Leicester from a range of other countries. We set out to explore with young people in four inner-city schools what they understood by community and how they felt about their relationship to their neighbourhoods, the city and the wider world. In particular we wished to gain insights into the opportunities they have to experience rules, rights, responsibilities and institutions. We examined evidence of their engagement with local communities.

It is often assumed that, as non-voters, young people are not involved or engaged in political processes. Consequently, little attempt is made to build on their existing political knowledge or experience and to use this as a foundation for citizenship learning in school. Disengagement from formal political parties is equated with widespread apathy, ignorance and complacency, despite evidence to suggest that many young people are finding alternative routes to political action (Roker *et al.* 1999). It is rarely acknowledged that, even among those of voting age, a decision not to vote may be a rational and considered political response rather than an expression of apathy.

Young people's interests may be overlooked because they are perceived as citizens-in-waiting rather than as citizens in their own right and thus they are seen as lacking equal status with other stakeholders. It is axiomatic in many areas of policy that user groups be consulted before key reforms are put in place. However, it was only in 2003 that the British government felt the need to demonstrate that it was consulting young people (DfES 2003). Whereas in Scotland young people were invited to contribute to the process of formulating programmes of citizenship education, in England no such consultation was organized. We argue for the importance of building on learners' existing political knowledge or experience, broadly defined, as a foundation for citizenship learning in school.

Young people are often stereotyped as lacking judgement, knowledge and manners, and those from minority ethnic backgrounds are often assumed to have further deficits. Black and minority ethnic students may be subject to labelling and stigmatizing on the basis of appearance (Jenkins 1996) and be considered as second-class citizens. Assumptions may concern nationality, residence status, language skills, capacity to operate effectively in society, religious affiliations and the compatibility of religious beliefs with social norms as defined by the majority community. Visible minorities are exposed to 'everyday racism' (Essed 1991) and 'street racism' (Parekh 2000). Since 11 September 2001, the popular press has contributed to arousing considerable antagonism towards Muslim women, portrayed as oppressed and refusing to accept modernity, and Muslim men, associated with hostility to Western society and sympathetic to terrorism. Individuals and groups have been harassed and mosques have come under attack in England as in many other Western countries. In Britain, Muslims have also been subject to enhanced and unwelcome police attention, including unjustified stop and searches, and arrests. Within the criminal justice system, Muslims are 9 per cent of the prison population but only 3 per cent of the general population. There is significant evidence of prison staff routinely engaging in the crudest forms of anti-Muslim racism (Commission on British Muslims and Islamophobia 2004).

When the police force or other public sector services make assumptions about and discriminate against members of ethnic minority groups on the basis of name or appearance, this amounts to institutional racism (Banton 1997; Macpherson 1999). Research from Canada confirms the findings of earlier ethnographic studies in English schools (e.g. Wright 1986, 1992) and the evidence we present in Chapter 4 that teachers are not immune from discriminatory judgements: '[in the school being studied] skin colour and its related physical traits serve perhaps more than any other characteristics to mark students ... Teachers often adjust their expectations of students on the basis of the latter's physical appearance' (Ryan 1999: 86). The implications of this can be seen in disciplinary practices, academic assessments, career guidance and in the disproportionate number of black and minority ethnic students excluded from schools (Osler and Hill 1999).

The disregarding of the strengths and experience of young people is the context in which, as we have previously demonstrated, those responsible for developing programmes of education for citizenship may assume that young people from ethnic minorities require extra instruction in national citizenship and even special programmes not required by the majority (Osler 2000c; Osler and Starkey 2001). They may fail to appreciate that young people are likely to bring considerable insights to their citizenship learning. Those from minority communities are likely to have understandings and experiences that challenge those of the majority. In particular they are likely to have experience of emancipatory politics and life politics.

Communities and identities

Our research project involved some 600 young people aged 10–18 who responded to a questionnaire. They were drawn from four schools in the city. We also collected further data from volunteers who took part in two workshops we ran at each school. Ours was an opportunity sample, but the demographic composition of the schools is in many ways typical of inner-city schools in Europe.

The schools were situated in two contrasting inner-city areas. In School A in Year 9 (aged 13–14 years) the vast majority of the students (87 per cent) described themselves as Indian, around 5 per cent as from other Asian backgrounds, 4 per cent as white and 4 per cent as being of mixed descent. The school has a relatively stable pupil population. More than 80 per cent of our sample had lived in Leicester for 12 years or more, that is, for all or most of their lives. Many of the parents of these students were formerly students at the same school, and for many families this is the third generation living in Leicester, their grandparents having migrated to Britain from East Africa during the late 1960s and 1970s.

By contrast, School B, an 11–16 comprehensive, has a very mobile school population: 78 per cent of our sample from Year 9 had lived in Leicester for four years or less. Around a third had lived in the city for less than two years and had therefore joined the school since Year 7. A significant proportion of these had arrived in Britain from overseas, many of them as refugees and asylum-seekers. There was greater ethnic diversity within the school population, with 60 per cent of the students describing themselves as Indian, 11 per cent as Pakistani, 7 per cent as Bangladeshi and 4 per cent as from other Asian backgrounds. A further 4 per cent described their heritage as African, 3 per cent as Caribbean, around 3 per cent as white and 4 per cent as being of mixed heritage. The self-descriptors of these students indicate considerable heterogeneity within each of these broad groupings.

School C was a primary school whose pupils usually graduated to School A. Two thirds of the sample described themselves as Indian, 17 per cent as being of mixed heritage and 12 per cent as white British. The proportion of mixed heritage children was significantly higher than in the secondary school which reflects a demographic trend noted in the 2001 census where increasing numbers of respondents identify themselves as being of mixed heritage. The pupils we worked with were in the final year, Year 6, aged 10 or 11.

School D, a college for 16–19-year-olds, drew on a wide catchment area and contained students from a variety of backgrounds, with white British being in the minority. All the groups we worked with and the population answering our questionnaire contained both boys and girls in approximate balance.

At School A all those participating in workshops were members of the school council who volunteered to participate in the project. They had therefore worked together before and knew each other quite well. In School B, workshop participants were selected and invited to participate by senior teachers. The young people were representative of the wider school population, in that they were drawn from a variety of religious and ethnic backgrounds, with some relatively new to the school. They did not all know each other well, although each student knew at least one other, being from the same tutor group. The younger children from School C were from the same class and knew each other well. The older students from the college, School D, volunteered from a sense of interest or curiosity. Some of the group were members of the college students' council.

We negotiated with the headteachers of the four schools to work intensively with a group of about eight students for two sessions about two weeks apart. We asked for a group that included boys and girls with a range of attainment. The students should be at ease working with two unknown adults. We explained that we would be conducting two workshops with the group, the purpose of which was to explore their understandings and experience of citizenship, justice/injustice and inclusion/exclusion. We also asked to administer a questionnaire to a whole year group. This covered questions of community, participation, identity and citizenship.

The format of the workshops was identical for each school, irrespective of age group. The first started with paired introductions where students in turn introduced their neighbour by name, particular interests and ambitions. This look to the future was then complemented by a consideration of their past and their background. They were invited to make notes about their own background and origins, in terms of geography and place; ethnicity and culture; and their experience, such as key events in their lives. The questionnaire drew heavily on a model developed by Richardson (Richardson and Miles 2003). This provided the opportunity to reflect on and share with us key aspects of their own identities.

In the workshops we facilitated a group discussion about two contrasting articles taken from a local newspaper as illustrative of aspects of citizenship. The first had the headline 'Hundreds demonstrate against asylum system'. It covered a march through the city centre organized by the Leicester Civil Rights Movement following the death by suicide of an asylum-seeker who was due to be deported to Iran. The second recounted the success of a three-year campaign mounted by a young local skateboarder to gain specialized facilities in his local park. Questions for discussion revolved round reactions to the stories; students' responses to the campaigns; personal involvement in anything similar; and suggestions for how other young people might be more engaged in political activity and make a difference.

The final activity of the workshop set up a research task for the students. Each participant was given a disposable camera and set the task of taking a set of photographs to illustrate 'me and my community'. They were given a deadline for handing in the film so that it could be printed in time for the second workshop.

The main activity of the second workshop was for each participant to create a poster entitled 'me and my community'. The elements of the poster were the photographs, captions and commentaries, and any other graphic material that the owner could find or generate that added to the effect. Each participant then presented the poster to the researchers and to the group, with opportunities for clarification, commentary and discussion. They agreed to leave the posters with us, as a source of data, and received their own set of the photographs.

The data that we generated by this process of interaction with the four schools is both quantitative and qualitative. Our qualitative data consists of field notes of the discussions, written responses to the activities in the workshops, the posters of photographs and commentaries and responses to open-ended questions from the general questionnaire.

Citizenship and community

The young people with whom we worked provided considerable evidence of feeling part of a range of communities. In Chapter 5, drawing on the work of the commission on the *Future of Multi-Ethnic Britain*, we identified three factors of community cohesion, namely: a feeling of belonging; a sense of gratitude and responsibility; and a shared symbolism (Parekh 2000: 50). We use these characteristics of community as a framework for the analysis of the responses.

A feeling of belonging

When asked in the questionnaire to name the main communities in Leicester, only a very few students (about 3 per cent) named a geographical location such as their neighbourhood. Although a third of the students failed to respond to the question, suggesting that they were perhaps unclear as to the meaning of the word 'community', over half the students responded unequivocally by naming religious or ethnic groups. This equation of community and culture was noted in a previous study as the dominant discourse in another multicultural inner-city area of England (Baumann 1996). It suggests that our respondents recognized that they themselves and others around them are defined significantly in terms of their belonging to religious and ethnic communities.

As well as these cultural communities, almost all the young people identified with their city, Leicester. The great majority refer to Leicester as where they come from. Many proudly mention their birthplace as the Royal Infirmary. A number also mention specific areas of the city. The neighbourhood is perhaps the locale with which young people more easily identify: 'The best thing about Leicester to me is the area [Belgrave] I come from. Everyone is really friendly' (Dipti, 17-year-old girl). The neighbourhood is seen as a resource to be celebrated whether in general terms or for the specific amenities available. The youngest respondents express this with enthusiasm:

> I love it. I like everything about it.
>
> > (Nadine,10-year-old girl)

> I like my area because of loads of close shops.
>
> > (Sunil, 10-year-old boy)

The locale is composed of significant places and people within the city. For the youngest in the study, the proximity of friends is very significant and school is a major source for creating friendships. Friends also provide security and caring:

> In my area I like that I have friends from school living across [from] my house.
>
> (Alyah, 10-year-old girl)

> These are some of my friends. I took this picture because they are safe to me.
>
> (Sunil, 10-year-old boy)

> These are my friends Hanisha, Priti, Satinder and Aisha. They are really nice, caring, kind and jolly all the time.
>
> (Jagdish, 10-year-old boy)

Safety and security are important for a sense of belonging, and the youngest informants also recognize the importance of those in the community who have a role in keeping them safe. This includes school staff: 'This is Sheila, a dinner supervisor. She is telling someone off, probably because someone was fighting' (Sandeep, 10-year-old girl). Older students also stress family, friendship and continuity as constituting community:

> This is the street on which I have grown up. All my friends live in the area.
>
> (Tariq, 17-year-old boy)

> All my relatives are no more than ten-minute walk away from where I live. So I get to see them quite often.
>
> (Meera, 17-year-old girl)

The family home is the fundamental place of belonging and so highlighted by many in their exhibitions, often with parents or family included:

> This is my mum standing outside my house.
>
> (Alyah, 10-year-old girl)

> This is my house. The blue one. I picked this photo because I really like my house.
>
> (Jagdish, 10-year-old boy)

> I've circled my house, well the porch anyway, on my little estate. It's only a small place but I like it that way. And the community is

very good and get on well. It's also very safe there (but my bike did get stolen last week).

(Sean, 16-year-old boy)

Community is also defined as the people and significant places in the neighbourhood. Rehana describes what she sees from her house and in her street. This includes the public facility of a park and two places of worship:

> This is St Peter's Church. I see lots of people go. I see weddings, funerals ... This is the big mosque in St Peter's. Lots of people go there every Friday to pray. The mosque is just behind my house. When it's a big day, I always go up in the attic to see people and I get a very good view. I quite like my community where I live because I get a good view of everything. I have very good neighbours – they are very friendly. At the bottom of my street I have a small park and pond. Old people go there for a walk, it's a small pond. In the summer little kids go there to play.
>
> (Rehana, 14-year-old girl)

This is a community in which Rehana feels at ease and where she recognizes people to be friendly. There is no sense of a hierarchy of esteem for the places of worship. Services in both church and mosque are observed as important public occasions attracting crowds, although she herself does not attend. In short, the community in which she lives is itself a community of communities (Parekh 2000). It consists of old and young people and contains communal, safe, public spaces. She is able to observe and gain a sense of perspective.

One young man who had arrived in Leicester fairly recently already felt at ease in the cosmopolitan neighbourhood where he lived and he compared it favourably with the more homogenous area where he previously lived in Zimbabwe. He is proud of the cultural diversity he experiences, and he identifies with his place of worship as providing a focus to his week and a sense of historical continuity. The other key institution in his neighbourhood is the community centre, which he associates with leisure and relaxation:

> My church is a very important place for me. I am not very religious but I love going to pray every Sunday. It's a really old building and on its other side there is our community centre. At my community centre is where people go and relax and chill. At the same centre there are clubs, karate, drama etc. I do karate at this centre and it is good fun. My street is called G. It's in Highfields, there are many people living there, people of many cultures, religion and race.

> I like my street people and these many cultures which are fascinating and you can learn more in life with many cultures surrounding you.
>
> (Morgan, 14-year-old boy)

Morgan clearly feels privileged to live in a multicultural area. He recognizes that his mixed community is a resource for learning. Many respondents consider Leicester to be friendly and diverse and there is perhaps a tendency to idealize the city when presenting it to us. They are particularly proud of the diversity that for them constitutes the essence of their city. Religious buildings are the outward and visible signs of this multiculturalism, but the availability of secular places of entertainment is also seen as an asset:

> Leicester is a multicultural city so I took a picture of a church but I was too busy to go down Belgrave Road to take pictures of temples and mosques.
>
> (Wayne, 12-year-old boy)

> Leicester is a multicultural city, so everyone gets along with everyone. In terms of facilities everything is near, such as my college and ex-secondary school. As for entertainment we have everything.
>
> (Meera, 17-year-old girl)

> Leicester is called the 'multicultural capital' as a lot of communities live together.
>
> (Mohamed, 17-year-old boy)

Since citizenship is a feeling of belonging, these young people are acutely aware of themselves as citizens. The greatest source of pride in their city is the fact that it is a multicultural community and they are firmly committed to a diverse society composed of a variety of religious and ethnic communities. They recognize the factors that make for security in their communities, starting with a home and friends and extending to those adults, teachers and supervisors that have responsibility for their welfare. They are aware of some places that enable people to enjoy their fundamental human rights, such as the right to rest and leisure, represented by parks and community centres (*UDHR*, Article 24) and freedom of thought, conscience and religion (*UDHR*, Article 18) symbolized by various places of worship. Although they do not articulate these rights, it will not be difficult, in a formal educational setting, to help them make the connection between their neighbourhoods and these universal principles.

Gratitude towards and responsibility for the well-being of the community

Expressions of gratitude are common throughout the responses. Parents and relatives are often singled out as significant influences and their specific contributions to education and upbringing acknowledged:

> My mum has made a difference to me because she tells me what to do and what not to do. She also explains things to me.
>
> (Mohit, 12-year-old boy)

> My parents have brought me up being able to do what I believe in. Don't have many restrictions.
>
> (Ayleen, 14-year-old girl)

> My grandmother has made the difference in me because she was very religious and she taught me a whole lot of stuff about God and I changed completely.
>
> (Anant, 12-year-old boy)

Several of the respondents chose to photograph their teachers. The older students wrote explicitly and positively about the encouragement of their parents, their peers and their teachers:

> Parents have influenced me to aim for the highest and the best, always encouraging me to do well in education because they never had the opportunities to do so. Teachers have influenced my way of thinking.
>
> (Meera, 17-year-old girl)

> Parents have influenced me in being truthful, honest and always aiming to do well. My friends have influenced in doing well.
>
> (Dipti, 17-year-old girl)

> Friends, sharing their opinions, has meant I have formed very strong opinions of my own.
>
> (Anita, 17-year-old girl)

The caption to one photo is 'my primary school' and the commentary reads: 'Grew up here. This place has educated me and started me off in life. I will never forget this. Medway Primary School will always be a part of me' (Tariq, 17-year-old boy).

With feelings of belonging to communities and of gratitude, comes a recognition that this entails responsibilities. Even the youngest recognize the importance of taking responsibilities within their school. One of the photos has this caption: 'This is the door monitors Aisha and Natalie. Sometimes I help out doing the door. I took this photo because I want people to see people doing this' (Jagdish, 10-year-old boy). Even at this age Jagdish is concerned to encourage others to take on responsibilities within the school community. Other young respondents express concerns for particular problems in their neighbourhood and some express a willingness to take responsibility for tackling these issues. One is concerned with vandalism and road safety. She chose to take a picture of overturned traffic cones with the commentary: 'This picture shows carelessness in the roads' (Nadeera, 12-year-old girl). Another is concerned for the quality of her environment: 'I don't like all the litter people throw on the floor and I'm willing to do something about it' (Ravinder, 10-year-old girl). Others have a sense of responsibility to wildlife as important to the local environment. A picture of some birds in a bush was labelled: 'I believe wildlife preservation in a city is very important' (Sean, 16-year-old boy).

Several respondents recognize their debt to public or municipal facilities, including parks, libraries and sports centres:

> This is very important to me because I live opposite the park. I have a lot of childhood memories, e.g. feeding the birds every morning.
> (Dipti, 17-year-old girl)

> All my childhood memories! Played in this park with all my cousins and friends. This park is very important to me as it is my childhood.
> (Meera, 17-year-old girl)

> This is my local library which I'm a member of. I visit it to study or revise for tests and borrow books when I'm bored.
> (Ayleen, 14-year-old girl)

> This is very important to me because when I'm down and depressed I visit the library to read.
> (Dipti, 17-year-old girl)

The young people use and value facilities provided by the local council. They do not explicitly acknowledge the political dimension of what they are reporting, namely that the facilities they use are supported through taxation and that they are free at the point of use. The fact that they express the importance of these facilities to their lives, both now and over time, provides a further opportunity for formal citizenship education to link with their lived experience.

A number of the young people had also gained an understanding of services and procedures through experiences such as visits to hospitals, housing and social security offices, and dealings with police and immigration officers, where they were often supporting and sometimes interpreting for an adult. Some were required to present a case or act as an advocate. Individuals were gaining and practising skills for citizenship and these examples, together with others where young people gave informal help to neighbours and family members, illustrate sites of learning for citizenship in homes and the community that can be built upon in schools.

A sense of responsibility is also expressed in the act of raising money for charities, often with the support of the school and often with an international perspective. The funds raised locally go towards a national campaign mediated by television and intended to provide assistance towards development projects in countries with a much lower per capita income than Britain: 'The reason I am bald in this picture is because I was raising money for Comic Relief' (Mohan, 10-year-old boy). Others had been engaged in fundraising efforts for a variety of causes including earthquake victims in Gujarat: 'I did a three-day sponsored silence for breast cancer a year ago. I mainly did this because I had just found out that a friend's mother had died as a result of this and it brought it closer to home' (Anjali, 17-year-old girl). Some demonstrate solidarity in the community by being regularly involved in helping others: 'Done a lot of voluntary work with disabled people, especially children. Makes me appreciate what I have and what I'm capable of' (Anita, 17-year-old girl).

While Mohan has learnt about the work of Comic Relief and other voluntary agencies, both from television programmes and through follow-up at school, Anjali acknowledges the learning experience she has had in the community from personal knowledge of someone with a fatal disease. Anita has a strong sense of responsibility to others and her voluntary work is also a powerful learning experience for her.

Many of the young people were working collaboratively to solve problems and achieve a just, peaceful and democratic community. A recent instance involving several of our participants was a campaign to save a local school, including writing to their MP and collecting signatures for a petition.

Contrary to prevailing stereotypes, the young people we spoke to clearly articulated a sense of belonging and community and a sense of responsibility that extends beyond local and national horizons. There is much for programmes of education for citizenship to build on. It would be mistaken to think that these young people are deficient in their citizenship and sense of belonging. Schools can still, however, play a very important role in helping them to explore the political issues behind their lives and activities in the community.

Shared symbolism

Communities are formed around shared symbolism and teaching about the communal symbols is a task shared by families and by the formal education system. In multicultural societies there are public secular symbols and those that represent or are meaningful to particular groups or traditions within the communities. One of the youngest participants presented certain architectural features as representing secular Leicester: 'This is the clock tower in the city centre. I took this picture because it is the best place people meet' (Sunil, 10-year-old boy). This is recognition that the city centre is a public space where young people and adults are able to meet freely. The clock tower is a landmark in the centre and surrounded by a pedestrianized area. It is therefore a very useful meeting place available to all. Referring to a piece of public sculpture nearby, Sunil wrote: 'This is a really nice statue in the city centre. I took this picture because I like sport'. Leicester has a number of top-level teams in various sports and this is recognized in this piece of public sculpture. Members of all Leicester's communities can identify with this sporting tradition.

Alongside these widely recognized public symbols in the city centre there are lesser-known but nonetheless significant places within neighbourhoods. Sunil also highlighted the significance and the symbolism of a tree, specially planted in a local park in memory of a young boy who had died of cancer the previous year: 'I took this picture because my friend's brother died and they planted this to remember him'.

Whereas Sunil chooses to highlight secular symbols, several other students emphasized their pride in belonging to a religious community. The students delighted in explaining to each other and to us their family traditions and practices. The youngest respondents did not always distinguish between rituals that are religious in nature and others which are secular family traditions around hospitality and eating:

> I like being a Hindu. [Our] traditions – speak Gujarati; go to temple every Sunday, every Friday have takeaway.
>
> (Dinesh, 10-year-old boy)

> We have Sunday dinner every Sunday.
>
> (Nadine, 10-year-old girl)

> I'm Hindu – celebrate Diwali; pray every day. Like religion, food's good.
>
> (Mohan, 10-year-old boy)

Many respondents provided detailed accounts of their religious practice and observance. Religious buildings figured prominently in the posters including those of the youngest participants:

My Mosque. Some people from my Mosque.

(Alyah, 10-year-old girl)

This is a Hindu temple called a Mandir. I took this picture because it is special.

(Sunil, 10-year-old boy)

The five pictures on the left are all Mandir. I pray here.

(Mohan, 10-year-old boy)

I am a Sikh and I go to the temple and pray – and we celebrate important things like Vashaki, mostly.

(Sandeep, 10-year-old girl)

This is the teachers of my religious group. I go every Sunday. We learn about living and God one hour. It's better than watching Sunday television.

(Ranjit, 14-year-old boy)

This is Ram Mandir near Belgrave Road. I go to a religious class every Saturday.

(Asha, 13-year-old girl)

Several were keen to communicate the significance of religious places and explain the symbolism to those from different traditions:

This is an outside view of the Swaminarayan Hindu Mission. I go every Sunday for religious studies. I've drawn a Hindu symbol ... [This is] the local temple showing statues of Hindu gods. This is an inside view. The photo is of Pramukh Swami Maharaj. The picture on the left is Sahajanand Swami [God]. Next to him is his ideal saint, Gunatitanand Swami.

(Mohit, 12-year-old boy)

An older respondent stresses the importance to him of his place of worship: 'This helped create my beliefs and values. I visit the mosque about three times a day. The mosque is a very special and sacred place. All people come together and pray to God' (Tariq, 17-year-old boy). This is a clear example of a lifestyle choice. The student identifies with his Muslim faith and involves himself in the life of the mosque. Given the extent of

Islamophobia or anti-Muslim discrimination in Britain following the events of 11 September 2001, his life politics are likely to lead to attention to emancipatory politics. As a young British citizen, Tariq is entitled to equality of treatment, but this may require more effort on his part than for someone from the majority community.

The workshops we offered specifically invited the young informants to communicate their understandings of community to an audience, including ourselves as outsiders to some of their communities. The didacticism of the responses is impressive. The young people were clearly concerned to ensure that their audience understood aspects of community that were important to them.

These articulations of feelings about communities and explanations of practice and ritual illustrate the case for listening to young people and involving them in the teaching and learning process. Young people learn much from each other and this is particularly valuable in the case of education for citizenship where members of a class may be able to provide first-hand accounts of communities and of secular and religious symbols. We argue that learning for citizenship is much more complex than the programmes of study for the National Curriculum suggest. These preface each aspect of the syllabus with: 'pupils should be taught about' and 'pupils should be taught to' (DfEE/QCA 1999a). This seems to place the onus on the teacher rather than on the learning process, albeit organized by the teacher. An alternative formulation such as 'pupils should learn about ...' would be more coherent with active learning and student-centred approaches.

Changing and evolving communities

Communities evolve and adapt. Individuals and groups reflect on the ways in which the community is developing and may well adopt a critical stance. Political parties, pressure groups or factions may articulate different visions of the future. Individuals may be expected to make choices. Communities often have formal mechanisms and structures within which these debates can be held. At a national level this may be a parliament and there are regional and local councils that make decisions about resources and spending within their areas. Churches, temples, synagogues and mosques have meetings and councils where debates about the future take place and decisions are taken. School communities have governing bodies and, in many cases, a school council. All of these are sites of political activity.

Communities also evolve as members come and go, opt in and opt out. Communities are dynamic social groups with fluid boundaries and a capacity to welcome new members (Parekh 2000). Individuals contribute to the development of their communities. As we have suggested before, education for citizenship involves awareness of the past and of the history of the community. It implies working in the present and looking to the future. Individuals and groups have constantly to decide what is important to preserve and what needs changing (Osler and Starkey 1996). In talking to the young people in our research study we found that they were engaged with these processes and, through their critical reflection, contributing positively to the development of their community.

Reflecting on and reviewing community development

Our respondents had began to articulate political awareness of the need for change and improvement. They confidently express what is important to them and what needs to be changed. One particular topic of concern is the state of the immediate environment. Mohan (10) objects to: 'litter condition, amount of pollution'. Alyah, in the same class, is anxious about what occurs in her neighbourhood after dark: 'In my area I don't like that sometimes at night when you're about to fall asleep people start to make loud noises and keep us awake'.

An older student, Anita (17), who has lived in the same house on a council estate all her life, reports 'a lot of crime, attacks, drugs'. However, she has overcome her anxieties: 'My parents are quite scared, but I'm used to it'. These three students evaluate their environment, whether the physical conditions (litter, pollution, noise) or the social environment of fear linked to violence and crime.

We have noted religious affiliation as an important element in the identities of the students we worked with. Many were starting to challenge traditional structures and expectations, evaluating them in the light of other values they held, particularly a strong sense of a right to equality. Several of the students identifying themselves as coming from a Hindu background simultaneously expressed their pride in their culture and religion and contested the inequalities inherent in the caste system and in traditional gender roles:

> In my culture, I don't believe in some of the Indian values, like the caste system, women doing all the cooking, fasting, and so on. But overall, I'm proud of my culture.
>
> (Meera, 17-year-old girl)

> In my religion, I don't like the fact that parents are more lenient with their sons and stricter with the daughters.
>
> (Anjali, 17-year-old girl)

I don't like the way parents put pressure on their children and how
they expect a lot from girls and not boys.

(Dipti, 17-year-old girl)

Sean, (16), from an Irish background, resents the pressure on him for
religious conformity, but nonetheless takes pride in what he calls his
origins: 'Ireland plays a part in my life. [I'm] open to all, not part of anything, prefer to decide for myself what I believe rather than taking on one
particular belief. Look at all beliefs. Believe that fear is an issue in belief.
Shouldn't be. Pressure also'. Both his parents and three of his four grandparents are from Leicester, but the influence of his Irish grandfather, whom
he describes as a 'strong Catholic' has been very significant. He is now
working out his own sense of identity and beliefs.

Anita (17) is also exploring her own relationship to religious belief.
From a Hindu family, she describes herself as an 'Asian atheist'. She has
been influenced by her sister, who left home at age 17 to marry a Muslim
and converted. Her parents, although strict, have been impressed at the
couple staying together for 13 years and have come to accept the situation.

In this way the life choices of young people influence the dynamics of
the community. They may trigger inter-generational conflicts, but these
usually resolve themselves and older generations may learn from the experiences of the young as well as vice versa.

Commitments to equality are also expressed in forthright criticisms of
manifestations of racism in the community:

I'm White, English. [I] hate the idea of small, all white village communities, very parochial. [I] hate [expressions like] 'half-caste' and
'coloured'.

(David, 16-year-old boy)

What I dislike is the stereotypes put on Asians and getting racist
comments from others who are not educated to understand.

(Mohamed, 17-year-old boy)

I learn about how people treat my brother because of the way he
looks. How stereotypical people are. He always tells me to stick up
for myself and be independent.

(Najma, 14-year-old girl)

From these comments it is clear that there are strong feelings that
racism corrodes social relations as do violence and crime. They are antithetical to a sense of community. Such convictions have the potential to
inspire action. It is also clear that religion remains a strong influence for
many, but that where traditional religion is perceived as conflicting with

ideas of equality and freedoms, it is challenged. These factors suggest that communities are dynamic and evolving, being influenced by other communities with which they are in contact. One important role for education is to help young people develop skills of intercultural evaluation by considering which features it is important to retain and which require to be changed.

Evolving personal identities

The students were invited to write about how they defined themselves in terms of ethnicity, culture, colour or race. They described their multiple and evolving identities. A number stressed their bilingualism. Many chose to explain their values, sometimes drawing on religious beliefs. Some chose to explain that theirs was an inter-faith family. For example, after her parents' divorce, Asha (14) continued to live with her mother, a Sikh, but she herself was brought up a Hindu. For many, religion was an identifier, even when they professed to be not very religious:

> I am Methodist. Don't really believe in God.
>
> (Ayleen, 14-year-old girl)

> I am Hindu, born in Leicester and proud of being a Hindu.
>
> (Wayne, 12-year-old boy)

> I'm Asian and my religion is Islam. I live in a multicultural area with Christians, Sikhs, Muslims and Hindus.
>
> (Najma, 14-year-old girl)

Pride in religion is often tinged with a sense that there is an external threat to the liberal multicultural community that they feel part of. This provokes strong expressions of support for a culture built on equality and respect for human dignity:

> I believe in God. I am a Hindu, my language is Gujarati and I like my religion. I HATE people who are RACIST! I don't have a problem with people who have a different culture than me. I mix with other religions. I am a very strong believer in God.
>
> (Nadeera, 12-year-old girl)

> I'm proud of my religion and I don't care if my colour is different because we are all equal.
>
> (Ravinder, 10-year-old girl)

A minority chose to identify themselves without reference to religion, or by stressing that they drew inspiration from a number of religions. These students tended to identify with geographical locations, notably countries where their families still have connections:

> Born and grew up in Leicester. Parents – dad from Uganda, mum from India. All my family before then lived in India. Mum's side of the family still do. Lived in same house all my life.
>
> (Anita, 17-year-old girl)

> Mum born in Malaysia, dad born in Zimbabwe. I was born in Leicester. Grandma and Grandad were born in India.
>
> (Alyah, 10-year-old girl)

All but two of the total sample from the workshops identify with other places as well as Leicester, even when it is the only place they have lived. This identity tended to be reinforced when there had been an opportunity to travel. Indeed, travel and the opportunity to spend time in another country were often highly significant learning experiences:

> I was born in Keighley in West Yorkshire. I lived there for nine years and moved to Leicester when I was in Year 5. My parents are both from Bangladesh and I visited Bangladesh in 1995 and moved to Leicester in 1996.
>
> (Najma, 14-year-old girl)

> I was born in England. I grew up with my parents. My parents and my grandparents are both from Bangladesh. And we speak Bengali. I have been to Bangladesh and it is a nice place with a beautiful countryside. The place I lived in there was a very nice place. It was very quiet and the neighbours we had were really kind and friendly. What I liked most is the sun always used to shine and how it was really hot.
>
> (Rehana, 14-year-old girl)

> My dad and grandparents were born in India. Me, my Mum and my sisters were born in England. I have stayed in India for two months and I liked staying there.
>
> (Sandeep, 10-year-old girl)

These romantic views of the country of family heritage contrast with other less favourable perceptions. Jagdish, who visited India at age 5, mostly remembered the rain and ants. Anjali (17) visited her mother's country, India, but 'did not really like it there as it was very hot and sometimes smelt really bad'. Likewise, Anita (17), who speaks Gujarati, found Gujarat itself a disappointment, describing it as 'roots, not home'. A young student who was born in India but grew up in Leicester has no doubts about where he prefers to be: 'I don't like India because it is quite smelly. I like where I live, in Leicester, because it is modern, convenient and simply the best!' (Mohit, 12-year-old boy).

While many students were aware that at one point members of their family had been forced to migrate because of political circumstances, including threats to their lives, some had first-hand experience of political violence. One had recently returned to Leicester after his family fled from Malawi. He had lived in the city for less than a year, after growing up in East Africa: 'I am from Malawi and I was born in Leicester in the General Hospital. My father and mother are from Malawi and my grandmother is from India. We left Malawi because almost every day people were getting shot in their houses and one of them was my neighbour' (Abdul, 14-year-old boy).

Migration, within or between countries, is not always the result of political factors. Changes in family circumstances, particularly parental separations, often meant a change of home:

> I was born in Dominica [the Caribbean] but I came to England when I was only three. First I lived in Highfields with my mum and dad, then they split up and I lived with my dad in Beaumont Leys.
>
> (Thabo, 14-year-old boy)

> I was born in Manchester and [lived there] until I was six months old. I moved from Manchester because my mum and dad had a divorce. My mum, dad and granddad are from Africa and my grandma is from India.
>
> (Asha, 14-year-old girl)

Many students were able to reflect on the various factors shaping their world view:

> I have been influenced by a lot of things, mainly religion, parents and elder peers. Also my travelling experience has also taught me things about life. Peers and people I look up to have influenced me greatly and, have helped me understand wider issues, or things that I haven't understood. The main person who has influenced me is a Black guy, and through talking to him I have understood my own and other people's culture.
>
> (Mohamed, 17-year-old boy)

Learning for citizenship certainly takes place in the community and many people take on the role of teachers even if they are not employed by schools. Their contribution to the community may be made through a place of worship, a community centre or a sports club. These informal teachers complement the work of teachers engaged in the formal sector of education.

Life politics

The majority of young people we worked with identified strongly with their city and their local neighbourhood. Education for cosmopolitan citizenship is about enabling learners to make connections between their immediate contexts and the national and global contexts. It is not an add-on but rather it encompasses citizenship learning as a whole. It implies a broader understanding of identity, including national identities. It also requires recognition that British identity, for example, may be experienced differently by different people.

Young people in Leicester, like those in many parts of the country, feel privileged to experience Britain as a multicultural society and proud of a community that values the past but looks to the future: 'I like living in Leicester because it is multicultural. I like the fact that even though we live in Britain our culture is kept alive' (Asha, 15-year-old girl). Culture is about people in a community. Asha is a member of a number of communities in Leicester and, like the other respondents, she identifies with a range of places and communities, within and beyond Leicester and the UK. These young people clearly have the potential to see themselves as members of a world community based on common human values. They are committed to equality and they celebrate diversity.

Our research suggests that many young people bring with them to their schooling values of care for others and feelings of responsibility, as well as experiences that equip them with knowledge and skills for citizenship. Their perspectives are in many cases best described as those of cosmopolitan citizens.

That said, in one school there was also significant hostility to refugees and asylum-seekers. This was in spite of the fact that some young people were aware that their own grandparents and parents had arrived in Leicester as refugees. Some were willing to defend the rights of current refugees and asylum-seekers and one, for instance, had gone out of her way to befriend asylum-seekers from Kosovo in a local hostel. In spite of initial prejudices we nonetheless found an open approach to discussion on this issue and a willingness to engage in dialogue.

We have shown how young people of all backgrounds may have confident and complex identities. They often have a sense of responsibility and of civic commitment. As well as demonstrating strong affective ties, either to their immediate locality or to the city of Leicester, these young people identified a number of facilities within the city which they valued. These included public spaces such as libraries, schools, shopping centres and community centres.

They also respected the cultural heritage of the city, including religious buildings, statues and parks. They were committed to protecting the environment and were clear about how they would improve their city. In general they were concerned about other neighbourhoods which were perceived to be dangerous because of 'bullies' and 'racists'. They wanted more cinemas, fewer racists and fewer gangsters, whom they explained spoiled their own neighbourhoods, smoking drugs and hanging about in groups, extorting money and ruining parks.

All the young people we spoke with were committed to respecting diversity between people. In general they had considerable sensitivity to injustice. Not surprisingly they were more likely to understand how to respond politically to local issues than to injustices or inequalities in other parts of the world, to which the major response was to give charitably.

Practising cosmopolitan citizenship starts with the realization that decisions about lifestyle and personal identities are profoundly political. Certain lifestyle choices, concerned with clothing, religious observance or leisure, for example, may bring conflict with family members, school or the wider community. Life politics may well require involvement with the emancipatory politics associated with struggles for equal life chances. Schools have a key role to play in allowing young people to consider the implications of their choices, in exploring their rights and helping them to make connections.

7 Mainstreaming antiracism

Introduction

In this chapter we discuss how antiracism is essential to democracy. We argue that the linking of antiracism and democracy is essential to the realization of a non-racist society and that forms of antiracism which link it exclusively to multiculturalism are insufficient. Education for citizenship is potentially a significant means for achieving this. One obstacle to ensuring the success of citizenship education programmes is the tendency to depoliticize the concept of citizenship. Citizenship education needs to take into account the fact that citizenship itself is a highly charged political issue. Indeed, it is both a contested concept and a site of struggle. We illustrate this by examining the status of citizen of the European Union, exploring the limitations of European citizenship and the ways in which citizenship may serve to exclude.

Citizenship education is increasingly seen as a priority in Europe and internationally. One of the major barriers to the realization of full citizenship rights in Europe is racism and this is acknowledged in policies at national and at European levels. These limitations contrast with a generous European rhetoric of equality and human rights. In this chapter we consider the European policy of mainstreaming antiracism and compare national initiatives to promote race equality in Sweden and England.

The tensions implicit in education for citizenship are such that it is far from certain that such programmes can effectively contribute to combating racism. We argue that, while education for democratic citizenship is certainly a site for mainstreaming antiracism, programmes need to take into account the wide range of experiences that students bring to their studies. Within the context of Europe, many students experience racism, which serves to limit their citizenship rights and restrict their participation. Any programme of education for citizenship will therefore need to address these experiences and equip all students with the skills to effectively challenge racism. Second, programmes will need to consider structural and institutional inequalities and the ways in which these are reproduced in schools. For example, recent reports from England suggest that schools, by their admissions policies and their ethos, may unwittingly be racist in their practices (Macpherson 1999), serving to undermine social cohesion and contributing to social inequality (Cantle 2001). In France, the cumulative effect of individual choices by middle-class parents is that many schools are effectively segregated by ethnicity (Felouzis 2003). Schools, as well as being a means to combat racism and xenophobia, may also contribute to the problem. This raises questions of what schools offer by way of citizenship education and, equally importantly, how they offer it.

Mainstreaming the fight against racism requires both general policies and practices and specific antiracist initiatives. Within education we argue that there is a need both for general policies to promote inclusion, participation and children's rights and for specific initiatives to actively combat racism and other anti-democratic discriminatory practices. We contend that education for citizenship and mainstreaming antiracism depend on clear understandings of democracy and human rights. Anti-democratic values and practices need to be brought out into the open and combated in schools. Only when this happens can antiracism genuinely be mainstreamed within citizenship education.

A common European framework

In the established democracies of Western and Northern Europe there is anxiety that democracy itself is threatened by decreasing voter participation rates on the one hand and the activities of vociferous xenophobic populist parties on the other. In Central, Eastern and South Eastern Europe the concern is to build democracy in order to secure economic development, peace and stability. One response to these concerns is the promotion of education for citizenship.

In 1997, the Council of Europe, an inter-governmental organization of 44 member states, launched the Education for Democratic Citizenship (EDC) programme. The EDC programme aims to promote best practice and develop new models for citizenship education, including the drafting of a common European framework. The EDC programme is also designed to be 'instrumental in the fight against violence, xenophobia, racism, aggressive nationalism and intolerance' (Council of Europe 2000b: 5). The Committee of Ministers of Education of the Council of Europe considers that the programme has demonstrated 'how education for democratic citizenship can contribute to social cohesion through learning to participate in the life of society, to assume responsibility and to live together' (Council of Europe 2000b: 3).

The EDC programme thus emphasizes the key role of education in combating racism and xenophobia, acknowledging that these are barriers to democracy and social cohesion. However, this apparent consensus conceals debates about the nature of citizenship, about multiculturalism in society and about the place of antiracism in education. There are structural features that are likely to impede the effective implementation of citizenship education programmes. First, citizenship is a contested concept. Second, it is a site of struggle. Third, the reality for many living in Europe is that their status as non-citizens severely limits their capacity to participate.

Citizenship, conflict and struggle

Citizenship is a status, conferred by nation states, and carrying rights and responsibilities. In principle, democratic states in the liberal tradition guarantee human rights to their citizens. However, entitlement to human rights extends to all human beings, irrespective of their citizenship status. Thus education for citizenship needs to be more than just civic education, which informs students of their status and their responsibilities. This is acknowledged by the Ministers of Education of the Council of Europe, who, in their Resolution, refer to citizenship education as 'process-focused' (Council of Europe 2000b: 5). In other words, it is about creating a stronger, fairer, more cohesive and more democratic society. Given the gross injustices and social fractures present in even the most democratic states, this process is inevitably critical. In inviting young people to make judgements about the world around them, citizenship education is political and therefore controversial.

Citizenship has always been a site of struggle. It is a process and an ongoing project. Campaigners for the rights of women, people with disabilities and minorities continue to seek justice and equal citizenship rights. Inclusive citizenship is an ideal and its realization is a process. This process involves politics and power as well as education (Lister 1997). Teaching and research in citizenship education need to address these debates about the nature of democracy and democratic education (Arnot and Dillaboug 2000; Osler 2000a). Citizenship education is necessarily a trans-disciplinary activity.

One of the most significant sites of political controversy, and therefore struggle, in Europe is the development of multicultural or cosmopolitan democracies. Whereas nation states were constructed on the basis of patriotism and nationalism, they have evolved in many cases and citizens may now have multiple loyalties within and beyond the state. Citizenship within nation states confers the right to vote. In other words, it is linked to a measure of democratic control and to territory (Kaldor 1995: 71). However, globalization and the development of transnational entities such as the EU have given rise to the development of citizens' movements that now constitute a civil society transcending national boundaries. Such movements may campaign for third-wave rights such as sustainable development, peace and greater transparency. This movement of 'cosmopolitan democracy' builds on the existing principles of the liberal international order, namely democracy and human rights, to extend democratic principles to all public institutions within and across states (Held 1995a, 1995b; Lister 1997; Delanty 2000; Keane 2003).

Within a cosmopolitan democracy, citizens may build on and develop their social, political, cultural, religious and commercial links for the benefit both of the territory in which they live and of the global community. This is perhaps of particular significance to diasporic communities, separated by migration and national boundaries, but retaining a sense of cultural unity. The number of such communities is growing, and within schools across Europe students are increasingly likely to hold multiple identities and loyalties. However, those responsible for formulating education policy in Europe and in its member states have given minimal consideration to these developments. Where diversity is acknowledged it is not always seen as positive. Within the discourse on education for citizenship there is a tendency to categorize an increasingly diverse school population, and minority students in particular, as problematic (Osler 2000b; Osler and Starkey 2000, 2001; Starkey 2000).

The characterization of multicultural societies as problematic is precisely the terrain on which xenophobic political parties have chosen to operate. Far right and populist politicians spuriously link multiculturalism to crime, to insecurity and to loss of national identity. Such discourses are profoundly anti-democratic as they deny the basic tenets of liberal democracy, namely equality of rights and respect for human dignity.

European citizenship as a problematic concept

Citizenship as a status conferred by nation states is both inclusive and exclusive. Citizenship is one signifier of who is included in the reciprocal relationship of democratically governing (the voters) and being governed (Lister 1997). It therefore defines the majority of those who are included in democratic processes and also those who are excluded. Non-citizens may lack voting and other rights and are consequently ineligible to participate fully. Even more crucially, the status of citizen normally confers rights of residence and therefore freedom of movement into and out of the territory. In many cases, and particularly for citizens of less economically favoured countries, freedom of movement, even to visit family members, may be curtailed. Such restrictions operate disproportionately against black people in Europe.

In the case of the EU, the status of European citizenship is exclusive to citizens of the member states but even they do not have the power to elect a European government. The definition of European citizenship excludes two sets of people who might legitimately consider themselves to be citizens in Europe. The first group is made up of those residents who are not citizens of any member state of the EU. The number of such individuals has increased since the 1990s as a result of migration from zones of conflict within and beyond Europe and from poorer areas of the world. Many of these migrants are refugees. Their children are present in the schools of all EU member states.

The second excluded group consists of citizens of those European states that are not members of the EU. In 2004, 44 states were members of the Council of Europe. All these states are signatories of the *European Convention on Human Rights (ECHR)* and are therefore committed to democracy and human rights. They include long-established democracies; countries such as Spain, Portugal and Greece which have experienced dictatorship in the second half of the twentieth century; and newly-established nation states, such as Bosnia, Macedonia and Ukraine. In other words, citizens of 19 democratic European states, including countries with such diverse histories as Norway, Switzerland and Russia, while being citizens of Europe, are not entitled to the status of European citizen.

Education for European citizenship is likely to face challenges both from those excluded from it and from those radically opposed to it. In all European states there are radical national parties that characterize the creation of European institutions as a threat to a previous national autonomy and integrity. In many states such discourse is suffused with xenophobia and racism. Education for citizenship in Europe is therefore particularly controversial and it is inevitably confronted with the need to address racism.

Liberalism, human rights and antiracism

The major European institutions, the Council of Europe (founded in 1949), the European Community (founded in 1957), the European Court of Human Rights and the European Parliament are all explicitly committed to democracy, human rights and the rule of law. These institutions underpin a European culture based on an ambition to achieve peace and stability in a continent that suffered two horrendous wars in the first half of the twentieth century.

While many European states were founder signatories of the *Charter of the United Nations* (1945), there was simultaneously a strong movement to promote European unity and create European institutions based on the principles enshrined in the UN Charter and *Universal Declaration of Human*

Rights (*UDHR*) of December 1948. The earliest of these institutions was the Council of Europe whose member states are required to sign the *ECHR* (1950) which gives legal force to a number of the rights from the *UDHR*. The *ECHR* is explicitly derived from the *Charter of the United Nations* and from the *UDHR*. All member states of the European Community or Union are also signatories of the *ECHR* and the EU has developed its own *Charter of Fundamental Rights* (European Union 2000).

The European movement that gave impetus to the creation of these institutions can be traced back to resistance to fascist and Nazi attempts to achieve dominance over Europe in the 1930s and 1940s. Given that the Nazi ideology was founded on racism and a denial of the essential equality of human beings, its opponents are, by definition, committed to the promotion of antiracism and race equality. In this the UN and the Council of Europe share the same ideals. The *ECHR* was intended to strengthen, at European level, the work of the UN. The preamble to the *ECHR* is quite explicit about this: 'Being resolved, as the governments of European countries which are like-minded and have a common heritage of political traditions, ideals, freedom and the rule of law, to take the first steps for the collective enforcement of certain of the rights stated in the Universal Declaration'.

The founding principles of the Council of Europe are both regional and universal, as are those of the European Community and EU. Both the Council of Europe and the European Community are profoundly committed to antiracism. Racism is seen as being based on principles entirely antithetical to European and international values of human rights, dignity and equality. Racism is therefore not only undemocratic, but is in its essence the enemy of democracy. It threatens the stability of individual states and of the continent as a whole.

Europe and antiracism today

The Council of Europe, working with the European Commission, convened a number of preparatory meetings before the 2001 UN World Conference Against Racism. The governments of the member states of the Council of Europe made a formal declaration at the European conference 'All Different All Equal: from Principle to Practice' held in Strasbourg in October 2000. This declaration makes a strong case for antiracism as an essential element of democracy:

> Europe is a community of shared values, multicultural in its past, present and future;
> ... Full and effective implementation of all human rights without any discrimination or distinction, as enshrined in European and other international human rights instruments, must be secured;

... Racism and racial discrimination are serious violations of human rights in the contemporary world and must be combated by all lawful means;

... Racism, racial discrimination, xenophobia and related intolerance threaten democratic societies and their fundamental values;

... Stability and peace in Europe and throughout the world can only be built on tolerance and respect for diversity;

... All initiatives aiming at greater political, social and cultural participation, especially of persons belonging to vulnerable groups, should be encouraged

Among the specific measures recommended, education is seen as having a leading role. Governments committed themselves: 'to give particular attention to education and awareness-raising in all sectors of society to promote a climate of tolerance, respect for human rights and cultural diversity, including introducing and strengthening such measures among young people' (Council of Europe 2000a: 5).

At the World Conference Against Racism, the European Commission highlighted the need for both legislation and education:

> The fight against racism is now firmly rooted in European law. Specific reference to the fight against racism is contained in the Treaty establishing the European Community ... We know though, that there are many areas of discrimination that cannot be tackled by law. Practical action is needed to reach out to people and to help change the underlying prejudices that fuel racist attitudes and behaviour. Education is called to play a fundamental role in this endeavour.
>
> (Diamantopoulou 2001)

This is a key analysis, confirming that legislation, while important, needs to be accompanied by an educational programme designed to create a climate of human rights. By promoting equality, strengthening democracy and encouraging respect for human dignity, education can play a key role in overcoming the conditions in which racism flourishes. Ensuring that these values and dispositions are at the forefront of the public conscience requires that they permeate the whole education process. In other words, it is vital that antiracism be mainstreamed.

Mainstreaming antiracism in public policies

One outcome of the European Year Against Racism (1997) was the formation of a working group within the Commission to evaluate the extent to which policies and programmes contribute to antiracism. The group produced an *Action Plan Against Racism* (European Commission 1998) that was intended to complement specific antiracist measures. It had four strands:

- paving the way for legislative initiatives;
- mainstreaming the fight against racism;
- developing and exchanging new models;
- strengthening information and communication work.

The action plan was followed by a European Commission report, *Mainstreaming the Fight Against Racism* (European Commission 1999) which draws together various previous initiatives and highlights how EU policies and programmes can contribute to the fight against racism. It outlines two main means by which racism can be challenged: first, by presenting diversity in a positive light; and second, by creating favourable conditions for a multicultural society. The report proposes issuing directives designed to implement Article 13 of the 1999 Treaty of Amsterdam. The first directive aims to combat various forms of discrimination in the labour market. The second aims to combat discrimination on the grounds of racial and ethnic origin in other areas within the limits of the powers of the EU, including education, provision of goods and services, social protection and social advantages.

The European Commission defines the concept of 'mainstreaming' antiracism as having two main strands, namely specific actions and incorporation across the whole field of policy:

> [It] aims to integrate the fight against racism as an objective into all Community actions and policies, and at all levels. This means not only implementing specific measures, but deliberately using all general actions and policies to combat racism by actively and visibly considering their impact on the fight against racism when drawing them up.
>
> (European Commission 1999: 3)

Mainstreaming antiracism in European education programmes

An example of mainstreaming antiracism is the inclusion of specific criteria for awarding European funds. For instance, schools and universities apply to the European Commission's SOCRATES programme which annually funds hundreds of transnational cooperation projects. The criteria for selection include the following priority: 'Emphasis placed by the project on the promotion of *equality between women and men*, equal opportunities for *disabled persons* and contributing to *the fight against racism and xenophobia* (European Commission 2000: 23 emphasis added). The Commission notes that almost half the projects in some sections of this complex programme address these issues specifically (European Commission 1999). The section of the SOCRATES programme involving projects between schools, known as Comenius, is even more explicit in its intentions. It contributes to promoting intercultural awareness in school education in Europe by transnational activities designed to:

- promote enhanced awareness of different cultures;
- develop intercultural education initiatives for the school education sector;
- improve the skills of teachers in the area of intercultural education;
- *support the fight against racism and xenophobia*;
- improve the education of children of migrant workers, occupational travellers, Gypsies and Travellers.

(European Commission 2000: 35, emphasis added)

Among suggested themes for projects, the Commission proposes that: 'Broad thematic areas for the development of a Comenius School Project could, for example, include arts, sciences, environmental education, cultural heritage, European citizenship, use of information and communication technology, *fight against racism*' (European Commission 2000: 37, emphasis added). The Commission is thus able to demonstrate that the priorities set for its educational programmes support antiracism. This trend is also observable, to different degrees, in policies of individual member states. We examine now two examples.

British government policy, race equality and educational inclusion

In Britain, antiracist initiatives have followed the Human Rights Act 1998and in particular the report of the Stephen Lawrence Inquiry (Macpherson 1999) which identified institutional racism as a major cause of social exclusion. In setting up the Stephen Lawrence Inquiry and accepting its finding of institutional racism, the British government acknowledged the importance of political leadership in challenging racism and in creating a climate in which race equality is seen as the responsibility of all. At the time of its publication in February 1999, senior figures from a range of political parties went on record to acknowledge institutional racism in British society and the government pledged itself to a programme to eradicate racism. For instance, when presenting the report to the House of

Commons the then Home Secretary Jack Straw stated: 'The report does not place a responsibility on someone else; it places a responsibility on each of us. We must make racial equality a reality. The vision is clear: we must create a society in which every individual, regardless of colour, creed or race, has the same opportunities and respect as his or her neighbour' (Hansard (House of Commons) 1999).

The report of the Stephen Lawrence Inquiry defined institutional racism as:

> The collective failure of an organisation to provide an appropriate and professional service to people because of their colour, culture, or ethnic origin. It can be detected in processes, attitudes and behaviour which amount to discrimination through unwitting prejudice, ignorance, thoughtlessness and racist stereotyping which disadvantage minority ethnic people. It persists because of the failure of the organisation openly and adequately to recognise and address its existence and causes by policy, example and leadership. Without recognition and action to eliminate such racism, it can prevail as part of the ethos or culture of the organisation. It is a corrosive disease.
>
> (Macpherson 1999: para. 6.34)

The report drew attention to institutional racism in the police force, but it did much more than that. It effectively made clear that institutional racism is endemic in British society. The Home Secretary explained: 'Any long-established, white dominated organisation is liable to have procedures, practices and a culture which tend to exclude or disadvantage non-white people. The police service in this respect is little different from other parts of the criminal justice system, or from government departments ... and many other institutions' (Hansard (House of Commons) 1999). In making this statement the Home Secretary stressed that institutional racism is not confined to the police and criminal justice system but has a profound impact across society, affecting everyone. Educational institutions are not exempt from the pernicious effects of racism.

As well as being part of the problem, education is seen as part of the solution and the Stephen Lawrence Inquiry report recommended that schools play a key role in enabling the development of greater racial justice. Of the report's 70 recommendations, three address education. As well as proposing amendments to the National Curriculum so that schools might more effectively value cultural diversity and prevent racism, the Inquiry recommended that LEAs and school governors take a lead in ensuring that racist incidents be recorded and reported. It recommended that schools monitor exclusions by ethnicity and that the school inspection agency, the

Office for Standards in Education (Ofsted), be given a lead role in monitoring how schools are addressing and preventing racism. The government's response to the Stephen Lawrence Inquiry's recommendations (Home Office 1999) accepted them in principle and also identified citizenship education as a key means by which schools would address and prevent racism and encourage young people to value cultural diversity.

Mixed messages concerning racism and antiracism

Many British political leaders appear uncomfortable when addressing or even acknowledging racism. Since 1997, there have been mixed messages concerning racism and antiracism from Labour ministers. On the one hand, certain government policies on refugees and asylum-seekers, such as the distribution of vouchers rather than cash for food and other essentials, and particularly some statements by government ministers, are considered by many commentators to have undermined the status of these groups and fuelled racism (see e.g. Rutter 2005). On the other hand, other ministers have made powerful statements, stressing the need to adopt antiracist policies and practices. The following example is from a Home Office minister:

> Antiracism is not about helping black and Asian people; it is about our future – white and black. We all live in a multicultural society and we all have a choice: either we make a success of multicultural Britain or we do not. If we fail to address those issues, our children – white and black – will pay the price of that failure. That is why all of us, white and black, have a vested interest in the [Race Relations Amendment] Bill and in antiracism. We must make Britain a success as a multicultural society.
>
> (Hansard (House of Commons) 2000)

However, despite the acceptance of the need for schools to prevent and address racism through their curriculum and ethos, education ministers have avoided making positive statements on the role of schools in challenging racism in society. Nor has any education minister acknowledged the existence of institutional racism in the education service.

Antiracism and social policy

One of the first actions of the Labour government in 1997 was to set up a special unit to find policy solutions to the growing divisions in society. The Social Exclusion Unit (SEU) has produced a number of influential reports. Just one of these, *Minority Ethnic Issues in Social Exclusion and Neighbourhood Renewal* (SEU 2000), makes explicit the links between racial discrimination and social exclusion. Despite this report, as we explain in Chapter 4, the

British government does not generally or consistently recognize racial discrimination as a factor in social exclusion.

In 1999 the Department for Ecuationan and Employment (DfEE) introduced the Ethnic Minority Achievement Grant (EMAG) as the main funding mechanism for addressing the specific educational needs of children from minority communities. The EMAG budget is over £150 million per annum. Previous funding arrangements had been seriously criticized by inspectors as providing inadequate and short-term funding which led to difficulties in recruiting and retaining specialist teachers, with the quality of the teaching being 'variable' (Ofsted 1999: 21). Evidence submitted to the Commission on the Future of Multi-Ethnic Britain suggests that although much of the thinking behind the new arrangements is sound, many of the criticisms of the former funding arrangements still apply. The Commission concluded that 'It appears unlikely that the grant will have substantial impact on the patterns of underachievement' identified by the Commission (Parekh 2000: 150).

A preliminary analysis of LEA EMAG plans indicated that some authorities were, in fact, setting targets for the improvement of various ethnic groups which, if achieved, would widen the gap in performance and increase inequality. In these authorities the target percentage increase for those groups whose average performance was lowest was smaller than the target percentage increase for the highest achieving group (Gillborn and Mirza 2000). Our own analysis, conducted on behalf of the Department for Education and Skills (DfES), also considers LEA action plans and student attainment (Tikly *et al.* 2002). It suggests that LEAs are setting targets which, if achieved, will close the performance gap between some ethnic groups. Our study suggests that some groups, notably African Caribbean students, have not been given the resources and support to enable them to close the attainment gap. The data available did not permit us to examine gender and ethnicity together as factors which impact on attainment. Our study was not the full-scale evaluation of EMAG promised by the government in 1997, and this plan to evaluate the impact of EMAG appears to have been dropped.

Policies, with some exceptions, tend to focus more broadly on reversing social exclusion, rather than directly addressing racial inequalities (Alibhai-Brown 1999: 7). So, for example, targets were set to cut the overall number of permanent exclusions from school by one third by 2002. However, these failed to address the disproportionate number of exclusions of pupils from particular communities, notably African Caribbean boys and girls. There is clear research evidence that suggests that when schools and LEAs are successful in cutting exclusions from over-represented groups, they in fact do so across the board. Particular groups will remain disproportionately vulnerable to exclusion and require specific targets and strategies, which are likely to produce better results overall (Osler and Hill 1999).

The Race Relations (Amendment) Act 2000

The most significant specific element of the British government's policy on race equality is the implementation of the Race Relations (Amendment) Act 2000. The Act places a positive duty on public bodies, including schools, to promote race equality. It is no longer sufficient for public bodies simply to avoid discrimination; the Act requires them to introduce policies and practices that actively promote race equality. A number of schools and LEAs appear to be addressing the attainment gap in response to this legislation (Osler *et al.* 2003).

Absence of discrimination is a prerequisite if individuals and communities are to flourish within a multicultural society, but it is insufficient to guarantee the full participation of all citizens within such a society. Diversity also needs to be 'given public status and dignity' and politicians need to work together with other citizens to 'develop a new social and cultural policy capable of nurturing ethnic identities' (Parekh 1991a: 197). In other words: '"British" must be seen as fully including the ethnic minority communities. But the minority communities being seen as British does not imply their denying their "ethnic" origins and identity' (Figueroa 2000: 59–60). What is needed is a vision of multiculturalism that recognizes that each individual has multiple identities. This new multiculturalism needs to be founded on human rights and must be inclusive of all, including white communities (Osler 1999; Osler and Starkey 2000).

Modern Britain is often referred to as a multicultural society. What this usually means is that the processes of post-war immigration have led to the development of 'visible' minority communities. The term 'multicultural' is often used synonymously with 'ethnic minority' or 'non-white', so that communities or neighbourhoods which are referred to as multicultural are usually assumed to have significant numbers of African, Caribbean or South Asian residents. The concept of multiculturalism is often exclusive of white communities, which may mistakenly be assumed to be culturally homogeneous.

Recent constitutional reform, including the establishment of a Scottish Parliament and Welsh Assembly, and the development of a new settlement between Britain and Northern Ireland, have led to increased interest and debate on what it means to be British and how citizenship is related to national and regional identities. So, for example, what does it mean to be British and Scottish? Meanings of nationality and national identity are being re-examined and redefined. It is within this new political and constitutional context that a new vision of multicultural Britain may be forged.

The Race Equality Code of Practice for Schools

In order to enable British schools to implement the Race Relations (Amendment) Act 2000, the Commission for Racial Equality (CRE) issued schools with a statutory code of practice on the duty to promote race equality (CRE 2002). The duty requires public authorities, including schools, to:

- eliminate unlawful racial discrimination;
- promote equality of opportunity;
- promote good relations between people of different racial groups.

The guidance covers issues such as admissions policies and the collection and analysis of data by ethnic groups. Schools are expected to set targets for improving the performance of underachieving groups. It stresses that the policy must be applied irrespective of the number of ethnic minority children in the school:

> Race equality is important, even if there is nobody from an ethnic minority group in your school or local community. Education plays a vital role in influencing young people, because the views and attitudes they form as pupils or students will probably stay with them for the rest of their lives. Also, racist acts (such as handing out racist literature) can happen in schools with no pupils from ethnic minorities.
>
> (CRE 2002: 7)

The legislation requires schools to prepare a written statement of policy for promoting race equality. The *Code of Practice* provides an example of how one school set about drafting and using such a statement. All members of the school community, including parents and pupils, had opportunities to be involved. The draft policy was discussed in citizenship lessons and the pupil council was given responsibility, along with the school governors and the school's senior management, for monitoring the implementation of the policy.

The *Code of Practice* recognizes the importance of the school having a clear statement of values and the need for staff training in the implications of such a statement for their teaching and for the procedures and ethos of the school. The opportunity provided by citizenship education to engage pupils in dialogue about the race equality policy and the values of the school is also clearly signalled.

Inadequate curriculum guidance

Rather than supporting the *Code of Practice* on race equality, the official guidance for implementing citizenship education, sent to schools in England by the Qualifications and Curriculum Authority (QCA), fails to give any lead on how issues of race equality are to be addressed. The scheme of work for Key Stage 3 (ages 11–14) simply suggests that an audit of citizenship provision and a planning framework can be derived from a series of questions linked to the main headings in the programme of study (QCA 2001a).

There are just three thematic headings: 'Rights and responsibilities', 'Government and democracy' and 'Communities and Identities'. Under the third of these, the guidance suggests three topic headings, the first of which is 'Me and my local community'. The authors of the guidance list what they consider to be the relevant concepts from the official programme of study for this topic, namely: identity; community; local networks; local organizations; participating and contributing; diversity; difference. It is implied that the scheme of work for this unit could be based on a series of questions:

- What are my identities?
- What groups/communities do I belong to and how can I contribute to them?
- What do I think about my local community?
- What concerns my community and who influences it?
- What is the diversity and difference in my community and how is it celebrated?

These questions largely avoid a critical approach. It is true that the first question supposes a model of multiple identities, which suggests a cosmopolitan rather than nationalist model of democracy. The fourth question, about concerns, could provide an opportunity to raise issues of justice, equity or discrimination, but as formulated it does not invite this approach. The question of who defines and gives voice to the concerns of the community is inevitably contentious and political but it is not suggested by the current formulation. The questions seem to avoid issues of power within the local community. Perhaps it is felt that this may involve politically sensitive issues. However, citizenship education is the intended site within the curriculum for developing political literacy and it is anomalous for the scheme of work to shy away from this.

The topic heading 'National identities' is followed by some even less relevant questions. The knowledge to be acquired is defined by the key words: diversity; government; responsibilities; voluntary work; stereotyping and prejudice; media; national identity; legal and human rights and responsibilities. The structuring questions are:

- How can different communities learn from each other?
- How do I understand diversity and how is it represented locally, nationally and globally?
- How tolerant am I of diversity and difference?

- What are the legal and human rights and responsibilities that underpin society?
- What systems protect and enable our rights and responsibilities?

The existence of publicly recognized 'communities' is thus accepted uncritically. This may well imply that the authors of the guidance have a model based on a monolithic 'majority community' and differentiated 'minority communities'. Also implied in the formulation 'different communities' is some kind of separation whereas, in reality, communities are likely to overlap, with a significant number of individuals feeling a sense of belonging in several communities.

While there is to be consideration of diversity 'nationally', there is no examination of the concept 'nation', nor indeed 'state'. Although human rights are said to underpin society, there is no reference to the role of the state in protecting rights or to the concept of the state as a political entity transcending diverse ethnic and cultural groupings. None of the questions addresses the proposed topic of 'national identity' let alone nationalism, which involves the defining of national identity in restrictive terms for political ends. While the topic heading *'National identities'* is given in the plural, there is no indication whether this refers to different national identities within Britain, or whether it is an invitation to consider the concept of cosmopolitan democracy.

In fact the very concept of democracy is absent from the theme of 'communities and identities', being reserved for the theme 'government and democracy'. This has the effect of de-politicizing the essentially political notions of community and identity. It denies students the opportunity to consider how political parties and movements manipulate these notions in order to stoke racism, nationalism and xenophobia. By linking democracy only to government, the programme neglects possibilities for democratic participation of children and young people in other institutions including the family, the school and the workplace.

The failure of the curriculum guidance to engage with political issues, indeed its tendency to de-politicize multiculturalism, is a further example of the education service in Britain providing less than enthusiastic support to initiatives intended to be mainstreamed across all policy areas. The *Code of Practice* for schools from the Commission for Racial Equality (CRE 2002), which is the main instrument for implementing the requirements of the Race Relations (Amendment) Act within the education service, emanates not from the DfES but from the Home Office. It remains to be seen whether school inspectors, LEAs and schools are prepared to support its implementation wholeheartedly.

Sweden's national action plan to combat racism

A 'national action plan to combat racism, xenophobia, homophobia and discrimination' was agreed by the Swedish government in February 2001. While emanating from the Ministry of Industry, Employment and Communications, the document is an attempt to mainstream across all areas of government and it gives a significant role to education.

The Swedish government asserts that this action plan is among its highest priorities. It presents antiracism as an essential element in protecting and promoting democracy. The plan was drawn up in the light of:

> Acts of violence and harassment of a racist, anti-Semitic or homophobic nature. Those attacked have included individual immigrants, homosexuals, Jewish people and Roma (Romany), active anti-racists, and journalists, polemicists, police officers and politicians in their capacity as representatives of the democratic society. Crimes of this nature are also attacks on democratic governance and the fundamental principle of the equal worth of all people.
>
> (Government of Sweden 2001: 6)

Like the duty imposed on British schools under the Race Relations (Amendment) Act, Sweden also requires schools to promote race equality:

> The Education Act (1985:1100) states that educational activities shall be carried out in accordance with fundamental democratic values and that everyone who works in schools must promote respect for the worth of the individual and respect for our common environment. The Education Act was strengthened and sharpened in 1998. Everyone in the school system must now work actively to combat all forms of offensive treatment such as mobbing and racist behaviour.
>
> (Government of Sweden 2001: 34)

In fact, since the Education Act 1998 there is a requirement on Swedish headteachers to draft, implement, monitor and evaluate an action plan to prevent and combat all forms of offensive treatment of pupils and their staff in schools. However, the national action plan paper admits that not all schools and local authorities have presented 'quality reports' that evaluate the implementation of their antiracism action plan. Similar concerns have been noted in England (Osler and Morrison 2000).

One important initiative by the Swedish government was to declare 1999 as 'Basic Values Year' and to launch a 'Basic Values Project'. This has produced a handbook for schools that stresses the need to listen more to children and young people. It also provides guidance on the role of the school in promoting common values and directly combating those values that are inimical to democracy:

> Schools should not be value-neutral but should clarify basic values and tolerance limits. The principle of the equal worth of all people is a democratic value that cannot be interpreted away. In interpersonal relations there should be no distinction between the worth of different groups of people and attitudes which deny this principle – such as *Nazism, racism, sexism, and the glorification of violence – shall be actively brought out into the open and combated.*
> (Government of Sweden 2001: 36, emphasis added)

This policy of openly confronting expressions of racism and xenophobia contrasts sharply with the declared policy of the British government's adviser on citizenship education and the stance taken by the DfES and successive ministers in avoiding the use of the terms 'racism' and 'antiracism' (see e.g. Crick 2000). In Sweden, democracy is the fundamental value that underpins the constitution and hence also its schools. It follows that the promotion of antiracism as a measure to promote democracy can be presented as a national policy supported by all democratic parties.

In Britain, where there is no written constitution, there is no formally agreed set of basic values. This means that education in basic values has no touchstone. Values can be presented as party political and therefore the product of political bias. For instance, whereas Sweden's action plan aims to combat homophobia, the British government was unable, until 2003, to fulfil its commitment to repeal Clause 28 of the Local Government Act 1988 that has been widely interpreted as essentially homophobic.

With respect to education, the National Curriculum for England aims to pass on 'enduring values', but these are not made explicit, nor are they linked to human rights and democracy. It is hardly surprising, then, that the subject of citizenship in schools in England is perceived as itself open to accusations of bias and that those drawing up guidelines attempt to de-politicize the subject.

Ways forward

Mainstreaming the fight against racism in Europe requires both general policies and practices and specific antiracist initiatives. Within education there is a need both for general policies to promote inclusion and integration and also for specific initiatives to actively combat racism and other anti-democratic discriminatory practices. Programmes of citizenship education are a specific initiative through which antiracism can be promoted and realized in schools. A major obstacle to ensuring the success of such programmes is the tendency to de-politicize the concept of citizenship itself. This is particularly the case in Britain.

Whereas the values of Sweden are set out in its constitution and those of Europe are clearly set out in a number of instruments and treaties, notably the *European Convention on Human Rights*, the basic values of both Britain and England remain vague. This lack of clarity provides a political space that is colonized, in Britain, by xenophobic nationalists, hostile to Europe, and often prone to sexism and homophobia. From this space they may act to fundamentally undermine democracy.

Across Europe, the curriculum subject of citizenship can provide a forum in which anti-democratic values and practices can be, in the words of the Swedish policy document, 'actively brought out into the open and combated'. Only when this happens can antiracism genuinely be mainstreamed within citizenship education. The mainstreaming of antiracism requires an understanding that it is essential to democracy. As the example of Sweden illustrates so clearly, it is by linking antiracism to democracy rather than exclusively to multiculturalism that it can start to receive the widespread acceptance it requires.

PART 3
Democratizing Schools

8   Democratic schooling

Introduction

In most democratic societies, schooling is recognized as a key means by which young people are educated for citizenship. Yet schools remain essentially authoritarian in their structures and organization. Indeed, as Riley (2004) has pointed out, the criticisms which John Dewey levelled against schools at the beginning of the twentieth century, with classrooms housing 'rows of ugly desks' and promoting a process of passive listening and 'the dependency of one mind upon another' remains a common pattern. 'If Dewey were to visit many of our classrooms today, he would be disappointed at how little has changed' (Riley 2004: 52), despite the fact that education for citizenship and democracy has become recognized as a pressing concern across a range of countries internationally.

Dewey, in his book *Democracy and Education* ([1916] 2002) stressed the need for an education based on democratic dialogue and shared values in which young people (and their teachers) are encouraged to look outward to the world beyond their school and their national borders. He also placed considerable importance on the quality of interpersonal relationships with the institution of the school. Today, the UN *Convention on the Rights of the Child (CRC)* confirms children's rights as citizens, provides a framework for the establishment of shared values based on human rights and respect for the equal dignity of all children and, in its Article 29 makes explicit the right to an outward-looking education. Despite the *CRC*, and the work of many educators committed to democratic learning, the entitlement of all children to an education where their views are taken into consideration (*CRC* Article 12) and which is based on democratic dialogue is not yet realized.

This chapter examines the principles of democratic schooling and considers some of the tensions between these principles and the structures and legal frameworks of schooling. We propose a set of pedagogic principles which support the development of democratic learning for human rights. We then present two initiatives to promote learning for citizenship and democracy in a primary and secondary school, reflecting on the challenges which teachers face in striving to promote democratic schooling.

The application of democracy to schools, which are institutions that have evolved from authoritarian rather than democratic principles, is challenging and is therefore likely to give rise to political struggle and debate. Learners, staff, parents, governors and local, regional and national governments all have interests in the conduct and outcomes of schooling and these may very well be in tension. Democracy is a means of addressing and resolving social tensions within communities. The school, as a community, is a place of rich possibilities for experiencing and learning about democracy.

Schooling and democratic practices: some tensions

It has long been recognized that schools have a key role to play in educating young people for citizenship and democracy. In many democratic countries, including France, the Nordic states and the USA, this role has been explicit right from the introduction of mass education. For example, in a discussion of education for citizenship, diversity and human rights in England and the USA, Hahn notes that in the case of the latter:

> there has been a general consensus since the end of the nineteenth century that schools have a role in integrating immigrants and should educate young people for citizenship in a multicultural democracy. Citizenship education is recognized as a central purpose of schooling. The social studies curriculum, which draws largely on history and the social sciences, is viewed as a key vehicle for citizenship education. In addition, other curriculum subjects, school ethos, and out-of-school experiences also serve to teach young people about democracy, national identity, social cohesion and diversity.
>
> (Hahn 2005)

Citizenship education in France, as in many other countries, has at the beginning of the twenty-first century been subject to considerable revision and development. Yet a central concept of public education has always been the incorporation of citizens into a common political culture:

> Citizenship education in France is thus crucial to the whole notion of state schooling. The school is the Republic's primary institution for socializing its citizens. Indeed, it is the school, through its curriculum, that is entrusted with the mission of defining what it

means to be a citizen and of ensuring that there is a common understanding of the rights and obligations of citizenship. The basis of state education in France is initiation into a common culture through a single curriculum. It does not recognise difference, but rather starts from the premise that, within the Republic, all citizens are equal.

(Osler and Starkey 2004: 5)

In England, at the beginning of the twenty-first century, we are witnessing a change in the preparation of young citizens for life in a democracy. Whereas, until recently, education for citizenship was largely implicit, with the introduction of citizenship as a school subject, which is both assessed and inspected, the processes of education for democracy are becoming explicit. This would seem to be particularly appropriate at a time of constitutional reform, and notably at a time when the rights and responsibilities of everyone, whether or not they have citizenship status, and the government's responsibilities to the people, guaranteed under the *European Convention on Human Rights (ECHR)*, are incorporated into domestic law, under the Human Rights Act 1998. Citizenship education is becoming more explicit as the rights and duties of individuals and governments towards each other become more explicit.

Nevertheless, the statement of values and purposes underpinning the National Curriculum for England places greater emphasis on the 'spiritual, moral, social, cultural and physical development, and thus the well-being of the individual' than on the well-being of society. It notes almost as an afterthought that 'Education is also a route to ... a healthy and just democracy' (DfEE/QCA 1999a: 10). No link is made between individual well-being and democratic structures, either in society generally or within the institution of the school. There is not yet a consensus that schools have a vital role in preparing citizens for democratic living. As we noted in earlier chapters, there is no statutory framework for the participation of students in governing bodies or to enable their participation in the day-to-day running of their schools, through student councils or other representative structures. It is perhaps therefore unsurprising that, despite the introduction of citizenship as a curriculum subject from 2002, a government sponsored survey of schools in England found that: 'Students' depth of understanding of fundamental democratic values and institutions is limited' (Kerr *et al.* 2003: iv). One reason for this failure to learn about democracy may well be the discrepancies between the experiences of learners in many schools and the information they receive about democracy and democratic values in formal citizenship lessons: 'It is not simply that schools do not practise the human rights and democratic values they preach. It is that many schools consistently contravene them' (Alderson 1999: 194).

While education for citizenship and democracy has long been a central aim of schooling, there has often been a tension between this aim and the actual processes of schooling which, as we have seen, do not always promote inclusion and rights. The process of democratizing schools is often assumed to be one that focuses on school structures and culture, in line with the widely recognized principle, endorsed by European ministers of education, that: 'Democracy is best learned in a democratic setting where participation is encouraged, where views can be expressed openly and discussed, where there is freedom of expression for pupils and teachers, and where there is fairness and justice' (Council of Europe 1985).

In England, schools generally refer to the needs of individual learners, the quality of interpersonal relationships and equality of opportunity in their mission statements. It is less common for them to make explicit reference to human rights and democratic values. Moreover, as we have explored in earlier chapters, pressures of a content-heavy curriculum, national testing requirements and competition between schools are all likely to detract from opportunities to enable students to discuss, research and develop democratic skills.

Education and democracy

John Dewey ([1916] 2002) identified two key criteria for a democratic society that he applied to education. Dewey's first criterion for democracy is that the society has 'a large number of values in common'. He argued that the 'democratically constituted society' is one where social control is achieved as a result of a consensus about shared aims and values rather than through coercion. Dewey argues that 'the bond of union is not merely one of coercive force' ([1916] 2002: 97). There needs to be awareness of mutual interests between those who have power and authority and those affected by their decisions. Within any community, including school communities, where members recognize their mutual interests, voluntary cooperation is more likely to occur.

Dewey's second criterion is that there should be free association and interaction within and between communities. Interaction between social groups leads to opportunities to continuously revisit habits, processes and procedures. As Dewey puts it, the result will be: 'change in social habit – its continuous readjustment through meeting the new situations produced by varied intercourse' (Dewey [1916] 2002: 100). In other words, as social groups interact they will develop new perspectives, experiences and opportunities to develop and practise skills of intercultural evaluation. Dewey defines democracy in terms of opportunities for maximizing communication between individuals and groups: 'In order to have a large number of values in common, all the members of the group must have an equable opportunity to receive and to take from others. There must be a large variety of shared undertakings and experiences' (Dewey [1916] 2002: 97–8).

A democratic education therefore implies opportunities 'to receive and to take from others' and 'a large variety of shared undertakings and experiences'. Dewey thus makes a strong argument for comprehensive education because segregation, whether within or between schools, leads to the impoverishment of the communication and dialogue that are possible among the members of a school community. Democratic schools provide opportunities for students to work collaboratively on tasks in a range of diverse groups. The tasks are shared experiences and they are the occasion for discussion, negotiation, dialogue and communication. Democratic schools also provide opportunities for dialogue between school leaders and administrators, governors, teachers, ancillary staff and students. Democratic schools are outward-looking and value links and exchanges with other organizations. The school curriculum reflects this outward-looking approach.

Democratic dialogue in schools is an opportunity for all concerned to examine their values and their behaviours and to be responsive to the perspectives of others. Dewey's vision is of a cosmopolitan democracy in which the horizons of all members are constantly extended by opportunities to learn from those from other backgrounds. He concludes that:

> A democracy is more than a form of government; it is primarily a mode of associated living, of conjoint communicated experience. The extension in space of the number of individuals who participate in an interest so that each has to refer his own action to that of others, and to consider the action of others to give point and direction to his own, is equivalent to the breaking down of those barriers of class, race, and national territory which kept men from perceiving the full import of their activity.
>
> (Dewey [1916] 2002: 101)

In other words, in a democracy, the principle of reciprocity is fundamental. A citizen is required both to 'refer his own action to that of others' and also 'to consider the action of others'. Citizens are aware both of the impact of their own actions and of ways in which the behaviour and lifestyle of others may enrich their own. Democracy requires 'the breaking down of barriers of class, race, and national territory'. The cosmopolitan democracy needs to be nurtured in school. Dewey's vision is internationalist and he recognizes that this will require teachers to engage with controversial issues: 'It is not enough to teach the horrors of war and to avoid everything which would stimulate international jealousy and animosity. The emphasis must be on whatever binds people together in cooperative human pursuits and results, apart from geographical limitations' (Dewey [1916] 2002: 114).

The emphasis is on our common humanity. Schools are democratic in so far as they provide opportunities for all participants to learn from one another. This is a core principle. Indeed it is, for Nobel prize winner Amartya Sen, a universal principle: 'The practice of democracy gives citizens an opportunity to learn from one another, and helps society to form its values and priorities' (Sen 1999: 12). This in turn requires schools 'to take rights seriously as living ever-present realities which can only be addressed with integrity by people within relationships of mutual respect' (Alderson 1999: 196).

Thus democracy in schools is fundamentally about respect. Democracy as a fundamental principle of education may be in tension with authoritarian school structures but it should not necessarily threaten schools or undermine student discipline. Research suggests that increased student participation is, in fact, likely to enhance discipline (Osler 2000a; Taylor with Johnson 2002; Ekholm 2004). Within democratic schools there will be an opportunity for teachers and managers to explain their perspectives and the reasons – for example, for specific school rules and procedures. This does not mean relinquishing authority. Teachers and school managers have the responsibility to exercise their authority in the interests of improving educational opportunities for all children.

Democratic schools are not only likely to be better disciplined, but to be more effective in a number of respects. Harber (1995: 11) provides four key pragmatic reasons why democratic schools are more effective:

- rules are better kept by staff and students if democratically agreed;
- communications are enhanced;
- greater control by staff and students leads to an increased sense of responsibility;
- consideration of a range of internal and external interests and options enhances decision-making.

Democracy and pedagogic principles

The principle of democratic participation requires schools to examine their structures, organization and management. We have also identified the wide-ranging implications of the *CRC* for classroom organization, curriculum and pedagogy (Osler and Starkey 1996, 1999; Osler 1997a). An individual's understanding of pedagogy is likely to be closely related to a range of personal and cultural beliefs about the way children learn, what may be understood by individual intelligence, the subject matter, and the students in question. These beliefs, whether culturally based or related to our own biographies as teachers and learners, may or may not be challenged by the formal processes of teacher education. The rights enacted in the *CRC* suggest a number of principles, outlined below, which should be applied to the processes of teaching and learning.

Dignity and security (*CRC* preamble, 19, 23, 28.2, 29)

The student's right to dignity implies a relationship between teacher and student that avoids abuse of power on the part of the teacher, including the avoidance of sarcasm. In this relationship the teacher's own right to dignity should not be forgotten. Teachers need to establish, with their students, a classroom atmosphere in which name-calling and mockery are unacceptable. It is the teacher's responsibility to ensure that those who are most vulnerable are protected from bullying and have the opportunity to learn in a secure environment.

Participation (*CRC* 12, 13, 14, 15, 31)

The principle of participation runs through the *CRC*. Students should be given opportunities to exercise choice and responsibility in decisions which affect them at classroom level – for example, in the planning and organization of their own work. It is noteworthy that approaches based on choice, responsibility and negotiation which are regularly developed with very young children are often abandoned as they grow older. It is of course the case that inter-disciplinarity and a certain flexibility is built into the primary curriculum in the sense that the same teacher is likely to be responsible for several if not all areas of the curriculum. Although limitations on the choices open to older students are frequently explained in terms of curriculum constraints and subject specialization, they may also be closely related to teacher beliefs about the extent of children's autonomy and teacher control.

Identity and inclusivity (*CRC* preamble, 2, 7, 8, 16, 23, 28, 29, 31)

The preservation and development of identity, including the recognition of the multiple identities that individuals may develop, is a key right within education, yet one that is perhaps the most easily violated. Teachers need to ensure that they meet certain basic requirements, such as correct use and pronunciation of the child's name. Respect for individual children, their cultures and families is critical. This requires us to value diversity in the classroom and to recognize that diversity and hybridity are essential characteristics of all human communities. It means seeing children's characteristics, whether cultural, emotional or physical, as attributes to be built upon, rather than deficiencies. Education systems, schools and classrooms that deny or marginalize diversity are likely to discriminate against those who do not match the presupposed norm. Children whose social and cultural backgrounds are different from those of their teachers, and those with learning difficulties or disabilities, are particularly disadvantaged in such systems.

Freedom (*CRC* 12, 13, 14, 15)

Pedagogy needs to permit maximum freedom of expression and conscience. The exercise of the rights of freedom of expression, freedom of conscience and religion, and freedom of association and peaceful assembly all require a range of skills which need to be developed in the classroom. The right of children to have their opinion taken into account in decisions made about them similarly requires a pedagogy which promotes skills of expression and decision-making. Teaching and learning needs to be based on student-teacher and on student-student dialogue. It assumes a model of learning and development in which the learners will often be best suited to identifying their own needs. The model assumes that teachers are continually developing their own teaching skills and are also open to learn from the students. Freedom of expression will have certain limitations, in order to protect the freedoms, security and dignity of others.

Access to information (*CRC* 17)

The exercise of the right of freedom of expression is at least partially dependent on access to information and ideas, including information from the mass media and from a diversity of national and international sources. Teachers have a responsibility to ensure that not only does the child have skills of reading and writing to gain access to information but is able to critically interpret visual images in newspapers, video, internet sources and other media. Skills involved in the development of visual literacy include questioning, recognition of bias and discrimination and those skills associated with the design and production of visual materials – for example, a photo sequence or video. An appropriate pedagogy will permit students to identify issues about which they wish to learn more, analyse the mass media, encourage creativity, imagination, criticism and scepticism, and allow students to arrive at their own judgements. The selection and range of sources of information in the classroom is usually determined by teachers, within the confines of available resources. While the teacher is responsible for ensuring that the child is protected from materials injurious to their well-being, there is also an obligation to develop a pedagogy whereby children have access to information on a need-to-know basis and are encouraged to identify and express their needs.

Privacy (*CRC* 16)

The right to privacy, which is jealously guarded by so many adults, is often disregarded when we are dealing with children, in the context of the school, the staffroom and the classroom. Pedagogy should respect the child's right to privacy, with regard to family and home, and schools need safeguards, in the form of guidelines, to protect the child's reputation when sharing information about individuals. While recognizing that we often ask personal questions of children in order to build upon their own experiences, cultures and identities, as teachers we need to remember that there exists a power relationship between teacher and student which may sometimes cause children to reveal more than they might wish to do. The teacher should consider the context, and avoid situations where children may be asked to reveal personal information in public, as for example in a whole-class discussion. If the principle of the child's best interests is consistently applied as a primary consideration, this should not prevent teachers seeking information designed to protect a child judged to be vulnerable in some way.

These pedagogic principles have been developed for debate and for schools and groups of teachers to engage in a process of self-evaluation. We have drawn on the work of Covell and Howe (1995) to develop another self-evaluation tool 'Does your school environment give everyone a chance to enjoy their rights?' (see Appendix 4) which draws directly on the *CRC*. This tool for evaluating the degree to which the school is in keeping with the principles of the *CRC* can be used by both teachers and students.

Democratizing schools

Here we examine two examples of school-based initiatives to promote education for democracy and inclusion, both of which set out to transform school cultures and both of which began with curricular reform. In each case we draw on the work of a senior teacher at the school who led the initiative. Each project focused on promoting student participation and democracy. In each case we examine ways in which the school promoted shared democratic values and a democratic dialogue among students (Dewey [1916] 2002). We report on staff engagement with the processes of change and on their participation in decision-making related to the curriculum, but do not set out to analyse the degree to which the schools were democratically managed. Instead we focus on processes of democratization as they impact on students. Both examples highlight some of the tensions which prevail as teachers and students respond to the introduction of new democratic processes and yet continue to have expectations of each other and of schooling which are not based on democratic ideals. Both schools have been given pseudonyms.

Human rights education in an Irish primary school

At Gaelscoil, a multidenominational, coeducational primary school located in a city suburb in the Republic of Ireland, the principal, Colm Ó Cuanacháin, decided to take advantage of the considerable autonomy which Irish schools have to develop their own curricula in order to implement a human rights education programme. Gaelscoil is one of 139 Irish language schools established by the government in response to parental demand in a particular locality. It was the first Irish language school to be established as a multidenominational school, beyond the control of Church authorities and open to children of all religions and none. From its foundation in 1993 the school has been 'democratically run, with active participation by parents in the daily life of the school, with due regard however, for the professional role of the teachers' (Ó Cuanacháin 2004). Gaelscoil has just 200 children, aged 4–12 years. Most come from middle-class homes.

After consulting with the staff, board of management and children, the principal developed a policy and programme of human rights education. The goal was that children would experience human rights and active citizenship first hand (Ó Cuanacháin 2004, 2005). The project was an integrated whole-school initiative which focused on the processes of teaching and learning and the formal curriculum but which simultaneously sought to develop school structures and organization to ensure greater democracy. The goal was 'to promote the knowledge, attitudes and skills needed to equip the children to become active, informed and caring citizens' (Ó Cuanacháin, 2005).

The principal worked with each class teacher to develop relevant themes and lesson plans for their class, integrating this work with the broader work plan to be undertaken. There was a strong emphasis on participative methodologies which would allow learners to develop skills in democratic dialogue. As well as working to address the taught curriculum, the school reviewed assemblies and other features of communal life to ensure that they supported the teaching of human rights and the development of democratic learning. For example, each class established its own class contract and a school declaration of rights was initiated. As Ó Cuanacháin (2005) explains: 'Steps were taken to organise and manage the school in a human rights framework where discipline, school organisation, relationships, and learning take place in a shared democratic environment'. Consequently, each class took lead responsibility for the development of a particular whole-school project – for example, the school council and the establishment of a school court.

One of the challenges facing the project was teachers' lack of experience and training in active learning methodologies. To a greater or lesser degree this was addressed through the provision of an elaborate set of teachers' resources and regular staff discussions. It was possible, within a small school where all the staff had made an initial commitment to the project, for teachers to meet regularly and to discuss the programmes of work with their colleagues, both in specially structured meetings and on an informal basis. Nevertheless, the processes were extremely time-consuming, particularly in the start-up phase.

The formal curriculum was structured around a number of themes:

- junior infants: kind and sharing;
- senior infants: fair and not fair;
- first class: respect for others;
- second class: building an understanding of human rights;
- third class: UN *Convention on the Rights of the Child*;
- fourth class: *Universal Declaration of Human Rights*;
- fifth class: equality (including gender equity, antiracism and disability issues);
- sixth class: conflict and conflict resolution.

The content of the programmes of work drew on children's own experiences, and, as well as examining the school as a community, children were presented with material which drew on a range of international contexts.

The principal evaluated the project through interviews with colleagues, diaries from the teachers and a longitudinal survey of the children. Ó Cuanacháin (2005) notes:

> There was unanimous endorsement and welcome for the human rights education processes introduced to the school, by both the teachers and the pupils. Everybody who contributed to the action research reported that the processes had a positive impact. Teachers felt that the attitudes the process cultivated, and will cultivate through continuous reflective interaction with others, will enable the children to better live in a changing, more intercultural, more diverse, and more challenging society in Ireland and the world. All teachers reported that cooperation and understanding appeared to improve between the children and their classmates, with increased evidence of interest in relationships and communication.

Teachers' comments reflect a sense of excitement at being involved in a pioneering initiative and in a shared enterprise:

> I found it helpful that we were all doing some of these things for the first time because we could talk about problems in a way we mightn't normally.

> The process of developing a policy and a plan as a group gave me a sense of responsibility, a stake in it all, and that made the positive moments more rewarding. By adopting the same approach with the children I could see the same sense of ownership in them.
>
> (Gaelscoil teachers quoted in Ó Cuanacháin 2004)

Both teachers and children reported that children enjoyed learning through participation, eagerly anticipating the next human rights education class. Children and teachers also reported an improvement in school discipline, with children better able to understand and address issues like bullying. This is reflected in children's comments:

> It's a good idea to learn about human rights so that we will have a better school.

> It made bullies feel ashamed. It worked on me.

> I learned that you should be aware that other people have rights and not just you, and you should help people to know their rights.

> I learned how important rights are, and that there are many people whose rights are being violated right in front of our noses, and we don't care.
>
> (Gaelscoil students quoted in Ó Cuanacháin 2005)

Children's responses also revealed how they appreciated learning more about the wider world.

Not everything that was tried was successful, and one of the challenges facing the human rights education project was implementing some of the whole-school initiatives. Not all teachers were able to take a lead in developing these, while at the same time seeking to transform their own classroom practices and learning methodologies. For example, the idea of a school court, where the school would be able to address discipline problems in an open and transparent way, did not get off the ground. As one teacher observed: 'We didn't think through the whole-school dimension enough. It has implications that we weren't ready for. The school court is a wonderful concept, but it is an entire project in itself to get it up and running, accepted and understood, by teachers and by the children' (quoted in Ó Cuanacháin 2005).

Although the project was, in some ways, over-ambitious in setting out to achieve such far-reaching reform in a relatively short time-span, it does demonstrate that: 'a human rights school can thrive in the context of current Irish national curricula and government policy. The integrated approach adopted in the school for the action research project worked, and can work in other schools' (Ó Cuanacháin 2005).

The principal's evaluation of the project, which sought out teachers' and children's perspectives, suggests that during the course of the project democratic dialogue was extended among teachers, among children and between teachers and children. The whole-school initiatives, such as the school council and school assemblies, presented children with the opportunity to work collaboratively on shared projects and to share their learning and experiences with others with whom they may not otherwise have worked. This dialogue, together with the whole-school focus on human rights, suggests a process by which shared values were extended and made more explicit.

Education for citizenship and democracy in a London secondary school

South Docks School is an inner-city 11–16 school, situated in an area of London with high social and economic deprivation. Most of the students live in the immediate locality of the school and around half the students are entitled to free school meals. There is considerable ethnic and linguistic diversity in the school population, with 55 per cent of students speaking English as an additional language. In 1999 the staff campaigned for their school to have specialist citizenship status. Although the government initially declined to recognize citizenship as a subject for specialist school status, the school was given additional resources to develop as a pilot for the introduction of citizenship education. The initiative was led by Anne Hudson, assistant headteacher, on whose research this example is based (see Hudson 2005 for a fuller account).

An important feature of the school was the high level of staff solidarity and their commitment to social inclusion and challenging inequality. Also important was the relatively open style of school management, together with the headteacher's commitment to the project and his willingness to take risks. From the beginning, teachers were consulted about the introduction of citizenship education, and a number engaged enthusiastically in this process, with over 20 attending two residential weekends on a voluntary basis. Teachers broadly endorsed the need to teach the concepts developed in the Crick Report on citizenship education (QCA 1998) and, after reviewing opportunities for developing citizenship skills and understanding through other subjects, concluded that students should have specialist lessons in citizenship.

The school introduced a General Certificate of Secondary Education (GCSE) citizenship course for students in Years 10 and 11, with each unit of work encouraging students to investigate issues that concerned them and to engage in activities to promote change. So, for example, students wrote to the *Sun* and the *Mirror* newspapers commenting on their coverage of the

Iraq war and designed posters for the staffroom on fair trade and ethical consumption. For their assessed work they investigated issues of personal concern, such as mobile phone theft, the improvement of local leisure facilities, bullying and making local streets safer. They presented their findings to a range of people with influence and power, including police officers and their Member of Parliament (MP). Younger students were also given specialist citizenship lessons, engaged in fieldwork and made presentations of their findings to people in positions of power in the locality. By engaging with issues of personal and community concern and suggesting positive solutions to problems they were encouraged to develop a sense of agency and to influence policy. These young people were beginning to engage in a democratic dialogue not only with each other but also with people beyond the school community in positions of power and influence.

Hudson (2005) identifies three levels of social identity which were reinforced and developed by the initiative: *passive, active* and *politicized* (Bradley 2003). For many students the project encouraged them to engage enthusiastically in citizenship activities held on special days and provided a welcome chance to interact with members of the school community, such as those in other year groups, with whom they would otherwise not come into contact. Hudson argues that these students' identities remained *passive* but that the curricular activities reinforced students' sense of belonging within the school community. Many students went a step further, developing *active* identities and believing they could make a difference. For example, a number had shown considerable distrust in the police, but after engaging with police officers at school, students began to suggest how they might work as partners with the police to improve their community: '... by telling the police who the thieves are because everybody knows who they are that are scared to tell the police. Have neighbourhood watches. More cameras in places people often get robbed, and tell the mobile phone company to make better security on the phones' (Layton, Year 11 boy, quoted in Hudson 2005).

Others emphasized how they could influence people in positions of power:

> I think I can make a difference because I told my opinions to my group – we shared these with our year and an MP – and those people might then go on and do something about it or tell someone else, so making the community more aware of such problems in society and then in the world.
>
> (Keeley, Year 11 girl, quoted in Hudson 2005)

> A few weeks ago we did make some kind of difference by presenting our research and findings about mobile phone theft to the local MP. The way we made this difference was by bringing up important issues which everyone knew about to present to people in power

who can make that change which we desire ... many people agree-
ing means power and power means making changes.

(Joshua, Year 11 boy, quoted in Hudson 2005)

The School Council was revitalized as part of the citizenship initiative
and was recognized both within the school and beyond as a significant
element in enabling students to develop democratic skills and shape their
community. As one student observed: 'Everyone can make a difference by
spending the form time discussing what is wrong and what needs to be
done outside school. Some students can make a difference [and] if they are
part of the School Council it will get our points across to teachers who have
the main power if our views go ahead' (Martin, Year 10 boy, quoted in
Hudson 2005).

Significantly, some young people moved from participation in school-
changing activities to taking up positions of power and responsibility in the
locality. Hudson argues that many of those young people who served on
the School Council developed *politicized* identities. Students reflected on
their experiences as elected representatives in the school community:

I believe the three years that I've been in the School Council ...
we've improved more and we're getting more things that we want.
Because in the School Council in Year 7 and 8 I don't think we got
that much. But in these years we're really developing and getting a
lot of things that we want.

(Charlene, Year 10 girl, quoted in Hudson 2005)

I do think it's been effective because usually quite a lot of different
points come up at each meeting and lots of them get sorted out,
especially things to do with lessons and how teachers can improve
themselves.

(Theo, Year 9 boy, quoted in Hudson 2005)

Some of those who were on the School Council were later elected to a
local forum, the Council of Champions, which paralleled the borough's
official council. Community Champions could be as young as 12 years old,
and anyone aged 12 plus could vote. Four school students were elected.
These students really developed a sense of agency and efficacy:

I chose to stand for the Council of Champions because I felt I could
make a difference by putting my views and other people's views
into action. Like issues to do with education and safety and
housing issues ... I actually feel encouraged to do more things for

the community ... I've learned like how to go into the world to make a stand for myself.

(Luke, Year 7 boy, quoted in Hudson 2005)

Despite such positive results, some teachers remained anxious about the extension of student democracy and student voice. Hudson notes that a number of teachers held understandings of citizenship which placed much more emphasis on student responsibilities than on student rights:

I still think that they have difficulties with understanding the rights and the *responsibilities* part of it and my expectations were that they would become more involved in dealing with the responsibility side of it.

(Head of Year B, quoted in Hudson 2005)

I think the difficulty's been the balance between rights and responsibilities. Because I do think from the point of view of the staff they see certain pupils that have been very very assertive but still don't have an understanding that there has to be a payback or there has to be some sort of balancing out.

(Head of Department A, quoted in Hudson 2005)

These views contrast with those of some students, who suggest that they had learnt not only how to engage in democratic dialogue with adults in the wider community but with their own teachers:

I have learned that actually pupils can work with teachers and be on the same level and get respect and get what we both want and we can communicate and discuss things that we all want together. Instead of teachers making all the plans we can actually tell them how we feel about things. So that's what I've learned. That we can actually discuss things. I think I have become more mature now. And I understand where teachers are coming from.

(Chardelle, Year 10 girl, quoted in Hudson 2005)

In reflecting on her findings Hudson notes that the next stage of this initiative should be feedback to the teachers, highlighting the benefits students have identified. She also suggests that had teachers been provided with a human rights framework from the beginning and been invited to see citizenship in terms of reciprocal rights and responsibilities, their anxieties might have been reduced.

In the course of the project, democratic dialogue was extended among students, who were given exposure to local power-holders, and were encouraged to address issues within the school community, the wider local community and at a global level. The outward-looking curriculum engaged them in considering questions of fair trade, ethical consumption and media representations of the war in Iraq. These were not mere academic exercises, but encouraged some students to take an active role in the community and to express their opinions on matters of national and international significance in order to influence the democratic process.

Sustaining democratic practices

Democratic schooling requires dialogue and an outward-looking or cosmopolitan perspective. This dialogue enables the development of shared values and mutual respect between teachers, students and other members of the school community. Currently schools attempting to democratize face considerable challenges, since structures, legal frameworks and popular expectations are derived from authoritarian rather than democratic traditions. A contradiction remains between these authoritarian traditions and the expectation that schools will prepare citizens for democratic life. As the examples we have presented show, it is possible for individual schools to transform their practices and engage in processes of democratization. The two schools demonstrate how it is possible for school leaders with commitment and vision to promote democratic learning for human rights and empowerment. However, for such initiatives to be sustainable, schools also need appropriate legislative frameworks. One of the important features of democracy is the need for its constant renewal and development. Authoritarian schools undermine democracy. Education for democratic citizenship implies a review of power relationships within schools and the development of a new culture of schooling in which teachers and students work together to create democratic schools.

9 Rights and responsibilities

Introduction

We consider that education for citizenship should be a space where political claims can be debated and controversies examined rather than avoided. We also argue strongly that citizens have responsibilities to each other. However, there is a tendency in discussions on citizenship education to emphasize the responsibilities of young people rather than their rights. This effectively depoliticizes citizenship education, appealing to moral sentiments and ignoring social contexts.

While human rights are clearly defined in international instruments, human responsibilities have not been codified in the same way. There is certainly a well-established rhetoric of responsibilities and these are so prevalent that it is important to debate underlying meanings. In this chapter we examine human rights instruments and draw on the recommendations of various international commissions to explore the degree to which the international community may be moving towards a common understanding of agreed responsibilities. Our analysis is intended to promote debate about responsibilities and the degree to which they might provide a basis of shared values in education.

De-politicizing rights?

In many respects the content and pedagogy associated with human rights education is now well documented and supported by policy statements and internationally agreed texts.[1] While the promotion of human rights is essential for an inclusive democracy, discourses of human rights can seem threatening to those in authority, including, ironically, elected representatives. An unqualified discourse of human rights is often seen as provocative or potentially inflammatory. Advocating the promotion and implementation of human rights invites political controversy about the limits of human rights claims and about competing claims. A simultaneous reference to responsibilities is used as a way of de-politicizing the claims. The terms of reference for the Crick Report on citizenship education in England, for example, placed greater emphasis on responsibilities than rights: 'To provide advice on effective education for citizenship in schools – to include the nature and practices of participation in democracy; the *duties, responsibilities and rights* of individuals as citizens; and the value to individuals and society of community activity' (QCA 1998: 4, emphasis added).

In its evidence to the Crick committee, the British Youth Council also felt the need to qualify any suggestions of young people's entitlements to rights. It proposed that the curriculum: 'should consider the *responsibility* of belonging to society – the *rights* and *responsibilities* of citizens. It should look at children and young people's *rights* and *responsibilities* as citizens, and how these change as they grow older. It should also look at the law and the justice system and how it relates to their rights and *responsibilities*' (QCA 1998: 19, emphasis added).

The word 'responsibilities' can be used as a bland and de-politicized rhetorical device. We have therefore attempted to define and explore the concept in the context of citizenship, which is, by definition, a political space. In attempting to categorize and list responsibilities, it may be appropriate to legislate to enforce certain responsibilities (paying taxes, for instance) while other duties (e.g. voting) may have to be left to individual conscience and a collective social ethic. Our intention is to provide a starting point for debating the issue of responsibilities. We suggest that this debate is important to those drawing up policies and guidelines, including school behaviour policies in societies that are both multifaith and secular. Given the prevalence of a discourse of responsibilities, we review those definitions that have been proposed in international contexts and attempt a synthesis in order to provide a common understanding of the concept of responsibilities as has been achieved for the concept of rights.

Identifying responsibilities

Article 29 of the *Universal Declaration of Human Rights* (*UDHR*) states that 'everyone has duties to the community in which alone the free and full development of his personality is possible'. This explicit reference to duties, or what are now more usually referred to as responsibilities, as an essential element of a human rights framework has received relatively little attention in liberal democracies. Whereas it took three years, between the signing of the United Nations *Charter* and the final adoption of the *UDHR*, to define human rights to the satisfaction of all parties, no such attempt was made to define human responsibilities.

René Cassin attempted, in 1947, to include a formulation of duties in the *UDHR* (Cassin 1969). However, Eleanor Roosevelt argued that the principles of individual liberty, which had driven the war against Nazism and Fascism, were overriding. It was agreed to leave the formulation of duties until after the completion of the formulation of rights, but no commission was ever convened to undertake this task.

In fact, much current discourse of human rights automatically links responsibilities with rights. Giddens (1998: 66), for instance, proposes the maxim 'no rights without responsibilities'. In fact, to insist that there are no rights without responsibilities is problematic. All human beings have entitlements to rights. To deny certain individuals their rights (e.g. the right to a fair trial or the right to education) simply because they have failed to fulfil particular responsibilities is to undermine the basis of human rights.

The case for linking rights and responsibilities is made on the basis of reciprocity. Those who have rights have a reciprocal obligation to help others achieve their rights. A popular booklet for younger school children, inspired by a publication of the National Children's Rights Committee, South Africa, gives a number of examples, such as 'Children have the right to a clean environment ... and the responsibility not to pollute it' and 'Children have the right to live without violence ... and everyone has the responsibility not to be violent to others' (Save the Children 1999).

It is thus possible to derive responsibilities from rights, but in attempting to arrive at a definition in this way, it becomes clear that there is not a straightforward one-to-one equivalence between rights and responsibilities. The Geneva based International Council on Human Rights Policy (ICHRP) has undertaken some useful groundwork. It identifies three kinds of individual responsibilities, namely:

- duties on individuals in their roles as agents of the State to respect, promote and protect human rights;
- duties on individuals to exercise their rights responsibly;
- duties of individuals towards others and their community.

(ICHRP 1999: 15)

The first type of duties is an extension of the duties and responsibilities of states, since it refers exclusively to those working for the state in some capacity. The second category of duties falls within a human rights framework, as rights are clearly defined. An understanding of the limits of claims of human rights is an essential element in understanding human rights. It is consequently the third category, duties of individuals towards others and their community, that requires some definition and enumeration. In attempting to define responsibilities, our starting point is that entitlement to rights is never conditional on acceptance of responsibilities. For instance, the right to vote in elections for government cannot be restricted to those who conscientiously exercise their responsibility to inform themselves of the policies of the candidates.

International statements of responsibilities

The *African Charter on Human and Peoples' Rights* (1981)

The first attempt to define responsibilities in a human rights instrument was the *African Charter on Human and Peoples' Rights* (ACHPR), adopted in 1981 by the member states of the Organization of African Unity (OAU). The *Charter* defines duties and responsibilities. Article 25 follows the thesis whereby all rights have reciprocal responsibilities. It places an obligation on states to promote education for the rights in the *Charter* and to 'see to it that these freedoms and rights as well as corresponding obligations and duties are understood'.

There follows a section (Articles 27–9) which defines the duties and responsibilities of individuals, as opposed to those of states and of parents:

Article 27
1 Every individual shall have duties towards his family and society, the State and other legally recognized communities and the international community.
2 The rights and freedoms of each individual shall be exercised with due regard to the rights of others, collective security, morality and common interest.

This article lists the various collectivities, from family to international community, to which individuals have obligations. The precise nature of those obligations is defined in the following articles:

Article 28
Every individual shall have the duty to respect and consider his fellow beings without discrimination, and to maintain relations aimed at promoting, safeguarding and reinforcing mutual respect and tolerance.

The *Charter* here defines respect, tolerance and non-discrimination as responsibilities of individuals towards each other.

Article 29
The individual shall also have the duty:
1 To preserve the harmonious development of the family and to work for the cohesion and respect of the family; to respect his parents at all times, to maintain them in case of need.

This emphasis on the family as a unit and respect for parents is an expression of an ethical position prevalent in many religious traditions and in many societies. The family is also recognized as fundamental to society in Article 16 of the *UDHR*. However, in many societies the family is an institution that is undergoing radical change. There are increasing numbers of single-person households and diverse forms of family life. There may be a number of citizens, such as those looked after by the state, who have little experience of family life. As such it is not clear that this duty is as universal as human rights.

The duties that follow under Article 29 of the *ACHPR* concern the relationship of the individual to the nation and the state. Just as Article 29.1 privileges the family, so articles 29.2–6 privilege the nation.[2] Such an attitude of responsibility to the state of which one is a citizen can be seen as reciprocal given the duties and responsibilities of the state under human rights law. This set of duties can be summarized as:

- preparedness to serve the state, including defending it against internal or external threats;
- loyalty to fellow citizens by respecting national secrets and by paying taxes.

Commission on Global Governance

A list of universal responsibilities was drawn up by the Commission on Global Governance (CGG) in its report published at the time of the fiftieth anniversary of the UN (CGG 1995). The impetus for setting up the CGG came from former German Chancellor Willy Brandt soon after the fall of the Berlin Wall in 1989. It was subsequently endorsed by the then Secretary General of the UN, Boutros Boutros-Ghali. The CGG, chaired by Shridath Ramphal of Guyana and Ingvar Carlsson of Sweden, included members from nearly 30 countries, broadly representative of the world community.

The CGG distilled from all the human rights instruments available a list of eight fundamental universal rights and seven universal responsibilities. The list of responsibilities is as follows:

- contribute to the common good;
- consider the impact of their actions on the security and welfare of others;
- promote equity, including gender equity;
- protect the interests of future generations by pursuing sustainable development and safeguarding the global commons;
- preserve humanity's cultural and intellectual heritage;

- be active participants in governance;
- work to eliminate corruption.

(CGG 1995: 57)

Unlike the *African Charter*, this list does not situate individual responsibilities within the context of a nation or state. Thus, while both formulations refer forward to future generations, the *African Charter*, drafted at a time of nation building, confines its concerns to the territorial integrity of states. The CGG takes an altogether more planetary view. Its concern with global commons reflects struggles in the UN over drafting treaties on climate and the law of the sea.

Some of these formulations require context to make them meaningful. The notion of contributing to the common good requires a shared understanding of what that means. Every political party and movement and every religion is based on a vision of the common good that competes for attention and resources. A number of notorious leaders in the twentieth century, including Stalin, Hitler, Mao and Pol Pot, demanded duties from their citizens that required complicity in human rights abuses and genocide in the name of 'the common good'. The common good in the twenty-first century requires definition by reference to the goals of the UN, namely freedom, justice, development, democracy and peace. It is also a concept that must be treated with caution:

> citizenship (in a plural society) involves: commitment to the society in its diversity; openness to, and indeed solidarity with and respect for, the different other, in particular the 'ethnically' different; acceptance of the basic equal worth of all people, of the rights and responsibilities of all; and a rejection of any form of exploitation, inequitable treatment or racism. It means a taking account of difference where that is appropriate, but not where it is not. But none of this implies a blind commitment to 'the common good'.
>
> (Figueroa 2000: 57)

The seven universal responsibilities proposed by the CGG are only unproblematic in a liberal and pluralist political context. Humanity's cultural and intellectual heritage must be defined in its diversity, not in terms of 'one (public) fixed, homogeneous social and cultural heritage' (Figueroa 2000: 50). Such public definitions, linked to ethno-nationalism have been pretexts for violence, abuses of human rights and genocide. However, the cosmopolitan citizen will recognize a responsibility to preserving diversity as the essence of humanity.

The seventh responsibility, the elimination of corruption, is innovative in human rights discourse. It is not hard to justify, however, as corruption is corrosive of democracy which is the main guarantee of justice, equality and sustainable development. That said, there are other forces, notably racism, equally damaging to democracy, as we discuss in Chapter 7.

InterAction Council

Two years after the CGG, another group of former heads of state and government, convened by former Prime Minister of Japan Takeo Fukuda, presented a draft *Universal Declaration of Human Responsibilities* to the UN. In spite of the eminence of the members of the group, their work did not command universal agreement (ICHRP 1999). The draft *Declaration* contains 19 articles, which expand the seven principles of the CGG.

The *Declaration* is not, in fact, drafted in universal terms. Article 3, for instance, is based on a distinction between 'good' and 'evil', about which there is unlikely to be a universal consensus. Article 6 includes responsibilities of governments as well as of individuals. Article 11 is about the responsible use of wealth and Article 13 details the responsibilities of members of professions. Article 14 lists the responsibilities of the media. Articles 16 to 18 provide principles for sexual relationships, marriage and parenting. All these refer to limited rather than universal categories.

One original contribution to the thinking on responsibilities is the 'responsibility to develop their talents through diligent endeavour' (Article 10). This personal responsibility for self-improvement is likely to require opportunities provided by the state or the community, particularly educational and training opportunities.

European definitions

The Council of Europe has strongly promoted human rights education and from 1999 this has included a consideration of responsibilities alongside rights. It is likely that those promoting the policies were aware of the InterAction Council draft *Declaration*. The Committee of Ministers of Education adopted a *Declaration and Programme on Education for Democratic Citizenship, Based on the Rights and Responsibilities of Citizens* (Council of Europe 1999a). The ministers accept that there are 'common responsibilities in combating social exclusion, marginalisation, civic apathy, intolerance and violence'.

In the same year the Parliamentary Assembly adopted a Recommendation (1401) *Education in the Responsibilities of the Individual*. Drawing on expressions of fundamental values, particularly as expressed in the *ECHR*, the *UDHR*, the *European Social Charter* (Council of Europe 1961) and the *Framework Convention for the Protection of National Minorities* (Council of Europe 1995), the Assembly concluded that:

Everyone should, *inter alia*:

a   fully respect the dignity, value and freedom of other people, without distinction of race, religion, sex, nationality, ethnic origin, social status, political opinion, language or age; everyone must act towards others in a spirit of fellowship and tolerance;

b   act peacefully without recourse to physical violence or mental pressure;

c   respect the opinions, privacy and personal and family life of other people;

d. show solidarity and stand up for the rights of others;

e   in practising his or her own religion, respect other religions, without fomenting hatred or advocating fanaticism, but rather promoting general mutual tolerance;

f   respect the environment and use energy resources with moderation, giving thought to the well-being of future generations.

(Council of Europe 1999b)

This list introduces elements not present in the formulations of the *ACHPR* and the CGG, such as acting peacefully and respecting privacy. Acting peacefully is very much in the spirit of the *Charter* of the UN and is a logical extension of respecting dignity. Respecting privacy is a reciprocal responsibility to the right to privacy under the *ECHR*.

Showing solidarity and standing up for the rights of others corresponds to the CGG's concern that individuals should promote equity. There is also agreement on the importance of responsibility to future generations for the environment.

The formulation on the responsibility to practise religion 'without fomenting hatred or advocating fanaticism' seems to correspond to specific political concerns of the time of the Recommendation. A similar formulation is found in Article 15 of the InterAction Council draft *Declaration*. However, religious movements do not have a monopoly on such incitement. Political parties and the media may incite to hatred using entirely secular discourses. The responsibility to avoid fomenting hatred is covered by respecting the dignity, value and freedom of others. A draft responsibility that refers only to those who practise religion cannot be a universal.

Defining responsibilities: a synthesis

From an examination of these international attempts to define responsibilities, we have drawn up our own list of universal responsibilities. In the same way that we have, in Chapter 8, proposed a number of pedagogic principles that can be derived from human rights, we suggest that an agreed list of universal responsibilities is a starting place for the development of codes of behaviour and other policies in the context of education.

A   Individual and collective responsibilities to others
     Whatever their role or position, everyone should respect and promote the dignity and human rights of others. Everyone should:

   - consider the impact of their actions on the security and welfare of others;
   - show consideration for others and treat them with respect;
   - work for equity, including gender equity;
   - respect privacy;
   - act non-violently.

B   Contributions to communities at local, national and global levels.
     Everyone should:

   - work for freedom, justice, development, democracy and peace;
   - develop skills and talents and take advantage of educational opportunities;
   - respect the rule of law;
   - show solidarity and stand up for the rights of others;
   - actively participate in governance and in civil society;
   - work to eliminate corruption.

C   Responsibilities to future generations
     Individually and collectively everyone has responsibilities to practise sustainable ways of living and to preserve and enhance:

   - the diversity of humanity's intellectual and cultural heritage;
   - peaceful and creative social structures;
   - the life-sustaining resources of the global environment.

An audit of responsibilities

These universal responsibilities constitute a statement of ethical values for cosmopolitan citizens. As with other ethical codes, this one has no purpose unless it is studied and implemented. In the context of education for citizenship, and in addressing personal, social and health education, schools should provide opportunities for pupils and teaching staff, and other stakeholders, to consider and debate these principles as both individual and shared responsibilities. All members of a school community, the learners, the teachers and the support staff, should have opportunities to consider their responsibilities and the implications of these for their behaviour and lifestyle. Since they are proposed as universal responsibilities, they apply to adults and young people alike.

Consider the impact of their actions on the security and welfare of others

When many people interact in close physical proximity, as in schools, these considerations are particularly important. Although individuals have the responsibility to be considerate, the institution is greatly helped when approved practices and procedures are formalized. For instance, something as simple as keeping to the left on stairs or not running in corridors will contribute greatly to the security and welfare of others.

Show consideration for others and treat them with respect

Consideration for others requires thinking about the rights and needs of those who may be affected by what we say or do. The key principle is that the human dignity of others is to be respected. Teachers are careful to be as polite to and respectful of their students as they expect them to be. Everyone will take care that names are learnt and properly pronounced. Deliberate name-calling, like racist, sexist or homophobic comments or jokes, has no place in a community where respect and consideration are key principles of interaction.

Work for equity, including gender equity

In view of the right to equitable treatment, the institution needs to have policies that help to ensure equity. At the same time individuals have the responsibility to do their best to implement the policies. At a minimum this implies that both staff and students are familiar with equal opportunities issues and the policies that derive from them. Ideally, both staff and students should be involved in the formulation of such policies and all parties or their representatives should be involved in policy design and monitoring. Policies should cover the curriculum as well as the informal provisions of the school and its ethos. Gender equity should not be divorced from other equality issues such as those relating to race and disability.

Respect privacy

This is the obverse of the right to privacy. Those with personal and confidential information have the responsibility to share it only with permission and in the interest of obtaining help and support.

Act non-violently

While there is usually a need for some forms of coercion in rule-governed institutions, these should not include the use of force. Aggressive forms of speech and threatening behaviour short of actual physical violence are in themselves potentially violent behaviours and have no place in a learning community based on respect.

Work for freedom, justice, development, democracy and peace

These are the principles on which the UN is based. They can be achieved through opportunities in the curriculum, in extracurricular activities and in the whole ethos and management of the learning community.

Develop skills and talents and take advantage of educational opportunities

We all have the responsibility, throughout our lives, to develop our skills through formal and informal educational opportunities.

Respect the rule of law

Respecting the rule of law is not necessarily the same as accepting that individual rules are necessarily in the best interest of the wider community. Some rules may need changing, and it is part of the democratic process to campaign to change unfair or weak legislation.

Show solidarity and stand up for the rights of others

Beyond simply showing consideration for others, it is also appropriate in a democracy to take positive steps to ensure the rights of others are upheld.

Actively participate in governance and in civil society

Institutions are obligated to provide structures for participation. Individuals have a responsibility to be involved. Involvement can take many forms, and at its most basic may simply imply voting for a representative. The school has a responsibility to establish participative structures, such as school or class councils and students should be encouraged to consider issues and decisions that affect them. Such structures might share responsibility for the allocation of resources.

Work to eliminate corruption

Most schools are financed with public funds and those ultimately responsible for the institution must be accountable for the use of those funds. Democracy implies transparency in the use of resources and any use of the funds for purposes incompatible with the goals of the institution may be considered corrupt. All members of the institution, staff and students, should be aware of the possibility of corruption and know what steps are open to them if corruption is suspected. As with issues of security, measures of prevention should be in place. It is likely that work to eliminate corruption will be collective, perhaps involving unions or associations of parents, for example.

Responsibilities to future generations

All members of the institution will be committed to preserving its assets and protecting communal facilities. They will also have an education that helps them acquire a global perspective and an understanding of the concept of sustainable development. Schools will provide opportunities for pupils to become familiar with local Agenda 21 initiatives. The publication, *A Curriculum for Global Citizenship* (Oxfam 1997) provides detailed guidance and resources across the whole age range. There is more general guidance available in the *Declaration on the Responsibilities of the Present Generations Towards Future Generations* (UNESCO 1997).

Children's own understandings of rights and responsibilities

It is sometimes argued that, if informed about their rights, young people will begin to demand rights without acknowledging their responsibilities. Moreover, it is sometimes asserted that young people do not want responsibilities, and that they see these as the preserve of adults. Not only is this a fundamental misunderstanding of the nature of children's human rights, which are based on the principle of reciprocity, that is to say, respecting and upholding the rights of others (see e.g. Osler and Starkey 1996, 1998; Flekkøy and Kaufman 1997) but it is also, perhaps, to underestimate young people's capacity and willingness to acknowledge their responsibilities.

In a research project conducted on behalf of the UK Commission for Racial Equality into exclusion from school (Osler 1997a), young people were invited to give their opinions on improving school discipline. They acknowledged that they shared a responsibility with teachers for ensuring that the school was an orderly place where everyone had an opportunity to learn, and were eager to develop their own skills and capacities to resolve conflicts and to participate more fully in decision-making processes. Their consultation and involvement in our research, which set out to identify good practice in managing school discipline and minimizing school exclusions, produced a wealth of creative ideas which complemented those of their teachers and gave us new insights (see Chapter 3). In particular, pupils highlighted that if schools are to ensure the greater participation of young people in decision-making in line with the provisions of the *CRC*, schools must not only provide structures for participation (school councils, class councils etc.) but also equip children with the skills to participate (e.g. advocacy, counselling and listening skills, conflict resolution). Pupils saw structured opportunities for exercising their participation rights as a fundamental part of a well-disciplined school.

Understanding reciprocity

The twenty-first century world is a global village within which diverse traditions and cultures coexist and interact. This is a source of rich creativity but also, in the context of gross inequalities, a source of tensions and conflicts. Schools, particularly those in cities, are often microcosms, reflecting the global diversity of populations. Even when schools are more homogenous in their composition, they have to prepare their pupils to live and work in a heterogeneous world. For all these reasons education is crucially about helping young citizens to develop those values and skills that will help them contribute to the global priorities of peace, sustainable development and the means to achieve these, namely democracy and respect for human rights.

Institutions and individuals have rights and responsibilities. In the case of education, those involved as students, teachers or in support roles are expected to be aware of the key principles and guidelines set out in Article 26.2 of the *UDHR*. The study of this and the full text of the *UDHR* can inspire local statements of values, such as those contained in school mission statements and policy documents.

Much work has been done on the application of human rights values to education. There is a developing rhetoric stressing the essential reciprocity of rights and responsibilities. It is relatively easy to convince individuals that they have rights, for these are strong claims that they can make in the expectation that they will receive benefits, such as protection and the provision of services. Responsibilities, on the other hand, imply not receiving but giving; not individualism but a sense of the communal and the collective. This has been and continues to be a feature of many religious traditions and values. In an increasingly secular context, there is a continuing pedagogical challenge, namely to promote responsibilities linked to rights for the achievement of global priorities.

10 Changing leadership

Introduction

Discourses surrounding educational management and school leadership are changing. In particular, the terms 'diversity' and 'race equality' are being used in the context of school improvement and with reference to debates about school standards. This chapter considers some of the reasons for the changes in school leadership discourse and explores whether these developments reflect a changing professional culture among school leadership trainers and researchers. In particular, it considers the extent to which equality and diversity issues have been mainstreamed. We draw on the voices of headteachers and others who hold leadership positions within the English education service. We examine the perspectives of school leaders, particularly those who have made an explicit commitment to race equality and reflect on ways in which their voices and experiences can inform policy in this area. In particular, we focus on the professional and life experiences of school leaders from minority ethnic communities. We consider headteachers as citizens and leadership for race equality as an aspect of citizenship. Increasingly, schools are beginning to recognize the benefits of consulting with students and engaging them in decision-making. The chapter therefore concludes by drawing on the voices of learners, posing the question: what can children contribute to changing leadership in schools?

Ethnicity: a leadership blind spot?

Since the publication of the Swann Report (DES 1985) no educational management specialist in England could fail to be aware of the failure of the education system to achieve equitable outcomes for all ethnic groups. From the 1990s the government and school management specialists had clear statistical evidence, based on LEA and other studies, of differentials in achievement by ethnicity (Gillborn and Gipps 1996; Gillborn and Mirza 2000).

The first official report to provide a national picture of attainment by ethnicity at the end of primary schooling (Key Stage 2) and through to GCSE examinations at 16 (Tikly *et al.* 2002) confirmed inequalities in attainment between ethnic groups. The report was commissioned as the first step to fulfilling a government promise, made in 1997, to evaluate the impact of the Ethnic Minority Achievement Grant (EMAG), public funds specifically designed to address inequalities in attainment between children of different ethnic groups. The researchers examined the action plans and strategies of LEAs in England to raise attainment.[1] These action plans contain information about the targets and strategies used by LEAs to raise achievement as well as performance data relating to different minority ethnic groups in each LEA. The research compared the LEA plans with a quantitative analysis of changes in minority ethnic performance so as to give some indication of the effectiveness of these targets and strategies in raising minority ethnic achievement within each LEA and across all LEAs. There were some common factors in the plans of those authorities that were most successful in closing the achievement gap, namely:

- helping schools to monitor achievement (by ethnicity/gender) and to focus on groups who were underachieving;
- collating and disseminating good practice;
- setting effective targets for minority ethnic learners. (Tikly *et al.* 2002: 15)

The evidence from the report suggests that where there is effective leadership and support from LEAs and when specific efforts are made to work with local communities, schools are able to build upon this and begin to close the achievement gap.

There were wide variations in the relative achievement of students from each minority ethnic group across LEAs. For example, the percentage of Bangladeshi pupils achieving Level 4 and above in standard attainment tests (SATs) in English at the end of primary schooling ranged between 53 and 71 per cent depending on the LEA. The percentage of Caribbean heritage pupils achieving 5 or more A*–C GCSE grades at the end of compulsory schooling, ranged between 16 and 59 per cent. These substantial differences cannot be explained solely in terms of other differences in school populations, such as social class differences. They suggest that an LEA can have a considerable impact in supporting schools in realizing race equality and that LEAs might usefully learn from each other. Despite these interesting findings, government officials chose to publish the research report without a press release, so avoiding public discussion of the continuing inequalities in primary schools and beyond and on the impact which LEAs can make in closing the achievement gap. Effectively, by omitting to publicize these findings, central government lost an opportunity to exercise leadership in helping to raise attainment.

Despite evidence of gross inequalities between groupings of students according to ethnicity, there are few references to equity issues in the textbooks aimed at aspiring school leaders, published in the 1980s and the 1990s in Britain. Typically, an edited collection of articles in a book on school management contained one chapter on gender but, if you go to the index and look for gender, race or social class, these concepts are not explored to any significant extent elsewhere (see e.g. Bush *et al.* 1999). They do not form part of the analysis of most educational management specialists from this period. Many of these educational management books make no reference to race equality or diversity. This is curious, since at the time of publication, substantial black and minority ethnic communities had been established for several decades and, during the 1990s Britain was experiencing a wave of migration which required many schools to accommodate newly-arrived refugees and asylum-seekers.

The failure to address equalities as a key aspect of school leadership is of considerable concern given the huge differentials in attainment between different groupings of students, by ethnicity, gender and social class. Throughout the 1990s successive governments laid considerable stress on raising educational standards. Schools responded to this challenge and there was an overall improvement in test scores and examination results, as is evidenced by SAT and GCSE results. Despite the overall improvement, there remains a significant gap between national averages and the average attainment of young people from African Caribbean, Bangladeshi and Pakistani heritage (DfES 2002).

In England, the reluctance of school management experts to consider ethnicity as a factor in student attainment and therefore as a critical concern of school leaders was matched by a model of school leadership which remained predominantly white and male. Studies which examined the leadership experiences of women (Adler *et al.* 1993; Ozga 1993) and both women and men from minority ethnic communities (Osler 1997c) have not been widely drawn on by trainers and researchers to develop more inclusive models of school leadership. The predominant message to aspiring headteachers who are female and/or from black communities is that their experiences are marginal. A leading journal, *Educational Management and Administration,* failed during the 1990s to attract more than a handful of articles specifically addressing diversity or race equality and the majority of contributors failed to see these issues as central to their concerns. It was possible for an aspiring headteacher working in a culturally diverse city, such as Birmingham or Leicester, to register for a Masters' degree in educational management in the 1990s and to complete the course successfully without addressing equality and diversity issues.

Rhetoric and realities

Discourses surrounding educational management and school leadership have undergone a significant change. The words 'school improvement', 'race equality', 'standards agenda' and 'diversity' are now used together in the context of educational policy development and school leadership training. This is a new development. In the British context it is due, in part, to the Race Relations (Amendment) Act 2000, which places a duty on all public bodies, including schools, local authorities, government ministries and inspection agencies to *promote* race equality.

The changing discourse of school leadership training and research can also be explained, in part, by the improved official data on ethnicity and achievement, which is now available. The Pupil Level Annual School Census (PLASC) provides data which makes it possible not only to monitor attainment by ethnicity and gender, but also to identify schools and LEAs whose policies and practices are helping to close the attainment gap and achieve greater equity between groupings of students.

Following the implementation of the Race Relations (Amendment) Act, it is no longer sufficient for schools to prevent racial discrimination; they are required to actively promote equality. Our research (Osler *et al.* 2003) suggests that LEAs and schools have responded to the Act by introducing measures to address differentials in attainment by ethnicity. In doing so they have acknowledged their responsibilities to learners, but they have been much slower to address their responsibilities as employers and take steps to promote good race relations among staff. We found that 18 months after the implementation of the Act none of the three LEAs that we studied (a London borough, a large and culturally diverse metropolitan authority and a shire county with a relatively low number of minority ethnic employees) had taken adequate steps to address and prevent the racial harassment of teachers. Although the Act is, potentially, a key tool in the realization of racial justice, a 2003 survey by the Department of Trade and Industry (DTI) of public sector employers, to assess progress towards implementing the Act, found that over half of all schools, colleges and universities were unable to identify a single outcome to show any progress whatever (Richardson 2004).

Under the Act, Ofsted is required to inspect schools to ensure they are fulfilling their duty to promote race equality. Inspection is being used across a range of public services as a tool intended to promote and mainstream race equality. Indeed, Home Office Minister Fiona Mactaggart placed the Act within the context of the government's efforts to reform public sector services, arguing that: 'Improvements in race equality across the public sector support the wider government aim of public service reform' (2003: 36). However, the research evidence suggests that the processes of cultural change are slow. In response to the 1999 Stephen Lawrence Inquiry report the government gave Ofsted lead responsibility for monitoring how schools address and prevent racism. The same year, the CRE commissioned us to carry out research on Ofsted. While we concluded that the school inspection framework was robust enough to enable Ofsted to carry out its government assigned role, we found that inspectors were ill equipped to carry out the task. Nor did the then Ofsted leadership accept that the new responsibility lay properly within its remit (Osler and Morrison 2000). Three years after our study and over a year after the Race Relations (Amendment) Act came into force, the House of Commons Education and Skills Select Committee published a report on the work of Ofsted. It quoted evidence from the CRE:

> Ofsted has made a commitment to examine and report on school race equality policies, and schools' arrangements for meeting their other duties. We are, however, concerned that this message, and what it means in practice, is not getting through to all inspectors. For example, a head teacher of a predominantly white school contacted us to express concerns about Ofsted inspectors who recently inspected her school. The Head stated that the inspectors dismissed the work that she and her school had put into a race equality policy and meeting the positive duty as not particularly relevant because the school had a very small ethnic minority population ... [the head teacher] saw race equality as an important issue, because the school had a very small ethnic minority population ... [we] emphasise that the positive duty applies to all maintained schools, irrespective of their ethnic make-up.
>
> (House of Commons Education and Skills Committee 2003: 16)

The Select Committee recognizes the key role of headteachers as leaders in preparing all young people to espouse the principles of equality and diversity regardless of the degree to which the school population is itself ethnically diverse. All headteachers are required to show commitment to these principles. These are legal requirements which reflect the government's stated commitment to address institutional racism (Home Office 1999) following the publication of the Stephen Lawrence Inquiry report (Macpherson 1999).

Some specialists in educational leadership have identified limitations to school improvement in the context of social inequality, disadvantage and discrimination:

> Britain remains a deeply racist society. Discrimination is found in almost every aspect of the way in which our social, economic and educational lives are led. The significant successes of the school

improvement strategies of the past decade are raised attainment for all pupils but they have yet to come to terms with the fundamental divisions in our society. In many ways school improvement has tended to exacerbate the gap between the socially advantaged and the socially disadvantaged. It is increasingly understood that school improvement can only enhance life opportunities if a number of environmental factors are propitious. Poverty, dysfunctional family life, communities with low social capital and cultural impoverishment remain more potent forces than improving the technical aspects of schooling.

(West-Burnham 2004: 16)

West-Burnham's analysis is worth considering in some detail, for in many ways it reflects a genuine attempt to address diversity and equality. He begins by acknowledging the ways in which racism and discrimination permeate British public life, recognizing that educational processes are not exempt. Without reflecting on the impact of racism and discrimination on attainment, he then acknowledges how school improvement strategies have sometimes widened the attainment gap. He fails to acknowledge that in many cases these strategies have been applied without any consideration to the discrimination and racism to which some students are subject. He falls into a trap of dividing students into two binary groups, the socially disadvantaged and socially advantaged, implying that it is the 'socially disadvantaged' who not only suffer from poverty, but are also the ones who have dysfunctional family lives, low social capital and cultural impoverishment. The conclusion seems to be that the limitations of school improvement strategies can be explained in terms of these factors. Yet it is not only those on low incomes who are subject to family instability, and it is by no means clear to whom he refers when he claims some communities experience 'cultural impoverishment'.

He fails to reflect on whether the school improvement strategies he advocates actually seek to build the social capital of students and their communities and whether they include a curriculum which responds to and builds on the diverse cultural experiences of students. One of the reasons that school improvement strategies may widen the attainment gap is that they are often culture blind. If, indeed, he believes that some communities suffer from cultural impoverishment, might this not mean that their cultures and ways of living are not recognized or reflected in the school curriculum?

Finally, despite having acknowledged racism and discrimination, he fails to address the school's own moral and legal obligations to challenge these. The possibility that the school improvement strategies to which he refers may have been racism blind is not addressed.

A number of commentators, particularly those concerned with the education of children with special educational needs, have drawn attention to tensions between the government's standards agenda and its commitment to inclusive practices in schools (see e.g. Loxley and Thomas 2001). It is important to consider such tensions, since the goals of raising standards for all and that of ensuring equitable outcomes for minority ethnic students should, theoretically, be complementary. In practice, the standards agenda involves an extensive testing regime. From the early years of schooling, children (and their teachers) are subject to a long process of preparing and sitting for tests. Tests serve the function of informing us how successful schools are in meeting the needs of different groupings of students, providing information which can then be used to redirect resources to meet the needs of those who require additional support. However, the tests are problematic: they remain, first and foremost, a means by which schools are assessed. The government sees testing as a means by which schools' success or failure can be measured. Pressures on schools to 'raise standards' within a context where academic results are published in annual league tables have led them to compete for students. Rather than raise standards by addressing the needs of those who are educationally disadvantaged (and thus relatively expensive to educate), schools compete for high attaining students who can succeed with fewer resources. In this context, equity goals may take second place to pressure to ensure that the maximum numbers of students achieve good grades in public examinations.

At classroom level, many teachers feel pressured to teach for the tests, so limiting the curriculum. Learners also feel the pressure of tests: low-attaining students and those with specific learning needs may be obliged to follow a programme of teaching which does not meet their individual needs. For such students, repeatedly low grades may compound a sense of failure. Enabling all students to achieve their maximum potential should be compatible with the standards agenda. Yet educators are working within a specific legislative framework, where schools are expected to compete for potentially high-attaining students in a quasi-market. While recognizing that legislative reform may be necessary in order to ensure that schools are in a position to meet the needs of disadvantaged students, we maintain that equity is compatible with raising standards. Equitable teaching practices which direct resources towards the most disadvantaged and towards closing the attainment gap will impact on overall outcomes, thereby raising average standards. As a review of research examining issues of equity in schools in the USA observed:

> there is an inherent and crucial link, rather than a conflict, between the achievement of equity goals and the achievement of high academic standards. In many respects, the two movements

seek the same objective: educational outcomes that don't vary by gender, race, class or ethnicity. Standards propose that all students can succeed, no matter how disadvantaged or challenged they are.

(AAUW 1999: 7–8)

New research agendas?

A research project carried out by Hay Group Management sought to identify the values and beliefs that make up the cultures of effective schools (Hobby 2004). Researchers presented teachers with 30 'statements of values' that they were then asked to arrange in order of priority. The report positioned itself centrally within the school improvement movement, drawing on research on school leadership and effectiveness. Yet only one of the 30 statements touched on issues of justice and equality: 'creating opportunities for everyone – widening horizons – fighting injustice'. Teachers were not invited to consider equitable outcomes or broader questions of social and racial justice as part of the values framework of a successful school. It would appear that we have a long way to go before race equality is mainstreamed.

The new leadership discourse, which rhetorically links school improvement and diversity, does not draw on the substantial body of work on race equality in education which has developed in LEAs and among academic researchers since the 1970s. There is currently little cooperation between researchers engaged in educational leadership, management and policy (traditionally a prestigious area of work) and those who have been toiling for years (often on the periphery) to draw attention to issues of racial justice in our schools. Yet cooperation between these groups is vital if research is to be useful to those engaged as school leaders.

The National College of School Leadership (NCSL) has commissioned research on the leadership of schools whose student populations are characterized as ethnically diverse. The NCSL has also carried out some research into the leadership experiences of teachers from minority ethnic communities – for example, those from African Caribbean communities. Yet it is not clear that links are being made between these two research strands. The current model assumes a leadership which is white (and largely male) and a client group (i.e. students and parents) who are from other diverse backgrounds. The new leadership discourse appears to be drawing on the work of school leadership experts who have worked in international (postcolonial) contexts, such as Hong Kong and Singapore, but not on the experiences of black headteachers in Britain. The leadership experts explore diversity from a cross-cultural perspective which stresses cultural differences. The model of cross-cultural analysis proposed by school leadership experts seeking to explore societal and institutional cultures (Dimmock and

Walker 2002) does not address equalities and inequalities. While an international and comparative framework may be valuable in providing new insights, it would be unfortunate if new research commissioned by the NCSL focused on cultural differences and ignored institutional and structural inequalities which are well-documented by scholars and practitioners (e.g. Wright 1992; Osler 1997a, 1997c; Gillborn and Mirza 2000; Wright *et al.* 2000; Tikly *et al.* 2004).

For schools to address current inequalities and fulfil their duty under the Race Relations (Amendment) Act to promote race equality, they need school leaders (and inspectors) who have an understanding of structural inequalities in the education system and the skills and confidence not only to debate issues like institutional racism but also to introduce polices and practices which enable their colleagues to create more equitable classrooms. The danger of the current approach is that it assumes that schools are neutral places where leaders are required to 'cope with' or 'manage' diversity. Where inequalities are recognized these may then be explained in terms of cultural (mis)understandings. This framework is likely to generate research outcomes (and training materials) in which intercultural understanding rather than equity is the key concern. Difference is likely to be emphasized at the expense of equity.

School leaders and racial justice

If schools are to develop as inclusive communities then equality and diversity need to be acknowledged as twin principles. Our research (Osler and Morrison 2000, 2002) carried out with headteachers in the wake of the Stephen Lawrence Inquiry report (Macpherson 1999) suggests that headteachers had begun to recognize institutional racism in education and were anxious to do something to address it. Unfortunately, they were not always aware of how they, personally, might make a difference through their leadership. While some recognized the need to monitor student performance according to ethnicity and gender, others still felt it was enough to focus on *individual* students in order to make a difference: 'Our equal opportunities approach is very much to know what the needs of every individual child are, what every individual child should be achieving and to be tracking that' (secondary headteacher, quoted in Osler and Morrison 2000: 133). This headteacher had been moved by the findings of the Stephen Lawrence Inquiry and by the play *The Colour of Justice*. She confided that 'some of our staff do have a racist approach'. Her solution was: 'being very supportive when students want to have an Eid party or, you know, when groups of students want to do something very much, making sure that they are respected and valued for doing it ... you give that leadership and then that should percolate down' (Osler and Morrison 2000: 133).

The headteacher recognizes racist practices among her staff but her response is not to provide training for the teachers or consider disciplinary action but to place emphasis on cultural activities. By contrast, another headteacher in the same LEA placed considerable emphasis on group monitoring to identify structural inequalities and on ensuring that young people left school with qualifications which would enhance their future choices:

> as a school one of the biggest challenges we are facing is around achievement. How vast numbers of young people can see a point to education. There are increasing numbers here who present challenges in terms of their behaviour. Young people should be able to expand their experience here so that they have a choice in the outside world. I want young people to be able to benefit from their education here. They have to pass examinations, which is the currency in terms of having a choice. So yes, we have targets for different groups of youngsters to check that all are benefiting – monitoring by ethnicity and gender.
>
> (secondary headteacher, quoted in Osler and Morrison 2000: 134)

This headteacher was aware that there are structural inequalities in both the wider society and in school, disadvantaging students from particular ethnic groups. His analysis and practice extended beyond concern about individual students to addressing ways in which his school might disadvantage students from particular communities. He was aware that within the LEA, boys of African Caribbean and Pakistani heritage were more vulnerable to disciplinary exclusion than were their white peers. He was also aware that the average attainment of these groups was below that of their white male peers. Having identified this problem he was addressing it by directing resources into employing a community-based worker to meet with students who he believed were underperforming and/or vulnerable to exclusion. He had expected his school's differentials in exclusion rates to be raised by Ofsted inspectors and was somewhat taken aback when this proved not to be the case. In this school, monitoring was not a mere statistical exercise but part of a process of redirecting resources to achieve greater equity.

Headteachers recognized the importance of tackling racist behaviour among students, although the degree to which they felt able to take a leadership role varied. They also saw this work in the context of a wider local community:

> I think, actually, in schools like this, [where] there is a smaller percentage of children who come from ethnic minority groups, that you have to make a specific decision to include ... The curriculum content has to include things from the other cultures, so that you

do bring in the children who are in the minority ... I used to work in the inner city ... where there was a much higher percentage of children from ethnic minority groups in the school and you know the white population accepted them, I felt, fairly readily. I feel that here, on the odd occasion, we have had children where it is obvious that their parents are racially prejudiced and they have given their children those views, and therefore because we haven't had such a high proportion of children from those groups in the school, they would then become the victim, more readily so, of bullying. We obviously have to make sure that if we do hear of any of those kinds of incidents we act very, very strongly among those groups.

(primary headteacher, quoted in Osler and Morrison 2000: 134)

In this case the headteacher recognizes the wider role of the school in challenging racism and inequality. It is insufficient merely to address attainment; the school also has a role in achieving security for all its members. Unlike the Ofsted inspectors criticized above by members of the Select Committee on Education, she recognizes that the task of educating young people to understand the importance of racial justice is important in an area where there is less visible diversity.

School leaders as citizens

The evidence from our study of the life histories of black headteachers and those in senior management positions (Osler 1997c) reflects a commitment to and leadership for race equality based on life experiences. There is a blurring of the boundaries between professional and other community responsibilities. In this sense, black headteachers and senior LEA staff can be said to be exercising their citizenship through their professional lives:

As the LEA erodes, how are you going to actually effect change? And I think the answer is, encourage more black people to put themselves forward on governing bodies. Address meetings and encourage them to be involved. Advise parents on what questions to ask. I'm a resource, anyone in the community knows that they can ask advice. I do a lot of career counselling for black women in particular, through networking. It is a case of trying to work under the system as well as on the system. I think as isolated black people that's the only thing we can do. I would rather be in school as a headteacher. That is where you have influence and power.

(Yvonne, LEA adviser, quoted in Osler 1997c: 134)

Unlike West-Burnham (2004), who sees lack of social capital within certain communities as a 'potent force' undermining school improvement strategies but one which educators are, apparently, powerless to overcome, Yvonne sees the building of social capital, among parents and her black colleagues, as her responsibility as an educator. She believes she can make a difference; the boundaries of her professional and citizenship activities overlap and blur.

Relationships between black and minority ethnic leaders and local communities are often complex, with leadership roles often extending beyond the school and into the community:

> In the beginning, some of the parents, especially your own parents, Asian parents, as they are not used to seeing somebody [Asian] in authority, they wonder. They do wonder if it is the right person to go to. You want to prove to them that you are not there *just* to speak their language. Yes, you are one of them but you have got the qualifications and ability to be a head of school. Fortunately that situation has improved. The parents are [now] much more fluent, they have built up confidence. So the relationship with parents has developed. In inspection, that came out as a model of good practice at the school. I have acquired their respect.
>
> (Anju, special school headteacher, quoted in Osler 1997c: 137)

> My position is an extremely difficult one. There is a demand that the black community expect of you, you have got to be absolutely perfect; you have got to be able to solve all their problems, you have got to be there to answer all their prayers. At the same time, the white communities out there are watching you, make one error and they will shoot you down and they will get you. So I am in a no-win situation; I have got to be better than better.
>
> (Frank, secondary headteacher, quoted in Osler 1997c: 136)

These headteachers recognize the importance of working with communities and feel a heightened sense of responsibility to these communities, but their ethnicity, community connections and identities do not necessarily make this a more straightforward task for them than for their white colleagues.

There are a range of initiatives, both national and local, that aim to identify potential leaders in schools. Brown (2004) notes the work of the NCSL and others in this area and acknowledges the training and support of school leaders in school improvement processes, self-review and evaluation. Nevertheless, he concludes:

> Many school leaders are still unsure about what this means in terms of promoting genuine race equality practices in school. This

is in spite of the fact that there are appropriate audit tools available to schools, for example, 'Learning For All' from the CRE … Many feel confident in the generic areas of leadership and management but feel extremely insecure about equality issues in their schools.

(Brown 2004: 37)

The Raising African Caribbean Achievement (RACA) project in Birmingham worked closely with primary schools whose African Caribbean learners were achieving in line with or above national expectations. The most important factors contributing to their success in these schools were:

- leadership;
- partnership with parents;
- well structured pastoral systems;
- high teacher expectations;
- culturally relevant curriculum provision;
- effective use of data analysed by ethnicity (Brown 2004: 38).

We would suggest that the NCSL and other trainers and school leadership experts have much to learn from the experiences of minority ethnic school leaders and from the RACA project. In particular they need to recognize that the promotion of generic skills for leadership is unlikely to be adequate and that headteachers need to be supported in applying their leadership skills to work with parents and communities, in supporting their staff in developing a culturally relevant curriculum and in developing monitoring by ethnicity beyond data collection to interpretation of needs and targeting of resources.

Leadership involves a commitment to achieving racial justice and to genuine change. As one black headteacher expressed it:

I accepted that the system was not created for me, I just happened to be here. If the system is going to do anything for me I have got to make it do it. I have got to go in there and change it from within. I have argued with the more radical of my friends because they don't want any part of the system; they want to drop out of the system in many ways, but they want to attack it from the outside. To me that is confusion, if you are going to attack it, it means you must bother about it enough to want to change it. So it would make more sense to use those energies positively and constructively, and by that I mean getting into the system and getting into some positions of power wherever possible, and then changing it from there.

(Clifton, primary headteacher, quoted in Osler 1997c: 135)

Most importantly, a number of black leaders have a transformatory view of education:

> Teaching I consider to be a real mission, education does matter, and it matters for young black and white kids in inner-city Manchester, inner-city Birmingham, inner-city London. I can remember in my first school there were kids who were absolutely spaced out because they had never seen a black teacher before ... When I went into the classroom, the first thing I said was: 'I am not here to play, I am here to work and you are here to learn, so if you are going to play you can stand outside. Your parents are working hard in shit houses for you to be here, they are working anti-social hours and you are not going to mess about'. Now that sort of understanding of the potential of education I think has stayed with me and I think that is the most important thing. I understand what parents want, I understand that education is potentially liberating and useful.
>
> (Lesley, secondary headteacher, quoted in Osler 1997c: 136–7)

Our research into the Ofsted school inspection framework (Osler and Morrison 2000) suggests that some mainstream headteachers also recognize race equality as a key citizenship issue and one which requires political leadership:

> If race equality is an important moral issue in this country then I think the Ofsted inspection framework could be explicit about this. It's not explicit in the new framework. It can't be quantified in the hard-nosed way that some data can be, but if it's an issue for society then schools could be asked how they are responding to society's agenda.
>
> (Primary headteacher, quoted in Osler and Morrison 2000: 127)

Headteachers often see multicultural school communities as advantaged rather than exceptional. This contrasts with a model of school leadership where 'coping with' or 'managing' diversity is presented as an exceptional or special activity. These leaders avoid a somewhat colonial model in which outsiders are employed to manage diverse school communities and counteract disadvantage:

> I think that [the situation of predominantly white schools] is an important issue that sometimes is not taken seriously enough. I think [this school] has a built in advantage. It's in a multi-ethnic community, a community that has for a long time been multi-ethnic, so there's a sense that the people who live here, have

always lived here reasonably well together and so the multi-ethnicity of the community is always there. That is its natural state. I mean there's a school in the south of [the borough], which is a white school, in which there's been a sort of trickling of black pupils into the school. It's a white school, a white working class area, National Front, all those sort of things have been there. Now they are getting a lot of refugees because they are under-subscribed and therefore the issues for them are much more difficult to cope with than the issues for us. They are starting from a very different point and I think that any sort of inspection process would have to recognize that, recognize that there is the sort of racism which is long gone here.

(Secondary headteacher, quoted in Osler and Morrison 2000: 139)

School improvement and leadership: young people's perspectives

As we discussed in Chapter 3, recent research has highlighted the contribution which young people can make in improving schools (Osler 2000a; Rudduck and Flutter 2004). School leaders can draw on their experiences to inform their understandings of equality and diversity. Our research on girls and exclusion (Osler and Vincent 2003: 90) demonstrated how young people are often able to identify inequalities and injustice: 'Say there's a big group of us, like five black kids and six white kids, you can guarantee they'll pick out the black before they come to the white. They always think the black kids are bad ... have done something before the white kids have' (Katrina, white student, mainstream school, fixed term exclusions).

Not only can young people provide insights into teacher-student relationships but they may also have an understanding of the wider processes in operation. The following quote from a group interview with three students shows how they are aware of the ways in which schools (de)select students in order to enhance their reputation:

> *S1:* [Neighbouring school] ... they kick them out and then we get them.
> *S2:* Yeah, we have all them...and [neighbouring school] have all the clever ones that just don't make any trouble.
> *S3:* They probably want a good reputation.
> *S2:* This school tries to help. Like if people are bad, they take them out and sit and talk to them instead of kicking them out straight away. Like they try and make them do better.

(Osler and Vincent 2003: 116)

The extract illustrates students' understandings of how exclusionary practices operate and of the efforts that some schools will make to include students with problems. The students' discussion also revealed their resentment of the neighbouring school and their understanding of how schools' performances and reputations are significant in the competition to get the most able students. This understanding suggests that school leaders would benefit from engaging students in decision-making processes relating to discipline, student attainment and inclusion. As well as understanding exclusion processes and how systems work, the young women we interviewed were also able to suggest practical solutions to complex leadership challenges.

Ways forward

Education for citizenship requires effective management and committed leadership. It is not enough, however, to rely on the commitment of school leaders to education for citizenship, diversity and equality. School leaders and educational administrators need effective support and this implies both political leadership and appropriate training. Unfortunately, the discourses of educational leadership and management have not always highlighted the twin principles of equality and diversity or given sufficient or explicit emphasis to the role of schools in educating for citizenship.

In Britain and across Europe, new legislation requires headteachers to develop more inclusive schools, where the rights of all are upheld. This is the case whether or not communities are visibly diverse. The evidence suggests that headteachers will need support in fulfilling their legal obligations. Moreover, they are likely to need training and support as they strive to close the attainment gap between students from different groupings. Those responsible for research and training on school leadership would benefit from engaging with the considerable body of research concerned with human rights, equity and diversity in schools.

Old models of school leadership marginalize the personal and professional experiences of those leaders who are not white and/or male. New inclusive models of school leadership need to be developed, drawing on the experiences of those who have been at the margins. Changing leadership for equality, diversity and citizenship needs to build on the voices of those headteachers who are already practising citizenship by striving for greater justice and more democratic schools. Changing leadership will also need to give due weight to the experiences of students, whose insights can inform more inclusive models of schooling.

Appendix 1:
The Universal Declaration of Human Rights

Preamble
Whereas recognition of the inherent dignity and of the equal and inalienable rights of all members of the human family is the foundation of freedom, justice and peace in the world,
Whereas disregard and contempt for human rights have resulted in barbarous acts which have outraged the conscience of mankind, and the advent of a world in which human beings shall enjoy freedom of speech and belief and freedom from fear and want has been proclaimed as the highest aspiration of the common people,
Whereas it is essential, if man is not to be compelled to have recourse, as a last resort, to rebellion against tyranny and oppression, that human rights should be protected by the rule of law,
Whereas it is essential to promote the development of friendly relations between nations,
Whereas the peoples of the United Nations have in the Charter reaffirmed their faith in fundamental human rights, in the dignity and worth of the human person and in the equal rights of men and women and have determined to promote social progress and better standards of life in larger freedom,
Whereas Member States have pledged themselves to achieve, in cooperation with the United Nations, the promotion of universal respect for and observance of human rights and fundamental freedoms,
Whereas a common understanding of these rights and freedoms is of the greatest importance for the full realization of this pledge, Now, therefore, The General Assembly, Proclaims this Universal Declaration of Human Rights as a common standard of achievement for all peoples and all nations, to the end that every individual and every organ of society, keeping this Declaration constantly in mind, shall strive by teaching and education to promote respect for these rights and freedoms and by progressive measures, national and international, to secure their universal and effective recognition and observance, both among the peoples of Member States themselves and among the peoples of territories under their jurisdiction.

Article 1
All human beings are born free and equal in dignity and rights. They

are endowed with reason and conscience and should act towards one another in a spirit of brotherhood.

Article 2
Everyone is entitled to all the rights and freedoms set forth in this Declaration, without distinction of any kind, such as race, colour, sex, language, religion, political or other opinion, national or social origin, property, birth or other status. Furthermore, no distinction shall be made on the basis of the political, jurisdictional or international status of the country or territory to which a person belongs, whether it be independent, trust, non-self-governing or under any other limitation of sovereignty.

Article 3
Everyone has the right to life, liberty and security of person.

Article 4
No one shall be held in slavery or servitude; slavery and the slave trade shall be prohibited in all their forms.

Article 5
No one shall be subjected to torture or to cruel, inhuman or degrading treatment or punishment.

Article 6
Everyone has the right to recognition everywhere as a person before the law.

Article 7
All are equal before the law and are entitled without any discrimination to equal protection of the law. All are entitled to equal protection against any discrimination in violation of this Declaration and against any incitement to such discrimination.

Article 8
Everyone has the right to an effective remedy by the competent national tribunals for acts violating the fundamental rights granted him by the constitution or by law.

Article 9
No one shall be subjected to arbitrary arrest, detention or exile.

Article 10
Everyone is entitled in full equality to a fair and public hearing by an independent and impartial tribunal, in the determination of his rights and obligations and of any criminal charge against him.

Article 11
1. Everyone charged with a penal offence has the right to be presumed innocent until proved guilty according to law in a public trial at which he has had all the guarantees necessary for his defence.
2. No one shall be held guilty of any penal offence on account of any act or omission which did not constitute a penal offence, under national or international law, at the time when it was committed. Nor shall a heavier penalty be imposed than the one that was applicable at the time the penal offence was committed.

Article 12
No one shall be subjected to arbitrary interference with his privacy, family, home or correspondence, nor to attacks upon his honour and reputation. Everyone has the right to the protection of the law against such interference or attacks.

Article 13
1. Everyone has the right to freedom of movement and residence within the borders of each State.
2. Everyone has the right to leave any country, including his own, and to return to his country.

Article 14
1. Everyone has the right to seek and to enjoy in other countries asylum from persecution.
2. This right may not be invoked in the case of prosecutions genuinely arising from non-political crimes or from acts contrary to the purposes and principles of the United Nations.

Article 15
1. Everyone has the right to a nationality.
2. No one shall be arbitrarily deprived of his nationality nor denied the right to change his nationality.

Article 16
1. Men and women of full age, without any limitation due to race, nationality or religion, have the right to marry and to found a family. They are entitled to equal rights as to marriage, during marriage and at its dissolution.

2. Marriage shall be entered into only with the free and full consent of the intending spouses.
3. The family is the natural and fundamental group unit of society and is entitled to protection by society and the State.

Article 17
1. Everyone has the right to own property alone as well as in association with others.
2. No one shall be arbitrarily deprived of his property.

Article 18
Everyone has the right to freedom of thought, conscience and religion; this right includes freedom to change his religion or belief, and freedom, either alone or in community with others and in public or private, to manifest his religion or belief in teaching, practice, worship and observance.

Article 19
Everyone has the right to freedom of opinion and expression; this right includes freedom to hold opinions without interference and to seek, receive and impart information and ideas through any media and regardless of frontiers.

Article 20
1. Everyone has the right to freedom of peaceful assembly and association.
2. No one may be compelled to belong to an association.

Article 21
1. Everyone has the right to take part in the government of his

country, directly or through freely chosen representatives.

2. Everyone has the right to equal access to public service in his country.

3. The will of the people shall be the basis of the authority of government; this will shall be expressed in periodic and genuine elections which shall be by universal and equal suffrage and shall be held by secret vote or by equivalent free voting procedures.

Article 22

Everyone, as a member of society, has the right to social security and is entitled to realization, through national effort and international co-operation and in accordance with the organization and resources of each State, of the economic, social and cultural rights indispensable for his dignity and the free development of his personality.

Article 23

1. Everyone has the right to work, to free choice of employment, to just and favourable conditions of work and to protection against unemployment.

2. Everyone, without any discrimination, has the right to equal pay for equal work.

3. Everyone who works has the right to just and favourable remuneration ensuring for himself and his family an existence worthy of human dignity, and supplemented, if necessary, by other means of social protection.

4. Everyone has the right to form and to join trade unions for the protection of his interests.

Article 24

Everyone has the right to rest and leisure, including reasonable limitation of working hours and periodic holidays with pay.

Article 25

1. Everyone has the right to a standard of living adequate for the health and well-being of himself and of his family, including food, clothing, housing and medical care and necessary social services, and the right to security in the event of unemployment, sickness, disability, widowhood, old age or other lack of livelihood in circumstances beyond his control.

2. Motherhood and childhood are entitled to special care and assistance. All children, whether born in or out of wedlock, shall enjoy the same social protection.

Article 26

1. Everyone has the right to education. Education shall be free, at least in the elementary and fundamental stages. Elementary education shall be compulsory. Technical and professional education shall be made generally available and higher education shall be equally accessible to all on the basis of merit.

2. Education shall be directed to the full development of the human personality and to the strengthening of respect for human rights and fundamental freedoms. It shall promote understanding, tolerance and friendship among all nations, racial or religious groups, and shall further the activities of the United Nations for the maintenance of peace.

3. Parents have a prior right to choose the kind of education that shall be given to their children.

Article 27

1. Everyone has the right freely to participate in the cultural life of the community, to enjoy the arts and to share in scientific advancement and its benefits.

2. Everyone has the right to the protection of the moral and material interests resulting from any scientific, literary or artistic production of which he is the author.

Article 28

Everyone is entitled to a social and international order in which the rights and freedoms set forth in this Declaration can be fully realized.

Article 29

1. Everyone has duties to the community in which alone the free and full development of his personality is possible.

2. In the exercise of his rights and freedoms, everyone shall be subject only to such limitations as are determined by law solely for the purpose of securing due recognition and respect for the rights and freedoms of others and of meeting the just requirements of morality, public order and the general welfare in a democratic society.

3. These rights and freedoms may in no case be exercised contrary to the purposes and principles of the United Nations.

Article 30

Nothing in this Declaration may be interpreted as implying for any State, group or person any right to engage in any activity or to perform any act aimed at the destruction of any of the rights and freedoms set forth herein.

Appendix 2:
UNICEF UK's unofficial summary of the UN *Convention on the Rights of the Child*

Article 1
Everyone under 18 years of age has all the rights in the *Convention*.

Article 2
The Convention applies to everyone whatever their race, religion, abilities, whatever they think or say, whatever type of family they come from.

Article 3
All organizations concerned with children should work towards what is best for each child.

Article 4
Governments should work to make these rights available to children.

Article 5
Governments should respect the rights and responsibilities of families to direct and guide their children so that, as they grow, they learn to use their rights properly.

Article 6
All children have the right to life. Governments should ensure that children survive and develop healthily.

Article 7
All children have the right to a legally registered name, the right to a nationality and the right to know and, as far as possible, to be cared for by their parents.

Article 8
Governments should respect children's right to a name, a nationality and family ties.

Article 9
Children should not be separated from their parents unless it is for their own good, for example if a parent is mistreating or neglecting a child. Children whose parents have separated have the right to stay in contact with both parents, unless this might harm the child.

Article 10
Families who live in different countries should be allowed to move between those countries so that parents and children can stay in contact or get back together as a family.

Article 11
Governments should take steps to stop children being taken out of their own country illegally.

Article 12
Children have the right to say what they think should happen, when adults are making decisions that affect them, and to have their opinions taken into account.

Article 13
Children have the right to get and share information as long as the information is not damaging to them or to others.

Article 14
Children have the right to think and believe what they want and to practise their religion, as long as they are not stopping other people from enjoying their rights. Parents should guide their children on these matters.

Article 15
Children have the right to meet together and to join organizations, as long as this does not stop other people from enjoying their rights.

Article 16
Children have the right to privacy. The law should protect them from attacks against their way of life, their good name, their families and their homes.

Article 17
Children have the right to reliable information from the mass media. Television, radio, and newspapers should provide information that children can understand, and should not promote materials that could harm children.

Article 18
Both parents share responsibility for bringing up their children, and should always consider what is best for the child. Governments should help parents by providing services to support them, especially if both parents work.

Article 19
Governments should ensure that children are properly cared for, and protect them from violence, abuse and neglect by their parents or anyone else who looks after them.

Article 20
Children who cannot be looked after by their own families must be looked after properly, by people who respect their religion, culture and language.

Article 21
When children are adopted the first concern must be what is best for them. The same rules should apply whether the children are adopted in the country where they were born or taken to live in another country.

Article 22
Children who come into a country as refugees should have the same rights as children born in that country.

Article 23
Children who have any kind of disability should have special care and support so they can live full and independent lives.

Article 24

Children have the right to good quality health care and to clean water, nutritious food and a clean environment so that they will stay healthy. Rich countries should help poorer countries achieve this.

Article 25

Children who are looked after by their local authority rather than their parents should have their situation reviewed regularly.

Article 26

The government should provide extra money for the children of families in need.

Article 27

Children have a right to a standard of living that is good enough to meet their physical and mental needs. The government should help families who cannot afford to provide this.

Article 28

Children have a right to an education. Discipline in schools should respect children's human dignity. Primary education should be free. Wealthy countries should help poorer countries achieve this.

Article 29

Education should develop each child's personality and talents to the full. It should encourage children to respect their parents, their own and other cultures.

Article 30

Children have a right to learn and use the language and customs of their families, whether these are shared by the majority of the people in the country they live or not.

Article 31

All children have a right to relax and play, and to join in a wide range of activities.

Article 32

The government should protect children from work that is dangerous or might harm their health or their education.

Article 33

The government should provide ways of protecting children from dangerous drugs.

Article 34

The government should protect children from sexual abuse.

Article 35

The government should make sure that children are not abducted or sold.

Article 36

Children should be protected from any activities that could harm their development.

Article 37

Children who break the law should not be treated cruelly. They should not be put in prison with adults and should be able to keep contact with their families.

Article 38

Governments should not allow children under 15 to join the army.

Children in war zones should receive special protection.

Article 39
Children who have been neglected or abused should receive special help to restore their self-respect.

Article 40
Children who are accused of breaking the law should receive legal help. Prison sentences for children should only be used for the most serious offences.

Article 41
If the laws of a particular country protect children better than the articles of the *Convention*, then those laws should stay.

Article 42
The government should make the *Convention* known to all parents and children.

Articles 43–54
Are about how adults and governments should work together to make sure all children get all their rights.

Appendix 3:
UN Convention on the Rights of the Child: selected articles of particular relevance to education

Article 12

1 States Parties shall assure to the child who is capable of forming his or her own views the right to express those views freely in all matters affecting the child, the views of the child being given due weight in accordance with the age and maturity of the child.

2 For this purpose, the child in particular be provided the opportunity to be heard in any judicial and administrative proceedings affecting the child, either directly, or through a representative or an appropriate body, in a manner consistent with the procedural rules of national law.

Article 28

1 States Parties recognise the right of the child to education, and with a view to achieving this right progressively and on the basis of equal opportunity, they shall, in particular:
   (a) make primary education compulsory and available free to all;
   (b) encourage the development of different forms of secondary education, including general and vocational education, make them available and accessible to every child, and take appropriate measures such as the introduction of free education and offering financial assistance in case of need;
   (c) make higher education accessible to all on the basis of capacity by every appropriate means;
   (d) make educational and vocational information and guidance available and accessible to all children;
   (e) take measures to encourage regular attendance at schools and the reduction of dropout rates.
2 States Parties shall take all appropriate measures to ensure that school discipline is administered in a manner consistent with the child's human dignity and in conformity with the present Convention.
3 States Parties shall promote and encourage international co-operation in matters relating to education, in particular with a view to contributing to the elimination of ignorance and illiteracy throughout the world and facilitating access to scientific and technical knowledge and modern teaching methods. In this regard, particular account shall be taken of the needs of developing countries.

Article 29
1 States Parties agree that the education of the child shall be directed to:
   (a) the development of the child's personality, talents and mental and physical abilities to their highest potential;
   (b) the development of respect for human rights and fundamental freedoms, and for the principles enshrined in the Charter of the United Nations;
   (c) the development of respect for the child's parents, his or her own cultural identity, language and values, for the national values of the country in which the child is living, the country from which he or she may originate, and for civilizations different from his or her own;
   (d) the preparation of the child for responsible life in a free society, in the spirit of understanding, peace tolerance, equality of sexes, and friendship among all peoples, ethnic, national and religious groups and persons of indigenous origin;
   (e) the development of respect for the natural environment.

2 No part of this article or article 28 shall be construed so as to interfere with the liberty of individuals and bodies to establish and direct educational institutions, subject always to the observance of the principles set forth in paragraph 1 of the present article and to the requirements that the education given in such institutions shall conform to such minimum standards as may be laid down by the State.

Appendix 4:
Does your school environment give everyone a chance to enjoy their rights?

This questionnaire is a revised version of that appearing in Osler and Starkey (1998).

Young people and adults can both experience the denial of their rights and freedoms. The list below will enable you to judge quickly and easily whether the spirit of the *CRC* is followed in a variety of situations in your school.

	Always	Sometimes	Never
Provision			
1 Students and teachers have opportunities to learn about the UN *CRC* and to consider its implications for the school (Article 29).	☐	☐	☐
2 Girls and boys have equal access to all subjects and lessons (Articles 2, 28, 29).	☐	☐	☐
3. All tests take account of cultural differences in the school population (Articles 2, 28, 29.1c, 30).	☐	☐	☐
4 In the teaching of national history, due weight is given to women and minorities and to their versions of history (Articles 2, 13, 28, 29.1c, d, 30).	☐	☐	☐
5 Resources for sport (including equipment, activities, times of use) are equally accessible to girls and to boys (Articles 2, 28, 31).	☐	☐	☐
6 Extracurricular activities organized by the school are available to all regardless of ability to pay (Articles 2, 28, 31).	☐	☐	☐

	Always	Sometimes	Never
7 The school is accessible to people with disabilities (Articles 2, 23, 28).	☐	☐	☐
8 The curriculum is organized so that students may opt out of religious education and this possibility is made known (Article 14).	☐	☐	☐
9 Care is taken that students' names are recorded and pronounced appropriately (Article 7).	☐	☐	☐
10 Efforts are made to ensure regular attendance (Article 28).	☐	☐	☐
11 The school provides opportunities for students to express themselves through art, music and drama (Articles 13, 14, 29, 31).	☐	☐	☐

Protection

12 People are careful not to cause physical harm (Articles 19, 28.2).
   For example:

	Always	Sometimes	Never
a) adults are not allowed to hit young people;	☐	☐	☐
b) young people are not allowed to hit adults;	☐	☐	☐
c) young people are not allowed to hit each other.	☐	☐	☐
13 Students' lockers are considered to be private property (Article 16).	☐	☐	☐
14 Any personal files on a student kept by the school can be inspected by the student whose file it is and the parents, if appropriate. The file can be checked and corrected if necessary (Articles 5, 16, 17, 18).	☐	☐	☐

	Always	Sometimes	Never

15 The contents of any files, whether personal or vocational, may not be communicated to a third party without the permission of the student and her or his parents if appropriate (Articles 15, 16, 18). ☐ ☐ ☐

16 Any person receiving information from a school file accepts that they are bound by confidentiality (Article 16). ☐ ☐ ☐

17 No posters, images or drawings of a racist, sexist or discriminatory kind may be displayed anywhere on school premises (Articles 2, 17, 29.1b, c, d). ☐ ☐ ☐

18 People encourage each other to be tolerant, particularly of those who appear different (Article 29). ☐ ☐ ☐

19 When there is an incident that may lead to the exclusion of a student or disciplinary action, an impartial hearing is organized. In other words, all those involved get a hearing (Articles 28.2, 40). ☐ ☐ ☐

20 A student accused of breaking the rules is presumed innocent until proven guilty and carries on with classes (Article 28.2, 40). ☐ ☐ ☐

21 Where a student has infringed someone's rights – student or adult – reparation is expected (Articles 2, 19). ☐ ☐ ☐

22 Adults infringing students' rights are also expected to make reparation (Articles 2, 19). ☐ ☐ ☐

	Always	Sometimes	Never

Participation

23 In their school work, students have the freedom to express their own political, religious or other opinions, whatever the opinions of the teacher (Articles 12, 13, 14, 17). ☐ ☐ ☐

24 The student newspaper is treated like any other publication, subject to the law, but is not subject to additional censorship (Article 13). ☐ ☐ ☐

25 Young people have created or can create an independent student union, recognized by the school authorities as representing all the students in the school (Article 15). ☐ ☐ ☐

26 There are formal and informal mechanisms for learners to make a complaint or suggestions for improving the life of the school (Articles 12, 13). ☐ ☐ ☐

27 Young people have as much right to respect as adults (Articles 12, 19, 29.1c). ☐ ☐ ☐

28 Students and adults (including parents, teachers and administrative staff) are consulted about the quality of the teaching in the school (Article 5, 12, 18). ☐ ☐ ☐

29 There is an elected student council (Articles 12, 13, 15, 17). ☐ ☐ ☐

30 Students are represented on the governing body of the school (Article 12). ☐ ☐ ☐

Notes

Chapter 3

1   The UN *CRC* applies to everyone under the age of 18 years. In this
    chapter we examine the status and rights of those within this age
    group, sometimes using the words 'child' and 'children' as shorthand
    to cover all young people to whom the *CRC* applies.
2   Although the right to vote is a key democratic right, it is not in itself a
    marker of citizenship. For example, in the UK residents who have Irish
    or Commonwealth citizenship have particular voting rights.
3   The issue of exclusion from school is explored in more detail in
    Chapter 4 as is the case study of the student with Asperger Syndrome.

Chapter 5

1   Held (2004: 171) identifies eight paramount principles associated with
    cosmopolitan values, namely:

    1 equal worth and dignity;
    2 active agency;
    3 personal responsibility and accountability;
    4 consent;
    5 collective decision-making about public matters through voting pro-
      cedures;
    6 inclusiveness and subsidiarity;
    7 avoidance of serious harm;
    8 sustainability.

Chapter 9

1   These are collected in several language versions at www.hrea.org.
2   See Osler and Starkey (2001) for a discussion of the responsibilities of the individual to the nation.

Chapter 10

1   These plans were the mechanism by which LEAs applied for EMAG over a two-year period (1998–2000) and by which they demonstrated to the government how they intended to use the grant. The action plans do not allow reliable cause effect analysis to be carried out. Nevertheless, it is possible to identify, from the data, the strategies of LEAs that appeared in the early years of EMAG to be making the greatest difference in raising the achievement of minority ethnic pupils.

References

Adler, S., Laney, J. and Packer, M. (1993) *Managing Women: Feminism and Power in Educational Management*. Buckingham: Open University Press.

Alderson, P. (1999) Human rights and democracy in schools: do they mean more than 'picking up litter and not killing whales'? *International Journal of Children's Rights*, 7(2): 185–205.

Alibhai-Brown, Y. (1999) *True Colours: Public Attitudes to Multiculturalism and the Role of the Government*. London: Institute of Public Policy Research.

Alliance Israélite Universelle (1961) *Les Droits de l'Homme et l'Education*. Paris: Presses Universitaires de France.

Alton-Lee, A. and Praat, A. (2001) *Questioning Gender: Snapshots from Explaining and Addressing Gender Differences in the New Zealand Compulsory School Sector*. Wellington: Ministry of Education, Research and Evaluation (Internal) Unit.

American Association of University Women (AAUW) (1999) *Gender Gaps: Where Schools Still Fail our Children*. New York: Marlowe & Company.

Amnesty International (2004) *Annual Report*. http://web.amnesty.org/report2004/index-eng (accessed 24 July 2004).

Anderson, B. (1991) *Imagined Communities*. London: Verso.

Anderson-Gold, S. (2001) *Cosmopolitanism and Human Rights*. Cardiff: University of Wales Press.

Annan, K. (2000) *'We the Peoples': The Role of the United Nations in the 21st Century*. New York: United Nations.

Anwar, M. (1998) *Between Cultures: Continuity and Change in the Lives of Young Asians*. London: Routledge.

Archard, D. (1993) *Children, Rights and Childhood*. London: Routledge.

Archard, D. (2003) Citizenship education and multiculturalism, in A. Lockyer, B. Crick and J. Annette (eds) *Education for Democratic Citizenship: Issues of Theory and Practice*. Aldershot: Ashgate.

Armstrong, D. (2004) *Experiences of Special Education: Re-evaluating Policy and Practice through Life Stories*. London: RoutledgeFalmer.

Arnot, M. and Dillabough, J-A. (eds) (2000) *Challenging Democracy: International Perspectives on Gender, Education and Citizenship*. London: RoutledgeFalmer.

Arnot, M., David, M. and Weiner, G. (1996) *Educational Reforms and Gender Equality in Schools*. Manchester: Equal Opportunities Commission.

Arnot, M., Gray, J., James, M. and Rudduck, J. (1998) *Recent Research on Gender and Educational Performance.* London: The Stationery Office/ Ofsted.

Banks, J. (1997) *Educating Citizens in a Multicultural Society.* New York: Teachers College Press.

Banks, J. (2004) Democratic citizenship education in multicultural societies, in J. Banks (ed.) *Diversity and Citizenship Education: Global Perspectives.* San Francisco: Jossey-Bass.

Banton, M. (1997) *Ethnic and Racial Consciousness,* 2nd edn. London: Longman.

Bauman, Z. (2001) *Community: Seeking Safety in an Insecure World.* Cambridge: Polity Press.

Baumann, G. (1996) *Contesting Culture: Discourses of Identity in Multi-ethnic London.* Cambridge: Cambridge University Press.

Beck, U. (2000) *What is Globalization?* Cambridge: Polity Press.

Beiner, R. (ed.) (1995) *Theorizing Citizenship.* Albany: State University of New York Press.

Bernstein, R. (2003) Edward Said, leading advocate of Palestinians, dies at 67, *The New York Times,* 25 September., http://www.nytimes.com/2003/ 09/25/obituaries/25CND-SAID.html (accessed 21 July 2004).

Blackstone, T., Parekh, B. and Sanders, P. (eds) (1998) *Race Relations in Britain: A Developing Agenda.* London: Routledge.

Blunkett, D. (2004) Strength in diversity, speech given at seminar 'Challenges for Race Equality and Community Cohesion in the 21st Century', Institute for Public Policy Research, London, 7 July, http://www.homeoffice.gov.uk/docs3/race-speech.pdf (accessed 16 July 2004).

Bradley, H. (2003) *Fractured Identities: Changing Patterns of Inequality.* Cambridge: Polity Press.

British National Party (BNP) (2004) *Election Communication England South East Region June 10 2004.* Welshpool: BNP.

Brown, G. (2004) Leadership, race equality and schol improvement, *Race Equality Teaching,* 22(3): 37–9.

Bush, T., Bell, L., Bolam, R., Glatter, R. and Ribbins, P. (1999) *Educational Management: Redefining Theory, Policy and Practice.* London: Paul Chapman.

Cantle, T. (2001) *Community Cohesion: A Report of the Independent Review Team.* London: Home Office.

Cantwell, N. (1992) The origins, development and significance of the United Nations Convention on the Rights of the Child, in S. Detrick (ed.) *The United Nations Convention on the Rights of the Child: A Guide to the 'Travaux Préparatoires'.* Dordrecht: Martinus Nijhoff.

Carter, C. and Osler, A. (2000) Human rights, identities and conflict management: a study of school culture as experienced through classroom relationships, *Cambridge Journal of Education*, 30(3): 335–56.

Cassin, R. (1969) *From the Ten Commandments to the Rights of Man* (original source unknown) published at www.udhr50/org/history/tencomms.htm.

Castles, S. and Davidson, A. (2000) *Immigration and Citizenship: Globalisation and the Politics of Belonging*. Basingstoke: Palgrave (Macmillan).

Children's Rights Alliance for England (CRAE) (2002) *Report to the Pre-Sessional Working Group of the Committee on the Rights of the Child, Preparing for the Examination of the UK's Second Report under the CRC, March*. London: CRAE.

Chua, A. (2003) *World on Fire: How Exporting Free-market Democracy Breeds Ethnic Hatred and Global Instability*. London: William Heineman.

Cohen, A. (1985) *The Symbolic Construction of Community*. Manchester: Manchester University Press.

Commission for Racial Equality (CRE) (1997) *Exclusion from School and Racial Equality: A Good Practice Guide*. London: Commission for Racial Equality.

Commission for Racial Equality (CRE) (2002) *Statutory Code of Practice on the Duty to Promote Race Equality: A Guide for Schools*. London: CRE.

Commission on British Muslims and Islamophobia (1997) *Islamophobia: A Challenge for us All*. London: Runnymede Trust.

Commission on British Muslims and Islamophobia (2004) *Islamophobia: Issues, Challenges and Action*. Stoke-on-Trent: Trentham.

Commission on Global Governance (CGG) (1995) *Our Global Neighbourhood*. Oxford: Oxford University Press.

Connell, R. (1989) Cool guys, swots and wimps: the interplay of masculinity and education, *Oxford Review of Education*, 15(3): 291–303.

Connolly, P. (1998) *Racism, Gender Identities and Young Children: Social Relations in a Multi-ethnic Inner City Primary School*. London: Routledge.

Council of Europe (1950) *European Convention on Human Rights and Fundamental Freedoms*. Strasbourg: Council of Europe.

Council of Europe (1961) *European Social Charter*. Strasbourg: Council of Europe.

Council of Europe (1985) *Recommendation No R (85) 7 of the Committee of Ministers to Member States on Teaching and Learning about Human Rights in Schools*. Strasbourg: Council of Europe.

Council of Europe (1995) *Framework Convention for the Protection of National Minorities*. Strasbourg: Council of Europe.

Council of Europe (1996) *European Convention on the Exercise of Children's Rights*. Strasbourg: Council of Europe.

Council of Europe (1999a) Committee of Ministers of Education *Declaration and Programme on Education for Democratic Citizenship, Based on the Rights and Responsibilities of Citizens*, CM (99) 76. Strasbourg: Council of Europe, www.coe.int (accessed 30 July 2004).

Council of Europe (1999b) Recommendation (1401) of the Parliamentary Assembly *Education in the Responsibilities of the Individual*, Strasbourg: Council of Europe, www.coe.int (accessed 30 July 2004).

Council of Europe (2000a) *Political Declaration Adopted by Ministers of Council of Europe Member States on Friday 13 October 2000 at the Concluding Session of the European Conference against Racism*, Euroconf (2000) 1 final. Strasbourg: Council of Europe, http://www.coe.int/T/E/ human_rights/Ecri/2-European_Conference/1-Documents_adopted/01- Political%20Declaration.asp (accessed 23 July 2004).

Council of Europe (2000b) *Project on 'Education for Democratic Citizenship': Resolution adopted by the Council of Europe Ministers of Education at their 20th Session, Cracow, Poland, 15–17 October 2000*, DGIV/EDU/CIT (2000) 40. Strasbourg: Council of Europe.

Covell, K. and Howe, R.B. (1995) Variations in support for children's rights among Canadian youth, *International Journal of Children's Rights*, 3(2): 189–96.

Crick, B. (2000) *Essays on Citizenship*. London: Continuum.

Cuccioletta, D. (2002) Multiculturalism or transculturalism: towards a cosmopolitan citizenship, *London Journal of Canadian Studies* 17: 9.

Dadzie, S. (2000) *Toolkit for Tackling Racism in Schools*. Stoke-on-Trent: Trentham.

Davies, L. (1998) *School Councils and Pupil Exclusion*. London: School Councils UK.

Davies, L. and Kirkpatrick, G. (2000) *The Eurodem Project: A Review of Pupil Democracy in Europe*. London: Children's Rights Alliance.

Delanty, G. (2000) *Citizenship in a Global Age: Society, Culture, Politics*. Buckingham: Open University Press.

Department for Education and Employment (DfEE) (1999a) *Social Inclusion: The LEA Role in Pupil Support*, Circular 10/99. London: DfEE.

Department for Education and Employment (DfEE) (1999b) *Social Inclusion: Pupil Support*, Circular 11/99. London: DfEE.

Department for Education and Employment (DfEE)/Qualifications and Curriculum Authority (QCA) (1999a) *The National Curriculum for England: Handbook for Secondary Teachers in England, Key Stages 3 and 4*. London: The Stationery Office.

Department for Education and Employment (DfEE)/Qualifications and Curriculum Authority (QCA) (1999b) *The National Curriculum for England: Citizenship Key Stages 3–4*. London: The Stationery Office.

Department for Education and Skills (DfES) (2001a) *Code of Practice on the Identification and Assessment of Special Educational Needs*. London: The Stationery Office.

Department for Education and Skills (DfES) (2001b) *Schools: Achieving Success*, Cm 5230. London: The Stationery Office.

Department for Education and Skills (DfES) (2002) *Statistics of Education: Pupil Progress by Characteristics*. London: DfES.

Department for Education and Skills (DfES) (2003) *Learning to Listen.* London: The Stationery Office, http://www.cypu.gov.uk/corporate/participation/docs/19005LearngtoListen.pdf (accessed 27 July 2004).

Department for International Development (DFID) (2000) *Strategies for Achieving the International Development Targets: Education for All – The Challenge of Universal Primary eEducation, March consultation document.* London: DFID.

Department of Education and Science (DES) (1985) *Education for All: The Report of the Committee of Enquiry into the Education of Children from Ethnic Minority Groups (The Swann Report, Cmnd 9453).* London: Her Majesty's Stationery Office.

Dewey, J. ([1916] 2002) Democracy and education: an introduction to the philosophy of education, in S.J. Maxcy (ed.) *John Dewey and American Education,* Vol. 3. Bristol: Thoemmes.

Diamantopoulou, A. (2001) Address of European Commissioner responsible for Employment and Social Affairs to Plenary Session of the World Conference against Racism, Durban, 2 September, http://www.migrantsingreece.org/files/RESOURCE_18.pdf (accessed 15 July 2004).

Dimmock, C. and Walker, A. (2002) School leadership in context: societal and organisational cultures, in T. Bush and L. Bell (eds) *The Principles and Practice of Educational Management.* London: Paul Chapman.

Ekholm, M. (2004) Learning democracy by sharing power, in J. Macbeath and L. Moos (eds) *Democratic Learning: The Challenge to School Effectiveness.* London: RoutledgeFalmer.

Essed, P. (1991) *Understanding Everyday Racism: An Interdisciplinary Theory.* London: Sage.

Etzioni, A. (1995) *The Spirit of Community.* London: Fontana.

European Commission (EC) (1998) *Action Plan Against Racism.* Brussels: Communication from the Commission (COM) 183, 25 March.

European Commission (EC) (1999) *Mainstreaming the Fight Against Racism: Commission Report on the Implementation of the Action Plan against Racism,* http://europa.eu.int/comm/employment_social/fundamental_rights/pdf/origin/implem_en.pdf (accessed 19 July 2004).

European Commission (EC) (2000) *SOCRATES: Guidelines for Applicants.* Luxembourg: Office for Official Publications of the European Communities.

European Union (EU) (2000) *Charter of Fundamental Rights of the European Union,* www.europart.eu.int/charter/default_en.htm, (Accessed 13 October 2004).

Felouzis, G. (2003) La ségrégation ethnique au collège et ses conséquences, *Revue Française de Sociologie,* 44(3): 413–47.

Figueroa, P. (2000) Citizenship education for a plural society, in A. Osler (ed.) *Citizenship and Democracy in Schools: Diversity, Identity, Equality.* Stoke-on-Trent: Trentham.

Flekkøy, M. and Kaufman, N. (1997) *The Participation Rights of the Child: Rights and Responsibilities in Family and Society.* London: Jessica Kingsley.

Freeman, M. (1988) Taking children's rights seriously, *Children and Society*, 4: 299–319.

Freeman, M. (1992) Introduction: rights, ideology and children, in M. Freeman and P. Veerman (eds) *The Ideologies of Children's Rights.* Dordrecht: Martinus Nijhoff.

Fryer, P. (1984) *Staying Power: The History of Black People in Britain.* London: Pluto.

Gallagher, C. and Cross, C. (1990) Children Act 1989: an introduction, *Malajustment and Therapeutic Education*, 8(3): 122–9.

Giddens, A. (1991) *Modernity and Self-identity.* London: Polity Press.

Gillborn, D. and Gipps, C. (1996) *Recent Research on the Achievement of Ethnic Minority Pupils.* London: The Stationery Office.

Gillborn, D. and Mirza, H. S. (2000) *Educational Inequality: Mapping Race, Class and Gender, a Synthesis of Research Evidence*, HMI 232. London: Office for Standards in Education.

Gillborn, D. and Youdell, D. (2000) *Rationing Education: Policy, Practice, Reform and Equity.* Buckingham: Open University Press.

Government of Sweden (2001) *National Action Plan to Combat Racism, Xenophobia, Homophobia and Discrimination.* Stockholm: Written Government Communication 2000/2001: 59.

Gray, J. (2001) The era of globalisation is over, *The New Statesman*, 24 September.

Greenfield, N. (2004) Pump it up, *Times Educational Supplement Friday Magazine*, 27 February (see also www.ryanswell.ca accessed 30 July 2004).

Griffin, C. (1993) *Representations of Youth: The Study of Youth and Adolescence in Britain and America.* Cambridge: Polity Press.

Gutmann, A. (2003) *Identity in Democracy.* Princeton, NJ: Princeton University Press.

Gutmann, A. (2004) Unity and diversity in democratic multicultural education: creative and destructive tensions, in J.A. Banks (ed.) *Diversity and Citizenship Education.* San Francisco: Jossey Bass.

Hahn, C. (2005) Diversity and human rights learning in England and the United States, in A. Osler (ed.) *Teachers, Human Rights and Diversity: Educating Citizens in Multicultural Societies.* Stoke-on-Trent: Trentham.

Hall, S. (2000) Multicultural citizens, monocultural citizenship? in N. Pearce and J. Hallgarten (eds) *Tomorrow's Citizens: Critical Debates in Citizenship and Education.* London: Institute for Public Policy Research.

Hall, S. and Held, D. (1989) Citizens and citizenship, in S. Hall and M. Jacques (eds) *New Times: The Changing Face of Politics in the 1990s.* London: Lawrence & Wishart.

Hansard (House of Commons) (1999) *Debates 24 February*, vol. 326, col. 393, Jack Straw. London: The Stationery Office.

Hansard (House of Commons) (2000) *Debates 9 March*, vol. 345, col. 1281, Mike O'Brien. London: The Stationery Office.

Hansard (House of Lords) (2000a) *Debates 10 January*, vol. 608, cols 481–2, Lord Bassam. London: The Stationery Office.

Hansard (House of Lords) (2000b) *Debates 19 December*, vol. 620, cols 636, 638 and 639, Baroness Blackstone. London: The Stationery Office.

Harber, C. (1995) Democratic education and the international aenda, in C. Harber (ed.) *Developing Democratic Education*. Ticknall: Education Now.

Hart, S.N. (1991) From property to person status: historical perspective on children's rights, *American Psychologist*, 46(1): 53–9.

Held, D. (1995a) *Democracy and the Global Order: From the Modern State to Cosmopolitan Governance*. Cambridge: Polity Press.

Held, D. (1995b) Democracy and the new international order, in D. Archibugi and D. Held (eds) *Cosmopolitan Democracy: An Agenda for a New World Order*. Cambridge: Polity Press.

Held, D. (2001) *Violence and Justice in a Global Age*, http://www.open-democracy.net/debates/article-2-49-144.jsp (accessed 7 July 2003).

Held, D. (2004) *Global Covenant: The Social Democratic Alternative to the Washington Consensus*. Cambridge: Polity Press.

Hirst, P. (2002) *What is Globalisation?* http://www.opendemocracy.net/debates/article-6-28-637.jsp#one (accessed 23 July 2004).

HM Treasury (2003) *Every Child Matters*, Green Paper, Cm 5860, September. London: The Stationery Office.

Hobby, R. (2004) *A Culture for Learning: An Investigation into the Values and Beliefs Associated with Effective Schools*. London: Hay Group Management.

Home Office (1999) *Stephen Lawrence Inquiry: Home Secretary's Action Plan*. London: The Stationery Office.

House of Commons Education and Skills Committee (2003) *The Work of Ofsted: Sixth Report of Session 2002–03*, HC 531, 23 July. London: The Stationery Office.

Hudson, A. (2005) Citizenship education and students' identities: a school-based action research project, in A. Osler (ed.) *Teachers, Human Rights and Diversity: Educating Citizens in Multicultural Societies*. Stoke-on-Trent: Trentham.

Ignatieff, M. (1995) The myth of citizenship, in R. Beiner (ed.) *Theorizing Citizenship*. Albany: State University of New York Press.

Illich, I. (1971) *Deschooling Society*. Harmondsworth: Penguin.

International Council on Human Rights Policy (ICHRP) (1999) *Taking Duties Seriously: Individual Duties in International Human Rights Law – A Commentary*. Geneva: ICHRP.

Jawad, H. and Benn, T. (eds) (2003) *Muslim Women in the United Kingdom and Beyond: Experiences and Images*. Leiden: Brill.

Jeleff, S. (1996) *The Child as Citizen*. Strasbourg: Council of Europe.

Jenkins, R. (1996) *Social Identity*. London: Routledge.

Kaldor, M. (1995) European institutions, nation states and nationalism, in D. Archibugi and D. Held (eds) *Cosmopolitan Democracy: An Agenda for a New World Order*. Cambridge: Polity Press.

Kaldor, M. (2002) Cosmopolitanism and organised violence, in S. Vertovec and R. Cohen (eds) *Conceiving Cosmopolitanism: Theory, Context and Practice*. Oxford: Oxford University Press. Paper originally prepared for Conference on 'Conceiving Cosmopolitanism', Warwick 27–9 April 2000, www.theglobalsite.ac.uk (accessed 30 July 2004).

Kaldor, M. (2003) American power: from 'compellance' to cosmopolitanism?, *International Affairs*, 79(1): 1–22.

Keane, J. (2003) *Global Civil Society?* Cambridge: Cambridge University Press.

Kerr, D., Cleaver, E., Ireland, E and Blenkinsop, S. (2003) *Citizenship Eduction: Longitudinal Study First Cross-Sectional Survey 2001–2002*, RR416. London: Department for Education and Skills.

Klug, F. (2000) *Values for a Godless Age: The Story of the UK's New Bill of Rights*. Harmondsworth: Penguin.

Lansdown, G. and Newell, P. (eds) (1994) *UK Agenda for Children*. London: Children's Rights Development Unit.

Le Guide du Routard (2002) *Guide du Citoyen*. Meudon: Hachette.

League of Nations (1924) *Geneva Declaration of the Rights of the Child*. Geneva: League of Nations.

Lindsay, M. (1990) The Children Act: a consideration of the implications for children's rights, *Malajustment and Therapeutic Education*, 8(3): 167–73.

Lister, I. (1974) *Deschooling*. Cambridge: Cambridge University Press.

Lister, R. (1997) *Citizenship: Feminist Perspectives*. London: Macmillan.

Loxley, A. and Thomas, G. (2001) Neo-conservatives, neo-liberals, the new left and inclusion: stirring the pot, *Cambridge Journal of Education*, 31(3): 291–301.

Macpherson, W. (1999) *The Stephen Lawrence Inquiry*. London: The Stationery Office.

Mactaggart, F. (2003) Race equality and accountability, in R. Berkeley (ed.) *Guardians of Race Equality: Perspectives on Inspection and Regulation*. London: Runnymede Trust.

Marshall, T. (1950) *Citizenship and Social Class and other Essays*. Cambridge: Cambridge University Press.

Matsuura, K. (2000) Education pour tous contre diversité culturelle? *Le Monde*, 20 April.

McLaughlin, T. (1992) Citizenship, diversity and education: a philosophical perspective, *Journal of Moral Education*, 21(3): 235–50.

Meltzer, H., Harrington, R., Goodman, R. and Jenkins, R. (2001) *Children and Adolescents who try to Harm or Kill Themselves*. London: Office for National Statistics.

Newell, P. (1991) *The UN Convention and Children's Rights in the UK*. London: National Children's Bureau.

Norwich, B. (1994) *Segregation and Inclusion: English LEA Statistics 1988–1992*. Bristol: Centre for Studies on Inclusive Education.

Nussbaum, M.C. (1996) Patriotism and cosmopolitanism, in M.C. Nussbaum and J. Cohen (eds) *For Love of Country: Debating the Limits of Patriotism*. Boston, MA: Beacon Press.

Ó Cuanacháin, C. (2004) Human rights education in an Irish primary school, Unpublished Ph.D. thesis, University of Leicester.

Ó Cuanacháin, C. (2005) Citizenship education in the Republic of Ireland, in A. Osler (ed.) *Teachers, Human Rights and Diversity: Educating Citizens in Multicultural Societies*. Stoke-on-Trent: Trentham.

Office for Standards in Education (Ofsted) (1996) *Exclusions from Secondary Schools 1995/6*. London: Ofsted.

Office for Standards in Education (Ofsted) (1999) *Raising the Attainment of Minority Ethnic Pupils: School and LEA Responses*. London: Ofsted.

Organization of African Unity (1981) *African (Banjul) Charter on Human and People's Rights*. Addis Ababa: OAU.

Organization of African Unity (1990) *African Charter on the Rights and Welfare of the Child*. Addis Ababa: OAU.

Osler, A. (1989) *Speaking Out: Black Girls in Britain*. London: Virago.

Osler, A. (1997a) *Exclusion from School and Racial Equality*. London: Commission for Racial Equality.

Osler, A. (1997b) Exclusions drama turns into a crisis for blacks, *Times Educational Supplement*, 13 October.

Osler, A. (1997c) *The Education and Careers of Black Teachers: Changing Identities, Changing Lives*. Buckingham: Open University Press.

Osler, A. (1999) Citizenship, democracy and political literacy, *Multicultural Teaching*, 8(1): 12–15, 29.

Osler, A. (2000a) Children's rights, responsibilities and understandings of school discipline, *Research Papers in Education*, 15(1): 49–67.

Osler, A. (ed.) (2000b) *Citizenship and Democracy in Schools: Diversity, Identity, Equality*. Stoke-on-Trent: Trentham.

Osler, A. (2000c) The Crick Report: difference, equality and racial justice, *Curriculum Journal*, 11(1): 25–37.

Osler, A. (2002) Citizenship education and the strengthening of democracy: is race on the agenda? in D. Scott and H. Lawson (eds) *Citizenship Education and the Curriculum*. Westport, CT: Greenwood.

Osler, A. and Hill, J. (1999) Exclusion from school and racial equality: an examination of government proposals in the light of recent research evidence, *Cambridge Journal of Education*, 29(1): 33–62.

Osler, A. and Morrison, M. (2000) *Inspecting Schools for Race Equality: Ofsted's Strengths and Weaknesses: A Report for the Commission for Racial Equality*.

Stoke-on-Trent: Trentham.

Osler, A. and Morrison, M. (2002) Can race equality be inspected? Challenges for policy and practice raised by the Ofsted school inspection framework, *British Educational Research Journal*, 28(3): 327–38.

Osler, A. and Osler, C. (2002) Inclusion, exclusion and children's rights: a case study of a student with Asperger syndrome, *Emotional and Behavioural Difficulties*, 7(1): 35–54.

Osler, A. and Starkey, H. (1996) *Teacher Education and Human Rights*. London: David Fulton.

Osler, A. and Starkey, H. (1998) Children's rights and citizenship: some implications for the management of schools, *The International Journal of Children's Rights*, 6: 313–33.

Osler, A. and Starkey, H. (1999) Rights, identities and inclusion: European action programmes as political education, *Oxford Review of Education*, 25(1 and 2): 199–216.

Osler, A. and Starkey, H. (2000) Citizenship, human rights and cultural diversity, in A. Osler (ed.) *Citizenship and Democracy in Schools: Diversity, Identity, Equality*. Stoke-on-Trent: Trentham.

Osler, A. and Starkey, H. (2001) Citizenship education and national identities in France and England: inclusive or exclusive? *Oxford Review of Education*, 25(2): 287–305.

Osler, A. and Starkey, H. (2003) Learning for cosmopolitan citizenship: theoretical debates and young people's experiences, *Educational Review*, 55(3): 243–54.

Osler, A. and Starkey, H. (2004) Citizenship education and cultural diversity in France and England, in J. Demaine (ed.) *Citizenship and Political Education Today*. Basingstoke: Palgrave Macmillan.

Osler, A. and Vincent, K. (2002) *Citizenship and the Challenge of Global Education*. Stoke-on-Trent: Trentham.

Osler, A. and Vincent, K. (2003) *Girls and Exclusion: Rethinking the Agenda*. London: RoutledgeFalmer.

Osler, A., Watling, R. and Busher, H. (2000) *Reasons for Exclusion from School*. London: Department for Education and Employment.

Osler, A., Street, C., Lall, M. and Vincent, K. (2002) *Not a Problem? Girls and Exclusion from School*. York: Joseph Rowntree Foundation.

Osler, A., Wilkins, C. and Pardinaz-Solis, R. (2003) *Racial Harassment of Teachers: Research Report to the NASUWT*. Leicester: University of Leicester.

Oxfam (1997) *A Curriculum for Global Citizenship*. Oxford: Oxfam, http://www.oxfam.org.uk/coolplanet/index.htm (accessed 30 July 2004).

Ozga, J. (1993) *Women in Educational Management*. Buckingham: Open University Press.

Parekh, B. (1991a) British citizenship and cultural difference, in G. Andrews (ed.) *Citizenship*. London: Lawrence & Wishart.

Parekh, B. (1991b) Law torn, *New Statesman and Society*, 14 June.

Parekh, B. (2000) *The Future of Multi-Ethnic Britain: Report of the Commission on the Future of Multi-Ethnic Britain*. London: Runnymede Trust.

Parffrey, V. (1994) Exclusion: failed children or systems failure? *School Organisation*, 14(2): 107–20.

Plesch, D. (2002) *Sheriff and Outlaws in the Global Village*. London: Menard Press.

Preston, P. W. (1997) *Political/cultural Identity: Citizens and Nations in a Global Era*. London: Sage.

Qualifications and Curriculum Authority (QCA) (1998) *Education for Citizenship and the Teaching of Democracy in Schools*, final report of the Advisory Group on Citizenship (the Crick Report). London: QCA.

Qualifications and Curriculum Authority (QCA) (2001a) *Citizenship: Key Stage 3 Scheme of Work*. London: QCA.

Qualifications and Curriculum Authority (QCA) (2001b) *Citizenship: A Scheme of Work for Key Stage 3, Teacher's Guide*. London: QCA.

Qualifications and Curriculum Authority (QCA) (2002a) *Citizenship: A Scheme of Work for Key Stage 4, Teacher's Guide*. London: QCA.

Qualifications and Curriculum Authority (QCA) (2002b) *Citizenship: A Scheme of Work for Key Stages 1 and 2, Teacher's Guide*. London: QCA.

Refugee Law Project (2004) *Working Paper No. 11: Behind the Violence: Causes, Consequences and the Search for Solutions to the War in Northern Uganda*. Kampala: Refugee Law Project (2004), http://www.refugeelawproject. org/index.htm (accessed 13 July 2004).

Richardson, B. (2004) Rhetoric and reality, *Race Equality Teaching*, 22(3): 40.

Richardson, R. (1996) The terrestrial teacher, in M. Steiner (ed.) *Developing the Global Teacher: Theory and Practice in Initial Teacher Education*. Stoke-on-Trent: Trentham.

Richardson, R., and Miles, B. (2003) *Equality Stories: Recognition, Respect and Raising Achievement*. Stoke-on-Trent: Trentham.

Riley, K. (2004) Reforming for democratic schooling: learning for the future not yearning for the past, in J. Macbeath and L. Moos (eds) *Democratic Learning: The Challenge to School Effectiveness*. London: RoutledgeFalmer.

Robertson, Robbie (2003) *The Three Waves of Globalization: A History of Developing Global Consciousness*. London: Zed Books.

Robertson, Roland (1992) *Globalization: Social Theory and Global Culture*. London: Sage.

Rodham, H. (1973) Children under the law, *Harvard Educational Review*, 43(4): 487–514.

Rodway, S. (1993) Children's rights: children's needs: is there a conflict? *Therapeutic Care and Education*, 2(2): 375–91.

Roker, D., Player, K. and Coleman, J. (1999) Young people's voluntary and campaigning activities as sources of political action, *Oxford Review of Education*, 25(1 and 2): 185–98.

Roosevelt, F. D. (1941) *The Four Freedoms,* address to the 77th Congress, http://www.libertynet.org/~edcivic/fdr.html (accessed 26 July 2004).

Rudduck, J. and Flutter, J. (2004) *How to Improve Your School: Giving Pupils a Voice.* London: Continuum.

Rudduck, J., Chaplain, R. and Wallace, G. (1996) *School Improvement: What Can Pupils Tell Us?* London: David Fulton.

Rutter, J. (2005) Understanding the alien in our midst: using citizenship education to challenge popular discourses about refugees, in A. Osler (ed.) *Teachers, Human Rights and Diversity: Educating Citizens in Multicultural Societies.* Stoke-on-Trent: Trentham.

Ryan, J. (1999) *Race and Ethnicity in Multi-Ethnic Schools.* Clevedon: Multilingual Matters.

Sandel, M. (1996) *Democracy's Discontent.* Cambridge, MA: Harvard University Press.

Save the Children (1999) *I've got them! You've got them! We've all got them!* London: Education Unit, Save the Children.

Sen, A. (1999) Democracy as a universal value, *Journal of Democracy,* 10(3): 3–17.

Shaw, M. (2003) Excluded get new right of appeal, *Times Educational Supplement,* 12 December: 13.

Sinclair Taylor, A. (2000) The UN Convention on the Rights of the Child: giving children a voice, in A. Lewis and G. Lindsay (eds) *Researching Children's Perspectives.* Buckingham: Open University Press.

Smith, T. (1997) Preface, in J. Gardner (ed.) *Citizenship: The White Paper.* London: British Institute of International and Comparative Law.

Social Exclusion Unit (SEU) (1998) *Truancy and School Exclusion.* London: Cabinet Office.

Social Exclusion Unit (SEU) (2000) *Minority Ethnic Issues in Social Exclusion and Neighbourhood Renewal.* London: Cabinet Office.

Social Exclusion Unit (SEU) (2001) *Preventing Social Exclusion.* London: Cabinet Office.

Starkey, H. (2000) Citizenship education in France and Britain: evolving theories and practices, *Curriculum Journal,* 11(1): 39–54.

Taylor, M. with Johnson, R. (2002) *School Councils: Their Role in Citizenship and Personal and Social Education.* Slough: National Foundation for Educational Research.

Thorne, S. (1996) Children's rights and the listening school: an approach to counter bullying among primary school pupils, in A. Osler, H-F. Rathenow and H. Starkey (eds) *Teaching for Citizenship in Europe.* Stoke-on-Trent: Trentham.

Tikly, L., Osler, A., Hill, J. and Vincent, K. *et al.* (2002) *Ethnic Minority Achievement Grant: Analysis of LEA Action Plans.* Research Report 371. London: The Stationery Office on behalf of the Department for Education and Skills.

Tikly, L., Caballero, C., Haynes, J. and Hill, J. (2004) *Understanding the Educational Needs of Mixed Heritage Pupils*, research report RR549. London: Department for Education and Skills.

Tisdall, G. and Dawson, R. (1994) Listening to children: interviews with children attending a mainstream support facility, *Support for Learning*, 9(4): 179–83.

Tomaševski, K. (1999) *Report on the Right to Education: Addendum Mission to the United Kingdom of Great Britain and Northern Ireland (England) 18–22 October*. Geneva: UN Commission on Human Rights.

Troyna, B. and Hatcher, R. (1992) *Racism in Children's Lives*. London: Routledge.

United Nations (UN) (1945) *The Charter of the United Nations*, http://www.un.org/aboutun/charter/ (accessed 30 July 2004).

United Nations (UN) (1948) *Universal Declaration of Human Rights*. New York: General Assembly of the UN.

United Nations (UN) (1959) *Declaration on the Rights of the Child*. New York: United Nations.

United Nations (UN) (1986) *Declaration on the Right to Development*, Resolution 41/128. New York: General Assembly of the UN.

United Nations (UN) (1989) *Convention on the Rights of the Child*. New York: United Nations. www.unicef.org/crc/crc.htm, accessed 11 october 2004.

United Nations (UN) (1998) *Human Rights Today: A United Nations Priority*, UN briefing papers, www.un.org/rights/HRToday/ (accessed 30 July 2004).

United Nations (UN) (2002) *A World Fit for Children: Outcome Document of UN Special Session on Children, 8–10 May, 2002*, www.unicef.org (accessed 30 July 2004).

United Nations Development Programme (UNDP) (2002) *Human Development Report 2002: Deepening Democracy in a Fragmented World*. Oxford: Oxford University Press.

United Nations Educational, Scientific and Cultural Organization (UNESCO) (1995) *Integrated Framework of Action on Education for Peace, Human Rights and Democracy*. Paris: UNESCO.

United Nations Educational, Scientific and Cultural Organization (UNESCO) (1997) *Declaration on the Responsibilities of the Present Generations Towards Future Generations*. Paris: UNESCO.

United Nations Commission for Human Rights (UNCHR) (1994) *Human Rights: The New Consensus*. London: Regency Press.

Verhellen, E. (2000) Children's rights and education, in A. Osler (ed.) *Citizenship and Democracy in Schools: Diversity, Identity, Equality*. Stoke-on-Trent: Trentham.

Watts, J. (1977) *The Countesthorpe Experience*. London: Allen & Unwin.

West-Burnham, J. (2004) Leadership to raise standards, leadership for race equality – binary opposites? *Race Equality Teaching*, 22(3): 16–18.

Williams, R. (1983) *Keywords*. London: Fontana.

Wolpe, A. (1988) *Within School Walls: The Role of Discipline, Sexuality and Curriculum*. London: Routledge.

Wright, C. (1986) School processes – an ethnographic study, in J. Eggleston, D. Dunn and M. Anjali (eds) *Education for Some: The Educational and Vocational Experiences of 15–18-year-old Members of Ethnic Minority Groups*. Stoke-on-Trent: Trentham.

Wright, C. (1992) *Race Relations in the Primary School*. London: David Fulton.

Wright, C., Weekes, D. and McGlaughlin, A. (2000) *'Race', Class and Gender in Exclusion from School*. London: Falmer.

Index